"If leadership studies have taught us anything, it is the importance of staying in touch with the times and providing leadership that helps people negotiate these times. In his latest offering, Bob Whitesel talks about millennial leadership for the church—a way to lead the people of God to respond missionally to issues that emerge out of the postmodern milieu. Bob Whitesel has proven to be a reliable, clear-thinking, practical guide for complicated tasks such as this. If these fast-paced, ever-changing, unpredictable times have you as church leaders a bit disoriented, this book may provide just the right handles to regain your footing."
—Al Tizon, Associate Professor of Holistic Ministry at
Palmer Theological Seminary and director of Word & Deed Network
of the Evangelicals for Social Action

"As usual, Bob Whitesel brings fresh new insights to frustrating old problems for local church leaders. In this refreshing book, readers will find important keys to managing the complexities of both the 'organism' and the 'organization' of the contemporary church."
—Charles Arn, author, speaker, and president, Church Growth, Inc.

"Leading churches today is an even more complex challenge that it was in 'the good old days.' Bob Whitesel's fertile imagination merges perennial leadership wisdom with contemporary perspectives and metaphors to produce a very engaging resource. I hope this text influences the future of thousands of churches."
—George G. Hunter III, Dean and Distinguish Professor, Emeritus, School
of World Mission and Evangelism, Asbury Theological Seminary

"Dr. Whitesel in *Organix: Signs of Leadership in a Changing Church* gives wise insight and practical principles about millennial leadership. Whitesel's years of teaching, study, and practice come forth very clearly in this book. I was impressed by the book's freshness, clarity, and layout. Great job!"
—Joel Comiskey, Ph.D., president of Joel Comiskey Group,
www.joelcomiskeygroup.com

"Tired of cliché books, opinions, and theories on leadership? Organix is based on quantifiable research and qualified conclusions written by a man skilled in the art of both. For those interested in leading by faith not fear, through cooperation not control, and into a future not constrained by the past, this book will light the way."
—Dr. Mark DeYmaz, Pastor, Mosaic Church of Central Arkansas; Author,
Building a Healthy Multi-ethnic Church and Ethnic Blends

"Dr. Whitesel's well-researched book is lucid and forward thinking, providing a complete toolkit for the relational, spiritually impassioned church using images from graffiti to information clouds. He organizes and visualizes this toolkit in such a way that even distracted pastors or leaders will remember both the parts and the whole. It is one of the rare books that saves its best chapters for last. I highly recommend that churches work through this book together, reflecting upon their vision, their actual behavior within their cultures, and their call."

—Reverend Rebecca Ver Straten-McSparran, Founding pastor, Tribe of Los Angeles; Director, L.A. Film Studies Center

"American society is undergoing dramatic changes and so, too, is the church. Bob Whitesel offers an insightful and well-researched recipe for the cultivation of authentic, organic leadership for this new reality. This book functions not only as a helpful guide for a new generation of millennial leaders but also as a wake-up call and transformational challenge for all those clergy still embracing a 'modern' approach to congregational leadership."

—Scott Thumma, PhD, author of *The Other 80 Percent: Turning Your Church's Spectators into Active Participants*, Hartford Institute for Religion Research, Hartford Seminary

ORGANIX

Signs of Leadership in a Changing Church

Bob Whitesel

Abingdon Press
Nashville

ORGANIX
SIGNS OF LEADERSHIP
IN A CHANGING CHURCH

Copyright © 2011 by Abingdon Press

All rights reserved.

This book is printed on recycled, acid-free paper.

Library of Congress Cataloging-in-Publication Data

Whitesel, Bob.
  Organix : signs of leadership in a changing church / Bob Whitesel.
    p.   cm.
  Includes bibliographical references (p.   ).
  ISBN 978-1-4267-4082-4 (book - pbk. / trade pbk. : alk. paper)   1. Christian leadership.   I. Title.
  BV652.1.W453 2011
  253—dc23

                        2011025395

All scripture quotations unless noted otherwise are taken from the New Revised Standard Version of the Bible, copyright 1989, Division of Christian Education of the National Council of the Churches of Christ in the United States of America. Used by permission. All rights reserved.

Scripture quotations marked AMP are taken from the Amplified® Bible, Copyright © 1954, 1958, 1962, 1964, 1965, 1987 by The Lockman Foundation. Used by permission. (www.Lockman.org)

Scripture quotations noted CEB are from the Common English Bible. Copyright © 2011 by the Common English Bible. All rights reserved. Used by permission. www.commonenglishbible.com.

Scripture quotations marked KJV are from The Authorized (King James) Version. Rights in the Authorized Version in the United Kingdom are vested in the Crown. Reproduced by permission of the Crown's patentee, Cambridge University Press.

Scripture quotations from *THE MESSAGE*. Copyright © by Eugene H. Peterson 1993, 1994, 1995, 1996, 2000, 2001, 2002. Used by permission of NavPress Publishing Group.

Såcripture quotations marked (NIV) are taken from the Holy Bible, New International Version®, NIV®. Copyright © 1973, 1978, 1984, 2011 by Biblica, Inc.™ Used by permission of Zondervan. All rights reserved worldwide. www.zondervan.com. The "NIV" and "New International Version" are trademarks registered in the United States Patent and Trademark Office by Biblica, Inc.™

Scripture quotations marked "NKJV™" are taken from the New King James Version®. Copyright © 1982 by Thomas Nelson, Inc. Used by permission. All rights reserved.

11 12 13 14 15 16 17 18 19 20—10 9 8 7 6 5 4 3 2 1

MANUFACTURED IN THE UNITED STATES OF AMERICA

The "O" represents a prevailing concern for "others."

 Theta, the first letter of the Greek word *theos* stresses that "God" is the source of the burden for others and provides the power to help them.

 The prescription for health is a fitting descriptor for a millennial emphasis on first addressing the spiritual and physical health of leaders.

 A stylized *g* for "graffiti" illustrates the risky, colorful, and artful collages that help define millennial organizations.

 The "recycle" symbol stresses that millennial leaders recycle places, experiences, and people rather than discard them.

 An *n* represents emerging networks that connect people more quickly, efficiently, precisely, and continuously.

 The *i* embodies a human form and emphasizes "incarnation," a going "in the flesh" to serve others rather than sending surrogates.

 The Jerusalem cross with a ✖ in each quadrant represents four types of measurement observed in Jerusalem (Acts 2:42-47), which at their core point to Christ's work on the cross.

To Dr. Eddie Gibbs,
Scholar, fellow wayfarer, and friend

CONTENTS

FOREWORD

There are many voices and opinions today on church leadership, missional church, reasons for church growth, reasons for church shrinkage, modern church, postmodern church, post-postmodern church, video venues, and multisite churches. The list goes on and on. I actually love that there is so much thinking and innovation happening out there, but it can be confusing. What is confusing is knowing what is theory about all these various things and what is reality. You can read about missional churches and leadership, but the question I always want to know is, Is what I am reading theoretical? Or is it based on actual research and practice of what God is actually doing (or not doing) in churches? There is a big difference between the two. Opinions are easy. But what is important to me is this: how are these opinions actually taking form in the church? And are disciples of Jesus being made as a result of these ideas and theories?

One person I know who doesn't just write theory or opinions is Bob Whitesel. Bob has a lot of opinions, but they are based on careful research and interaction with churches and church leaders all across the country. The first time I met Bob was after he came to our church unannounced and was "spying" as a scout to see what we were doing. I found it wonderful that Bob came more or less undercover. He got to see us function as a church with no awareness that we had someone there who was writing about us. Later on he and I talked, and since then, he has visited our church multiple times.

What I know is that Bob does research, and then it is the research that shapes what he writes. He doesn't make opinions before he researches. And because Bob has visited and met with leaders of all different types of churches across the country, he has an incredible amount of insight. Insight that I know I really appreciate and want to learn from.

So as you read this book, you can be assured that you are reading not mere theory or someone's opinions. You are reading opinions and guidance about leadership and practical insights that are based on real examples. Most of us don't get to talk to as many leaders as Bob has or visit as many churches as he has. I know I read everything that Bob writes as his experience and research accelerate my learning tremendously. Learning is so important because leaders are learners. And this book is a learning experience.

As we live in our fast-changing world, I am glad Bob has written a book that focuses on ways to lead. It isn't easy. *Organix: Signs of Leadership in a Changing Church* gives us hope and insight about how not to shrink back because of how fast-changing it is, but instead to boldly lead and explore ways to lead. This is practical insight from a leadership scout who has been scanning the land and

reports to us what is happening and how to lead the church in ways that I believe
Jesus would be proud of as he entrusts us with the sacred role of shepherding and
leading his people.

Dan Kimball
Cofounder, Vintage Faith Church, Santa Cruz, California

ACKNOWLEDGMENTS

My journey into the study of millennial leadership began when Gary McIntosh sat on our couch and reflected on how leadership is changing. *But into what?* I wondered. Within months I found myself back at my alma mater, Fuller Theological Seminary, in Pasadena, California, working on a second doctorate that would enable me to lead churches to health and growth in the emerging millennial landscape. Along my journey I studied leaders such as Dan Kimball, Karen Ward, Al Tizon, Mike Breen, Doug Pagitt, Soong-Chan Rah, Aaron Norwood, Bil Cornelius, and a host of others, who became not just my focus, but also my friends.

Along this journey I have been thankful for my mentors at Fuller Theological Seminary, including Eddie Gibbs, Gary McIntosh, Ryan Bolger, and Richard Peace, along with Asbury Seminary's George "Chuck" Hunter III. An unexpected honor was to receive for my research the Donald A. McGavran Award for Outstanding Scholarship in Church Growth from Fuller Seminary's faculty.

I am also appreciative for the local support I received from my friends President Henry Smith, Provost David Wright, and Deans Jim Fuller and Ken Schenck, along with Professor Russ Gunsalus and Vice President Wayne Schmidt. In addition, I learned much from my colleagues in the field of consulting and church growth, discussing leadership case studies with Ed Stetzer, Charles "Chip" Arn, Tom Harper, Bob Logan, and Carl George.

My students at Wesley Seminary at Indiana Wesleyan University provided a final and very important assessment of my work. Most of my students are millennial leaders, and they offered important sounding boards as a sequence of icons emerged that would represent their leadership practices.

But I never could have finished this book without the love, prayers, and support of Rebecca, my wife of thirty-six years; our daughters and their husbands, Breanna, Mark; Kelly, Tory; Corrie, Dave; Ashley and C. J.; and the effervescence of our grandchildren Cate, Kai, Abbey, and Caprina.

And finally, these journeys into emerging leadership would have been impossible without an unseen hand of guidance and strength from my heavenly Father. Ever since I experienced the grandeur and consequence of his mission, participating in the *missio Dei* has been my passion.

Bob Whitesel, DMin, PhD
Wesley Seminary at Indiana Wesleyan University
www.BobWhitesel.com
James 1:26-27

INTRODUCTION TO

Θ℞GΔNIϪ

SIGNS OF LEADERSHIP IN A CHANGING CHURCH

*An organism, not an organization; a network, not a bureaucracy;
a community, not a building or institution . . .
because following a person is different than fitting into an
institution.*

—*A church planter in his report to the denomination*[1]

A NEW APPROACH TO LEADERSHIP IS EMERGING

A new approach to leadership is emerging, championed by younger leaders and taking hold in organizations that are connecting with people under the age of thirty-five. The leadership attitudes of these younger leaders vary greatly from their parents' leadership style. This book offers three distinctive features to help the reader understand these emerging leadership practices:

1. A sequence of icons aids in memory retention of these emerging leadership practices.[2]
2. Case-study research based on analysis and/or interviews with hundreds of pastors, seminary students, client churches, and young organizational leaders provides a real-world foundation for conclusions.
3. These strategies are written for leaders young and old, as well as for lay volunteers and professional clergy.

   a. Emerging leaders can see what other young leaders are doing.

   b. Leaders who have operated under an older paradigm can now look into this promising approach to leadership, and use it to connect with those under thirty-five years of age.

1

MILLENNIAL LEADERSHIP

This new style of leadership roughly coincides with the two decades before the start of the new millennium (2001) and the years since (that is, 1980–today). Some have called this style *emerging leadership*,[3] and others have labeled it *postmodern leadership*.[4] Each label has shortcomings. *Emerging* is not a good descriptor, for one day it will have emerged. *Postmodern leadership* is a contentious designation because some leaders take issue—and with some validity—to certain aspects of postmodernism.[5]

Since this leadership has emerged in the postmodern-influenced era surrounding the new millennium, *millennial leadership* produces a better and less contentious descriptor. And the term *millennial leadership* has been growing in popularity in both the church and the business worlds as a fitting term for this new outlook.[6] Although it has its limitations, *millennial leadership* is the best means to refer to a leadership style that is growing in popularity and effectiveness in the decades immediately before and after the start of the new millennium.

MILLENNIAL LEADERSHIP COMPARED TO MODERN LEADERSHIP

If a new millennial style of leadership is emerging, what came before it? The answer is a more autocratic style of leadership. Millennial leaders intend to discard portions and adapt other portions of this older model. An investigation into the differences between modern and millennial leadership is, in fact, the focus of this book. But let's start with an introductory and historical comparison.

Modern leadership coincides with the so-called modern era that began with the Enlightenment (ca. 1650) and continued into the early twentieth century. The style of leadership most associated with this modern era is an authoritarian command and control leadership that arose with the Industrial Revolution (ca. 1800).[7]

Millennial leadership first surfaced in the early twentieth century as a reaction against the autocratic leadership style that went before it. Millennial leaders are usually more collaborative, vision motivated, consensus building, people sensitive, and process driven. Harrison Monarth states:

> The archaic command-and-control approach is shelved in favor of a culture in which managers admit they don't have all the answers and will implement and support team decisions. This means managers become the architects of that team dynamic rather than the all-seeing purveyors of answers. The result is a culture of trust and employee empowerment that is safe.[8]

Figure A.1 highlights basic differences between modern leadership and the millennial leadership that has come after it. In the following chapters we will see that modern leadership is a style that is waning in influence today but is still embraced by many leaders over the age of thirty-five.

Figure A.1. An introductory comparison of modern and millennial leadership

Features	Modern Leadership[9]	Millennial Leadership
Height of influence	Industrial Revolution to 1960s	1920s to today[10]
Primary leadership technique	Command and control[11]	Vision and consensus[12]
Motivation	Outcome oriented[13]	People oriented[14]
Age of typical leaders who employ it	Born in or before 1974	Born in or after 1975

Though figure A.1 is a brief comparison of the eras and ages of modern and millennial leaders, these intervals are not rigid. Therefore, the fourth feature is labeled "age of *typical* leaders." Many people born in a modern generation may gravitate toward a millennial leadership style, as does this author. Therefore, do not regard figure A.1 as indicating inflexible boundaries, but see it as indicative of periods of influence by each leadership style.

To help the reader further understand the differences between modern and millennial leadership, each chapter of this book introduces one of eight leadership aspects, contrasting modern and millennial approaches to each aspect. The end result is a better understanding of both types of leadership, the effectiveness of each, and when each is warranted.

LEADERSHIP INFLUENCES ON GENERATIONS

Figure A.2 illustrates how this changeover to millennial leadership began roughly in the middle of Generation X. This figure also shows how older generations (including older parts of Generation X) usually lean toward modern leadership practices.[15]

Figure A.2. Modern and millenial leaderships' influence on generations[16]

Years of Birth	Age (2011)	Customary Label[17]
1945 and before	66+	*Builders:* They built the U.S. into a worldwide economic power.
1946–64	47–65	*(Baby) boomers:* A boom in births occurred after WWII.
1965–83	28–46	*Generation X:* The boomers labeled them for their perceived nihilistic outlook.
(1965–74)	(37–46)	*Leading Edge Gen X:* A subset of Gen X, they mirror boomers more than they do Millennials.

 Modern Leadership

 Millennial Leadership ▼

(1975–83)	(28–36)	*Millennial Gen X:* Another subset of Gen X, this group mirrors the Millennials more than boomers.
1984–2002	9–27	*Millennial Generation:* Formerly called Gen Y, they are the first electronically netted generation.

A BRIEF HISTORY OF ORGANIC MILLENNIAL LEADERSHIP

The term *organic* has often been attached to the idea of millennial leadership. This is a fitting term to describe the inter-reliant nature of healthy organizations. Yet many people mistakenly believe organic leadership and organic churches to be new concepts. The idea of an organic organization, and even an organic church, has been used in the fields of political science, sociology, and church leadership for some time. Let's begin to investigate organic leadership by studying what great thinkers have said about it.

ORGANIC LEADERSHIP IN POLITICAL SCIENCE

Antonio Gramsci coined the term *organic intellectual*, which remains a popular term to describe a leader who can explain difficult concepts to the average person. Leaders who have been cited as organic intellectuals include Martin Luther, John Milton, John Wesley, Vladimir Lenin, C. S. Lewis, J. R. R. Tolkien, Martin Luther King Jr., Ronald Reagan, and Bill Clinton, among others.[18]

ORGANIC LEADERSHIP IN SOCIOLOGY

James F. Engel described an organic organization as having five attributes: (1) a unified group, (2) having special talents, (3) growing via disciplined planning, (4) helping those within the organization, and (5) helping those outside the organization.[19]

ORGANIC LEADERSHIP IN CHURCHES

Though the term *organic church* has recently become popular,[20] it has been used to describe churches for some time. Howard Snyder (1975) described a healthy church as a "charismatic organism," which he defined as empowered by God and with most of its people involved in ministry.[21] Charles Singletary (1988) described organic church growth including "all sorts of sub-groups, small groups and networks so vital to the assimilation, nurture and mobilization of the membership. Organic growth involves the leadership and shepherding network of a church."[22] Alan Roxburgh (1998) described the Free Churches of the Reformation as a "recovery of an organic, lay lead church seeking to restore pre-Constantinian images of church and leadership."[23]

Neil Cole defines an organic church in more communal terms and as a reaction to the overorganized church. Cole states that an organic organization is "not defined by a meeting...[but] when we do have meetings, we do not presume to have an agenda, but to gather, listen to God and one another."[24] Frank Viola follows this communal emphasis, stating "an organic church is a group of Jesus followers who are discovering how to live by Divine life together and who are expressing that life in a corporate way."[25] Viola said that he "takes his cue from [T. Austin] Sparks," who

> When I asked a group of students in Fort Wayne, Indiana, to define an organic organization, one pastor blurted out, "Organic means something that doesn't have artificial additives, something that doesn't have preservatives."

reacted strongly against the overorganized church of his day, avowing, "God's way and law of fullness is that of organic life.... This means that everything comes from the inside. Function, order, and fruit issue from this law of life within.... Organized Christianity has entirely reversed this order."[26]

5

ORGANIC LEADERSHIP IN THE BIBLE

Although congregations are not described as organic churches in the Bible, the idea of a church as an organism of interdependent and inter-reliant parts is repeatedly emphasized in Scriptures such as Romans 12, 1 Corinthians 12, Ephesians 1, and Colossians 1. In 1 Corinthians, for instance, Paul insisted that the church's leaders emphasize this organic nature in order to unite their divided congregation.

WHAT IT IS NOT

Regrettably, some people are not familiar with this history and think an organic organization is equivalent to an organization without "additives." When I asked a group of students in Fort Wayne, Indiana, to define an organic organization, one pastor blurted out, "Organic means something that doesn't have artificial additives, something that doesn't have preservatives." Still, this is a modern misperception, perhaps driven by organic products in our food stores. Foods grown naturally without additives are often called "organic foods" to differentiate them from products with artificial additives. Yet *organic* does not simply mean something lacking artificial additives. We shall see shortly there are four conditions that define an organism, and any food (or organization) could be lacking outside additives and still not fit the definition. Therefore, the popular belief that *organic* means "unadulterated" misses the point and should be abandoned.

> *Organic* does not simply mean something lacking artificial additives.

From even this short overview it should be clear that organic leadership has to do with being closely integrated, effectively organized, and healthy. Thus, to be labeled organic, an organization and/or leadership should display the four conditions of a living organism.

THE FOUR CONDITIONS OF ORGANICS

Mary Jo Hatch is one of the leading management thinkers and scholars on organic organizations. She has studied hundreds of organizations and believes there are four root metaphors found in organic organizations and organic leadership.[27]

CONDITION 1: ORGANIC DEPENDENCY ON ITS ENVIRONMENT

Hatch writes, "An organic organization is dependent on its environment for the resources that support life." By this Hatch means that just like a living organism, an organic organization realizes that it needs those around it to sustain it. It is not a closed, self-contained system. It is rather a system that is closely connected to those it serves. An organic church is, in part, an organization that is connected intimately and tenaciously to those outside the organization. While many churches today are self-contained microcultures, an organic organization reaches out to and connects with its environment because it is designed to do so.[28]

> An organic church is, in part, an organization that is connected intimately and tenaciously to those outside the organization.

CONDITION 2: ORGANIC HARMONY AMONG THE PARTS

Hatch emphasizes that in an organic organization all parts are needed and they work together harmoniously. The Bible repeatedly uses this metaphor to describe a church as one body of many (contributing) parts (1 Cor. 12:12, 14, 20, 27), where "each of us has one body with many members, and these members do not all have the same function, so in Christ we, though many, form one body, and each member belongs to all the others" (Rom. 12:4-5 NIV), with the result that the "body of Christ may be built up until we all reach unity in the faith and in the knowledge of the Son of God" (Eph. 4:12-13 NIV).

CONDITION 3: ORGANIC ADAPTION TO THE SURROUNDINGS

This means that an organic organization adapts to different environments. Hatch emphasizes that organic organizations realize that adaption to a new and changing environment requires ongoing change. The organic organization expects change, plans for it, and accomplishes it. This is at the core of what it means to be an organism.

CONDITION 4: ORGANIC UNIQUENESS FROM OTHER ORGANISMS

Mary Jo Hatch reminds us that different species live in different environments and respond differently.[29] What works in one organic organization may not work in another organization because each organizational context is unique. While modern leadership tries to create irrefutable laws, rules, and statutes that should apply across con-

> Organic organizations realize that adaption to a new and changing environment requires ongoing change. The organic organization expects change, plans for it, and accomplishes it.

texts, organic leadership recognizes that each entity has a unique environment. Thus, organic leadership creates not laws or rules but principles and theories that must be applied indigenously by local leaders.[30]

For any organization, even a church, to be organic, it must live out all of the above conditions. In this book each chapter will contrast how these elements are lived out differently among modern and millennial leaders.[31]

WHAT DO THE ORGANIX SYMBOLS REPRESENT?

Each letter or icon of *organix* represents a different broad attribute of millennial leadership and contrasts how modern leadership and millennial leadership tackle each attribute differently. Icons aid with memory retention. Figure A.3 is a one-sentence introduction to each.

Figure A.3. A one-sentence introduction to organix

The "O" represents a prevailing concern for "others."

Theta, the first letter of the Greek word *theos* stresses that "God" is the source of the burden for others and provides the power to help them.

The prescription for health is a fitting descriptor for a millennial emphasis on first addressing the spiritual and physical health of leaders.

A stylized *g* for "graffiti" illustrates the risky, colorful, and artful collages that help define millennial organizations.

The "recycle" symbol stresses that millennial leaders recycle places, experiences, and people rather than discard them.

An *n* represents emerging networks that connect people more quickly, efficiently, precisely, and continuously.

The *i* embodies a human form and emphasizes "incarnation," a going "in the flesh" to serve others rather than sending surrogates.

The Jerusalem cross with a ✖ in each quadrant represents four types of measurement observed in Jerusalem (Acts 2:42-47), which at their core point to Christ's work on the cross.

WHY THE *X* IN ORGANIX?

There is a millennial propensity to alter the spelling of words to create distinction with like-sounding letters. It is in part to use such personalization that an *x* was substituted for the *c* in organix. Chapter 8's use of an icon of a cross reminds us who actually accomplishes the mission.

WHAT ARE WE LEADING?
(THE MISSIONAL TASK)

But what exactly is this divine and enormous task to which Christian leadership is called? It can be summed up in the Latin phrase *missio Dei*, "the mission of God."[32]

The *missio Dei* is God's mission to reintroduce himself and restore fellowship with his wayward offspring. It emphasizes that "mission is not primarily an activity of the church, but an attribute of God. God is a missionary God."[33] John Flett explains, "The Father sent his Son and Spirit into the world, and this act reveals his 'sending' being. God remains active today in reconciling the world to himself and sends his community to participate in the mission."[34] William Willimon summarizes,

> It is the nature of this God to reach out.... A chief defining content of this good news of God (1 Thess. 2:1, 8, 9; Rom. 1:1) is this sort of relentless reach. This God has a gregarious determination to draw all things unto God's self (John 12:23).... The church exists not for itself, but rather to sign, signal, and embody God's intentions for the whole world. God is going to get back what belongs to God. God's primary means of accomplishing this is through the church.[35]

Specifically because this *missio Dei* is God's work to reestablish a relationship with his offspring, it is presumptuous and incorrect to say that other offspring have this mission. Only God has such a grand mission because only he can accomplish it. Yet he enlists human participation in the task, as Jesus emphasized, "My food...is to do the will of him who sent me and to finish his work" (John 4:34 NIV). It is best to say humans "participate" in the *missio Dei*, assisting God as he calls and equips us for his extraordinary task of reconnecting people to a loving, seeking God.

> "God has a gregarious determination to draw all things unto God's self.... The church exists not for itself, but rather to sign, signal, and embody God's intentions for the whole world."
> —William Willimon

Humanity is created by God with a purpose in mind. Matthew 28:19 tells us that purpose is to help people discover and reconnect with their creator

God.[36] But why would God choose such fallible humans to experience and even participate in this magnificent mission? The answer is that God dearly desires fellowship with humans (James 2:23; Isa. 41:8; John 1:1-3) and has created us in his divine image, which draws us back to him and he to us (Gen. 1:26-27).[37]

THE STRUCTURE OF EACH CHAPTER

To help readers apply the lessons of this book and better participate in the *missio Dei*, each chapter has the same recurring sections:

SECTION 1: STORIES OF ENCOUNTERS BETWEEN MODERN AND MILLENNIAL LEADERS

Each chapter begins with a short story, drawn from real-life experiences but with the names changed and stories combined to respect the anonymity of client and student congregations. These stories underscore the differences between modern and millennial leaders' approaches.

SECTION 2: EXAMPLES OF MODERN LEADERSHIP

The story sets the stage for an investigation of modern leadership practices gleaned from interviews, case studies, and research. A chart depicts distinctive modern leadership actions.

SECTION 3: EXAMPLES OF MILLENNIAL LEADERSHIP

Next, examples, principles, and insights illustrate how millennial leaders react differently, and often more helpfully and holistically, than modern leaders. A chart compares three attributes of millennial leadership with three corresponding elements of modern leadership discussed in section 2.[38]

SECTION 4: HOW TO CULTIVATE MILLENNIAL LEADERSHIP

The fourth section of each chapter is the most important. This section provides step-by-step actions that can help leaders grow in millennial understandings and attitudes.

SECTION 5: QUESTIONS FOR PERSONAL AND/OR GROUP STUDY

At the end of each chapter are questions suitable for personal study and group reflection. These questions are especially helpful for leadership teams that are leading new churches, attempting to turn around existing churches, or studying the principles and practices of tomorrow's leadership.

SECTION 6: NOTES AND RESOURCES TO DIG DEEPER

The reader may wish to investigate some topics and themes further. At the end of the book I have provided chapter notes on foundational research that can lead the reader to the original sources.

THE PURPOSE OF THIS BOOK

This introduction began with a quotation by a young church leader who described his church to denominational leaders as "an organism, not an organization; a network, not a bureaucracy; a community, not a building or institution . . . because following a person is different than fitting into an institution."[39] The purpose of this book is to help today's leaders understand such thinking, to provide an overview of future leadership, and to suggest practices a leader can employ to move toward more effective leadership. Yet it is not my intention to offer these leadership insights to grow bigger egos or bigger churches. My purpose is to learn how God's Holy Spirit is moving among Christian leaders today so that the body of Christ may better participate in the *missio Dei*, God's mission to reunite with his creation.

If the gospel we hear is not good news to the poor and freedom for the oppressed, then it is not the gospel of Jesus, no matter how many followers there are.

—*Shane Claiborne, co-founder of the Potter Street Community*[1]

	Modern Leadership	Millennial Leadership
O **Others**	1. Others and their allegiance drive the leader.	1. Others and their needs drive the leader.
	2. Others are resources to be managed.	2. Others are souls to be nurtured.
	3. Others are led by vision.	3. Others are led by integrity.

WHERE DOES MILLENNIAL LEADERSHIP START?

Leadership is a interdependent mixture of intuition, experience, and inspiration. And precisely because of this extraordinary fusion a starting place becomes difficult, if not impossible, to assign. An easy entry point is one of the most common behaviors of millennial leaders, represented first by an O in chapter 1, and then by a Θ (Greek: *theta*) in chapter 2.[2]

STAYING POWER

As the weekend retreat ended, two influential elders of Clarkston Church[3] drew me aside. "We've decided to call for Pastor Gordon's removal," began Julian. "It's not that we haven't tried," continued Rosa, "but Gordon is single-minded and stubborn. This weekend has been one long sales job. He's just trying to get us to buy his vision for a new building." Within a week I received an e-mail announcing that the elders were bringing Gordon before the council for removal. As I thought back to my two years working as a consultant with this church, I marveled how quickly things had changed.

Two years ago, Gordon was fresh out of seminary and following a popular pastor at Clarkston Church named Joan. Joan had turned a dying church of forty attendees into a growing congregation of more than 120 worshipers. Tapped as her successor, Gordon had graduated from seminary after forty years of running an investment program for his denomination. This was his first pastorate, and I remember the passion he brought to his new vocation.

Two years later, the enthusiasm was gone, replaced by a spirit of pessimism and duress. "They wanted me to change things," recalled Gordon in a phone conversation later that day. "And they gave me free rein. So I took it. They are forgetting that we grew a lot my first year."

"But last year was different," I interjected.

"Sure, they've got their own unrealistic ideas about how things should be done," continued Gordon. "They don't have the training. I do! They saw my way worked the first year. They should have listened to me last year too."

Rosa, in her mid-seventies, and Julian, in his early thirties, formed an odd partnership aligned against Gordon. "We both feel that Gordon won't support our ideas to help townspeople," began Julian. "We're the poorest area in the county, and Gordon just wants to focus on building a new sanctuary."

"He's afraid the new building won't be built if we use our money to help the needy here in Clarkston," added Rosa. "He's forgotten our history as a denomination that looks after the poor." Later Julian summarized: "Gordon is getting his ideas from what bigger churches are doing in bigger cities and the stuff he learned in seminary. He doesn't listen to our input. But we're more familiar with what people need around here because we live here. And he still doesn't."

Gordon recently confided, "Look, Bob, I've got three years until I can retire with some denominational benefits. No one wants to hire a pastor my age. So help me convince my board to do things my way for just three more years. Then I can retire. The church can hire someone else to beat up, and everyone will be happy."[4] Gordon didn't have three years. He barely had three months.

O STANDS FOR "OTHERS"

Among tomorrow's leaders there is a passion not for themselves or their own accomplishments but for helping those most in need: the underprivileged, disadvantaged, and deprived. To understand this empathy, let us first look at what modern leadership has evolved into, for this will help us understand the millennial reaction.

THREE PERILS OF MODERN LEADERSHIP REGARDING OTHERS

	Modern Leadership	Millennial Leadership
O **Others**	1. Others and their allegiance drive the leader.	1. Others and their needs drive the leader.
	2. Others are resources to be managed.	2. Others are souls to be nurtured.
	3. Others are led by vision.	3. Others are led by integrity.

MODERN PERIL 1: OTHERS AND THEIR ALLEGIANCE DRIVE THE LEADER.

In the modern leadership world, numerous books extol leadership as the pinnacle of human ambition.[5] And many of these books measure the leader's success in terms of how many follow her or him.[6] Harvard leadership professor Barbara Kellerman said, "The modern leadership industry, now a quarter-century old, is built on the proposition that leaders matter a great deal and followers hardly at all."[7] Another leadership writer warned, "Many in leadership positions today believe that their leadership should be measured by how many people look to or depend on them."[8] A result has been that modern leaders often measure success by the number of followers who meet the needs of the organization (or meet the needs of the leader).

> "The modern leadership industry, now a quarter-century old, is built on the proposition that leaders matter a great deal and followers hardly at all."
> —Barbara Kellerman

Subtle clues abound in the church world, such as when the leader's name is proudly displayed on church signage and in advertisements. Doing this builds a church on a person rather than a community and inadvertently fosters a cult of personality. Another damaging result is that the non-church community can view the leader as the most important person in the congregation. Leaders exacerbate this problem when they use possessive terms: "My church is located on Second Street," "*my* board does this," or "*my* youth pastor does that." Ownership, self-importance, and dominance are the subtle insinuation, announcing that if you want to be part of this church, you should view yourself as a possession subject to an earthly person rather than to Christ.

MODERN PERIL 2: OTHERS ARE RESOURCES TO BE MANAGED.

A type of management arose during the Industrial Revolution that valued workers for their labor, not for their worth. In 1913 Frederick Taylor described this as "scientific management"[9] and famously intoned, "The worker must be trimmed to fit the job."[10] To legitimize his conclusions, he conducted time and motion studies to show how jobs could be better performed at the workers' expense. Modern managers embraced this research to prove that by manipulating people, work can be done faster and more efficiently (oftentimes, however, at the expense of the workers' input, self-worth, and dignity).

The human resource movement rose in reaction,[11] where fulfilling a worker's needs and aspirations was seen as equally important. But this approach came to view humans as little more than just another "resource" to be allocated, deployed, and/or deleted.[12] After a century of these trends, modern leadership often became too focused on propping up the organization and/or the leader at the expense of the people it managed or served.[13]

An autocratic leadership model emerged in many churches that paralleled the business world where all major decisions passed through a central leader.[14] Known in the business world as the sole-proprietorship model, this is a mom-and-pop business approach where all-important decisions pass through "pop," the figurehead leader. In the church this figurehead is usually a professional clergyperson. But this creates a bottleneck in the decision-making process, stalling growth for several reasons. First, growth stalls because of the time needed to get a decision approved by a senior leader. Second, volunteers may feel their input is not trusted because the volunteers must "convince" a figurehead, far removed from the work, of the merit of the volunteers' ideas. Third, the figurehead will often respond by using past experience to criticize the new idea. Leaders become trapped in an experience trap and dismiss the innovations of others.[15] Volunteers such as Rosa and Julian often feel they do not measure up to the leader's expertise. They feel unappreciated, unacknowledged, and eventually a commodity.

MODERN PERIL 3: OTHERS ARE LED BY VISION.

"Everyone keeps talking about vision statements. They spend too much time on these things. Great Commission, Matthew 28:19, that's our mission!" said Leonard Sweet.[16]

An abundance of books today deal with how to fine-tune a church's vision.[17]

Yet very little church growth occurs because of a more accurate vision or mission statement. Rather, I have observed churches preoccupied with scrutinizing the language of their statements. Wrangling over words in our statements preoccupies congregations with the minutia of church language, disregarding the important language of good deeds to a non-church community.

Similarly, when conflict arises (as it will in the church), a leader may be tempted to retreat to her or his vision, using it as a weapon to demote the vision of others. Often, the leader may try to win over others by scheduling a vision retreat, which more aptly might be called a "vision-selling retreat." Then, if others are not won over, leaders such as Pastor Gordon may focus on Jesus' warning that "my Father is the gardener. He cuts off every branch in me that bears no fruit" (John 15:1-2 NIV).[18] Usually, this indicates the leader wants certain people (who don't agree with the leader) to exit the congregation, which in a worst-case scenario can lead to congregants being forced out. This can be exacerbated if the leader has come to see one's vision as superseding any corporate vision. This malady allows the leader to dismiss others' foresight for ministry.[19] Such a leader develops a type of people blindness.[20]

THREE ATTITUDES OF MILLENNIAL LEADERSHIP REGARDING OTHERS

	Modern Leadership	Millennial Leadership
O **Others**	1. Others and their allegiance drive the leader.	1. Others and their needs drive the leader.
	2. Others are resources to be managed.	2. Others are souls to be nurtured.
	3. Others are led by vision.	3. Others are led by integrity.

MILLENNIAL ATTITUDE 1: OTHERS AND THEIR NEEDS DRIVE THE LEADER.

Tomorrow's leaders have a healthy reaction to what modern leadership has become. One such reaction is a growing emphasis on serving others. But a parallel result can be that the leader feels overwhelmed by others' needs. At first glance, being overwhelmed by the needs of others might seem a detriment to leadership. But actually, this is a healthy and honest appraisal of the dire situation of so many in need.

Emerging leaders bemoan the unmet needs in the world. Their parents lived in a world of utopian promises. They had banished the Axis powers of World War II. Science and hard work seemed to be making the world a safe, ideal, and better place. But Generation X and the Millennials who followed saw no such grand hope. Despite their parents' best intentions to create a "perfect world," an emerging dislocation has divided rich from poor, wives from husbands, and residents from refugees. Generation X and the Millennials sense this is due to the failure of their parents' unrealistic perfectionism and overconfidence. They seek to help others rise above this morass.[21]

> Despite their parents' best intentions to create a "perfect world," an emerging dislocation has divided rich from poor, wives from husbands, and residents from refugees. Generation X and the Millennials sense this is due to the failure of their parents' unrealistic perfectionism and overconfidence.

It is little surprise that millennial leaders embrace a solidarity with Jesus' anguish when he cried, "Jerusalem, Jerusalem, you who kill the prophets and stone those sent to you, how often I have longed to gather your children together, as a hen gathers her chicks under her wings, and you were not willing" (Matt. 23:37 NIV). They share empathy with Jesus when "he looked out over the crowds, his heart broke. So confused and aimless they were, like sheep with no shepherd. 'What a huge harvest!' he said to his disciples. 'How few workers! On your knees and pray for harvest hands!'" (Matt. 9:36-38 THE MESSAGE).

The millennial leader understands that one may need to relinquish his or her job and move on if this would better meet the burgeoning needs of others.[22] Millennial leaders do not cling to promises of pensions, monies invested, and so forth when the needs of others are at stake. The dire situation of persons in need motivates the emerging leader, not the opportunity for ministerial status, success, or security.

MILLENNIAL ATTITUDE 2: OTHERS ARE SOULS TO BE NURTURED.

At one time, there was a line of thinking that autocratic leaders could more effectively lead an organization than any other type of leader.[23] Churches led by autocrats will sometimes grow rapidly in times of crisis or hardship,[24] but in the long term rapid church decline often results through firings, unresolved conflict, lack of accountability, and group exits.[25] An autocratic leader can help a church survive a time of crisis, but once that crisis ends, the same autocratic attitude can rapidly drive down church growth.

Groundbreaking research in the 1930s demonstrated that successful leaders usually practice a style of "democratic" or "consensus-building" leadership.[26] Not surprisingly, millennial leaders prefer a consensus-building style of leadership. "We build from the bottom up, where people, not leaders, receive the most attention," one young leader in England told me. "Your generation builds from the top down, but that doesn't create health... or unity." Millennial leaders sense that if there is disagreement, a synthesis must be discovered.[27] Sometimes synthesis is fostered by choosing to disagree, other times by compromising, but always through a type of nurturing.

MILLENNIAL ATTITUDE 3: OTHERS ARE LED BY INTEGRITY.

Authenticity and relevance are important to millennial leaders.[28] Authenticity consists of consensus, honesty, and evaluation.[29] The "relevance revolution" connotes sensitivity to local needs and fair-minded goal setting.[30] Both ideas are important, but integrity holistically describes most of these aspects. Integrity carries the theme of honesty, respect, and consequence, all with a corresponding consistency.

Fostering such integrity usually begins with an honest self-appraisal. Does the leader think more of oneself than he or she should? Does the leader promote his or her identity or ideas? Jesus bristled when encountering such haughtiness, criticizing such religious leaders of his day for the same reasons he might censure modern leaders. To his disciples, Jesus warned:

> They [the Pharisees] package it [God's good news] in bundles of rules, loading you down like pack animals. They seem to take pleasure in watching you stagger under these loads, and wouldn't think of lifting a finger to help. Their lives are perpetual fashion shows, embroidered prayer shawls one day and flowery prayers the next. They love to sit at the head table at church dinners, basking in the most prominent positions, preening in the radiance of public flattery, receiving honorary degrees, and getting called "Doctor" and "Reverend." (Matt. 23:4-7 THE MESSAGE)

The leader's response should be an unpretentious and stable demeanor.[31] Dan Kimball, cofounder of Vintage Faith Church in Santa Cruz and a leading thinker within the emerging church movement, once worked with a church with a very senior pastor-centric leadership culture. Much of the decision making was top-down, and this negative experience led him to deemphasize his importance at the church he cofounded. Dan still has significant input at the new church, but he encourages an atmosphere of team leadership. "I saw how a senior leader can become the main personality in an organization, and I didn't want that to happen here," was Dan's summation. "I want us to lead as a team, connected to those we serve."[32]

NURTURING THE THREE ATTITUDES REGARDING OTHERS

NURTURING MILLENNIAL ATTITUDE 1: OTHERS AND THEIR NEEDS DRIVE THE LEADER.

1.a. *Live among them.* A key to knowing the needs of others is to experience life with them. Leaders who become out of touch with those they serve experience churches that stop growing in attendance.[33] For example, a church leader might move out of a church's neighborhood as the church attendance grows and live in a different culture (usually a more suburban and affluent one) than do the congregants. David McKenna states, "By leaving the ghetto behind, the church has implied that its mission is meaningless to the poor, the hopeless and the wretched—except when an ocean separates the church from the ghetto."[34] Yet by living among them, a leader not only demonstrates solidarity with the poor but also continues to experience (and understand) their needs firsthand. John M. Perkins, a sharecropper's son who went on to found a well-known urban ministry, believes living among the needy is key to understanding and not patronizing them. "Living involvement," Perkins said, "turns poor people from statistics into our friends."[35]

> "Living involvement turns poor people from statistics into our friends."
> —John M. Perkins

1.b. *Learn from and with them.* One hundred years of church growth study in North America have shown that the more seminary training pastors received, the less likely they were to grow a church.[36] The culprit was not the training, but how the pastor came to depend on other seminary-trained leaders for ideas and innovations.[37] In other words, as pastors went through seminary, they began leaning more on the advice of other seminarians rather than leaning on the input of the people they served.[38]

To prevent this, the millennial learner learns *from* and *with* the people he or she serves. Aaron Norwood, pastor of the Bridge in Phoenix, orchestrated the purchase of a homeless shelter for the church's office. Norwood feels that having their office and ministry meetings in a homeless shelter keeps them connected to those they serve. "I learn so much from my friends in our addiction recovery program about faithfulness, perseverance, humility, and vulnerability," states Norwood. "As I teach them each week from Scripture, they interpret it back in such a rich and challenging way. As a leader, this ongoing conversation with them grows me tremendously."[39]

Seminaries are discovering the power of two-way communication through student-congregant collaboration. Many seminaries offer online seminary education, so seminarians can remain in their local church and immediately apply the lessons they learn. And some seminaries even require students to get input and advice from local congregants on their homework before they turn in their assignments.[40] Such collaborative actions are required if leaders are to indigenize the lessons they study.

> As pastors went through seminary, they began leaning more on the advice of other seminarians rather than leaning on the input of the people they served.

1.c. *Prepare to "sift out" the bad since both good and bad are in each culture.* At the intersection of Christ and culture there is innovation, but also pitfalls. Canadian researcher Michael Fullan said, "Change is a double-edged sword. Its relentless pace these days runs us off our feet. Yet when things are unsettled, we can . . . create breakthroughs not possible in stagnant societies."[41] The millennial leader understands that close fellowship with people outside the church can foster new innovations, but also immoral enticements. God recognizes this, too, and God "acts redemptively with regard to culture, which includes judgment on some elements, but also affirmation in other areas, and a transformation of the whole."[42] The church leader is not just a student of Scripture, but also an assessor of the culture into which he or she must translate it.[43] This requires the millennial leader to sift out what goes against the good news and retain what affirms it. "What does the gospel have to say to our culture? What elements does it affirm, what does it reject, what does it accommodate, and which need to be redeemed?"[44]

NURTURING MILLENNIAL ATTITUDE 2: OTHERS ARE SOULS TO BE NURTURED.

2.a. *Look for and nurture the potential in others.* Millennial leadership has a keen sensitivity to the potential that God has put into all of his creation. Emerging leaders see God's people as created in the image of God (Gen. 1:27), which means they recognize that because the Holy Spirit is within laypeople too (Joel 2:28-29; Acts 2:17), it will be together that a vision forward is discovered and attained.

But millennial leaders recognize at the same time that everyone has shortcomings and struggles. Millennial leaders often develop organizational unity by retelling stories about how anyone, even someone with shortcomings, can rise to the top. Citing their own personal journeys, leaders recall that though unqualified, it was circumstance, opportunity, and the help of others that allowed them to succeed.[45] Thus in millennial churches, those who might be overlooked by a more dignified Christian community are welcomed, affirmed, and put to use. As a result, the millennial leader embraces the biblical admonition to

> take a good look, friends, at who you were when you got called into this life. I don't see many of "the brightest and the best" among you, not many influential, not many from high-society families. Isn't it obvious that God deliberately chose men and women that the culture overlooks and exploits and abuses, chose these

"nobodies" to expose the hollow pretensions of the "somebodies"?...Everything that we have—right thinking and right living, a clean slate and a fresh start—comes from God by way of Jesus Christ. (1 Cor. 1:26-31 *The Message*)

2.b. *See learning in others as important as their performance*. This is related to 2.a. The millennial leader will give followers permission to fail. As Jesus did not harangue but heartened his disciples when they failed (Matt. 17:16-19), so too the millennial leader recognizes that failure is a powerful learning tool (Matt. 17:20-21; Mark 9:29). The millennial leader is not frustrated, angry, or even surprised when failure occurs. He or she sees this not just as a part of life, but as an important element of instruction. In reflecting on his church's office in a homeless shelter, Aaron Norwood states, "I have a sense that the call of the spiritual leader must be helping people internalize that they are in fact 'His Masterpiece' (Eph. 2:10) and that their value is based on their Creator/Redeemer, and not results."[46]

2.c. *Solicit others' input*. An article titled "The Power Trip" in the *Wall Street Journal* pointed out while nice people are more likely to rise to power, once they get there, they become less compassionate.[47] The millennial leader instinctively recognizes the lure of a power trip and solicits frequent input from those one serves. Today's successful leaders regard followers' input as equal to their own insights.[48] Further, good leaders nurture "effective talkback" where followers are free to talk back to the leader with the truth.[49]

2.d. *Obtain followers who complement your weaknesses*. In the increasing complexity of the new millennium one person's insights and skills are inadequate for holistic leadership. Not surprisingly, millennial leaders surround themselves with people who complement them.[50] For example, if the leader is a strong visionary (sometimes called a "strategic leader"), he or she will often have a right-hand person who is good at number crunching (often called a "tactical leader").[51] If the leader is not a people person, a complementary colleague will relish interacting with others. In the complexity of the millennial world, team leadership is not an option, but a standard.[52] The author of *The Leadership Jump: Building Partnerships between Existing and Emerging Christian Leaders* summarizes: "We have begun to see that effectiveness depends less on the heroic leader and more on the collaborative efforts of a number of people to create a team environment where together they can move the company, organization or ministry forward."[53]

> "The first Christ-suffering which every man [and woman] must experience is the call to abandon the attachments of the world."
> —Dietrich Bonhoeffer

NURTURING MILLENNIAL ATTITUDE 3: OTHERS ARE LED BY INTEGRITY.

3.a. *Live a simple life*. It is not the number of followers or the number of luxuries that characterizes tomorrow's leadership. In a world increasingly stratified

22

by haves and have-nots, tomorrow's leader is known by an ability to connect across such chasms and bring people together. To achieve this, millennial leaders sense the need not to be pretentious or showy. Even if they attain stature, millennial leaders still resonate with the common person because they are in essence common. Before his execution in a Nazi prison camp, Dietrich Bonhoeffer wrote movingly about this:

> The cross is laid on every Christian. The first Christ-suffering which every man [and woman] must experience is the call to abandon the attachments of this world.... When Christ calls a man, he bids him come and die. It may be a death like that of the first disciples who had to leave home and work to follow him, or it may be a death like Luther's, who had to leave the monastery and go out into the world. But it is the same death every time—death in Jesus Christ, the death of the old man at his call.[54]

3.b. *Live a natural life*. Don't try to copy the leadership styles of others. Don't even try to copy the leadership styles of this book. You can't. This book is a compilation of dozens of stories and observations about millennial leaders. Instead, create a collage of ideas, characteristics, and tools that are relevant to you and to the people you serve.[55] As we saw in the introduction, a natural connectedness to those you serve is part of what it means to be organic.

3.c. *Live a well-thought-out life*. The millennial leader resists quick decisions, easy answers, and come-what-may attitudes. He or she recognizes the propensity of modern leaders to be recklessly optimistic and excessively hasty. The millennial leader develops a more unhurried and circumspect attitude toward God's plans. Aaron Norwood writes,

> Planning, praying, and preparing for each day are so fundamental to who I am as a follower of Christ. My all-too-often experience is that daily "winging it" always leaves out prayer and scripture. And, long-term thoughtlessness keeps me from planning meaningful times with my family. To hold to these priorities means carefully and daily thinking about them.[56]

A leader knows that participation in God's mission will bring triumphs and hardships. The millennial leader's levelheadedness is fostered by an attitude that recognizes that the leader's personal vision can always be tainted by pride, self-importance, and haste.

3.d. *Live a life of honesty and openness about faults*. Millennial leaders often share openly their struggles and shortcomings, but they are careful not to do so in a sensational or inappropriate way. Being honest means that each struggle and shortcoming can help others relate to one's trials and triumphs. Yet this openness recognizes there is an audience where sharing personal faults is appropriate and other audiences where it is not. The millennial leader takes great pains to distinguish between the two.

3.e. *Live a life that models the* missio Dei. While the modern leader may try to attain a perfect life, the millennial leader is an open book of travels, travails, and triumphs. It is honesty coupled with resilience and persistence that demonstrates to others how the leader is reconnecting with God. This journey of return points others to the *missio Dei*: God's mission to redeem his creation and restore fellowship with it.

MOVING TOWARD MILLENNIAL LEADERSHIP: QUESTIONS FOR PERSONAL REFLECTION AND/OR GROUP DISCUSSION

The following questions are for personal reflection but can also be used in a group setting:[57]

1. *For personal and group reflection*: create an organix leadership journal by
   - selecting two items from each box, and
   - writing in it what you will begin to do over the next thirty days to move toward millennial leadership in these two areas.

O	Nurturing Millennial Leadership
Others	1. Others and their needs drive the leader. 1.a. *Live among them.* 1.b. *Learn from and with them.* 1.c. *Prepare to "sift out" the bad since both good and bad are in each culture.*
	2. Others are souls to be nurtured. 2.a. *Look for and nurture the potential in others.* 2.b. *See learning in others as important as their performance.*

2.c. *Solicit others' input.*

2.d. *Obtain followers who complement your weaknesses.*

3. Others are led by integrity.

3.a. *Live a simple life.*

3.b. *Live a natural life.*

3.c. *Live a well-thought-out life.*

3.d. *Live a life of honesty and openness about faults.*

3.e. *Live a life that models the* missio Dei.

2. *For group reflection:*
   - Share your responses to the chart above with your group (omitting answers/plans that are overly personal).
   - Take notes in your journal on the following:
     a. Does your group agree or disagree with your assessments and plans?
     b. What input did they give you regarding moving toward millennial leadership?
   - Then rewrite your plans in your journal using their input.

3. *For personal and group reflection:*
   - Revisit your notes in your journal every month for six months. Ask yourself:
     a. Are there areas where I am making progress? If so, describe them.
     b. Are there areas where I am still weak? What will I do to address this?
   - At the end of six months reread the chapter and update your plans.

God, kindle Thou in my heart within,
A flame of love to my neighbor,
To my foe, to my friend, to my kindred all.

—*Celtic prayer*[1]

	Modern Leadership	Millennial Leadership
 **God**	1. God makes the work easier for the leader.	1. God strengthens the leader for the work.
	2. God's presence is a sign of leadership.	2. God's presence is a sign of the leader's need.
	3. God celebrates the leader's work in the church's mission.	3. God examines the leader's participation in the *missio Dei*.

CAPTIVE

The microchurch is different, Joan thought. *And I liked it better!* Microchurch was Joan's pet name for a series of small churches she had pastored, the last of which had been Clarkston Church. Now she was the new pastor at Aldersgate Church. "Aldersgate," her husband had harrumphed on hearing of her appointment, "sounds like a prison!" And Joan was beginning to agree.

Joan felt more focused at the smaller churches she pastored prior to

Aldersgate. Aldersgate was a mid-sized congregation of more than 250 attendees with a generous salary and a paid support staff of three. Yet despite these advantages, Joan found her time increasingly captive to attending board meetings, smoothing ruffled feathers of important members, and generally spending less time with God.

Her status had changed as well. Her predecessor had been Jerry, a popular and active pastor in the community. And now Joan felt obligated to go to all the community board meetings her predecessor had attended. "I'm not me anymore," Joan lamented in one of our consultation sessions. "I've become a clone of Jerry, and I've lost the things that made me feel fulfilled: prayer walks, reading my Bible through every year, even my self-esteem. I'm more aware of my faults, too, for when I fail now, it affects a lot of people. Bob, do you think God is in this move? I'm not naturally who I was, and I can't take this pressure. How can I recapture those things I had when I was a small-church pastor? And if I can't, am I in the wrong place?"

Answers for Joan formed the first draft of this chapter as she longs to recapture at Aldersgate Church the more organic and spiritual leadership she had enjoyed at Clarkston Church.[2]

STANDS FOR "GOD"

Because the millennial leader is often overwhelmed by the magnitude of the need as well as the multifaceted challenges of leadership, she or he needs help beyond what humans can provide. And since we as followers of Christ participate in God's mission of reunification (the *missio Dei*), God must be the source for accomplishing it. The emerging leader seeks divine stamina, insight, power, travel companions, and even miracles to accomplish the task of meeting the needs of others on their routes back to a relationship with God.

This is not to say that humans create God to help them with their needs, but it is to say that God has placed in his creation a divine spark of compassion, and when that spark begins to grow, the leader recognizes that only in the Creator will a person find the source and power behind that flame. The needs of others will drive a person to God, for only God can supply the strength needed for the mission.

Theta (Θ) is the first letter of the Greek word for God (*theos*). A theta is this chapter's icon because of the magnitude of the mission and because of whose mission it is (God's). Though subsequent chapters will have only one meaning for each icon, this chapter's symbol (Θ) is a completion of the chapter 1 icon (O).

PERILS OF MODERN LEADERSHIP
REGARDING Θ (GOD)

	Modern Leadership	Millennial Leadership
Θ God	1. God makes the work easier for the leader.	1. God strengthens the leader for the work.
	2. God's presence is a sign of leadership.	2. God's presence is a sign of the leader's need.
	3. God celebrates the leader's work in the church's mission.	3. God examines the leader's participation in the *missio Dei*.

MODERN PERIL 1: GOD MAKES THE WORK EASIER FOR THE LEADER.

A viewpoint has risen within Christianity that believes if God is pleased with our efforts, he will make the work easier. Sometimes this is signified by a theology of abundance where a faithful leader should expect God to make the leader's path more affluent and unproblematic.[3] There are several flaws with this thinking.

Flaw 1: Blessings can overshadow buffetings. Often, churches are more familiar with the promises of blessings than they are with the warnings of buffeting. While there are scriptural promises that God will bless us, there are also warnings of difficulties that lie in following Jesus. Since prosperity writers often cite passages from 2 Corinthians,[4] let's look at a brief comparison of Paul's thoughts in this book.

Figure 2.1. A comparison of blessings and buffetings in 2 Corinthians

2 Corinthians	
Blessings	**Buffetings**
2 Cor. 9:8 (Amp):[5] "God is able to make all grace (every favor and earthly blessing) come to you in abundance."	2 Cor. 4:17-18 (*THE MESSAGE*): "Even though on the outside it often looks like things are falling apart on us, on the inside . . . not a day goes by without [God's] unfolding grace."

29

2 Cor. 8:9 (NIV): "For you know the grace of our Lord Jesus Christ, that though he was rich, yet for your sake he became poor, so that you through his poverty might become rich."	2 Cor. 11:23-28 (*THE MESSAGE*, where Paul is describing his life): "Beaten up more times than I can count, and at death's door time after time. I've been flogged five times with the Jews' thirty-nine lashes, beaten by Roman rods three times, pummeled with rocks once. I've been shipwrecked three times. . . . I've had to ford rivers, fend off robbers, struggle with friends, struggle with foes. I've been at risk in the city, at risk in the country. . . betrayed by those I thought were my brothers. . . . And that's not the half of it, when you throw in the daily pressures and anxieties of all the churches. When someone gets to the end of his rope, I feel the desperation in my bones."
2 Cor. 9:10-11: "Now he who supplies seed to the sower and bread for food will also supply and increase your store of seed and will enlarge the harvest of your righteousness. You will be made rich in every way so that you can be generous on every occasion."	

Conclusions:

a. God blesses his people spiritually (2 Cor. 4:18; 8:9) and physically (2 Cor. 9:10-11),

b. but blessings do not rule out buffetings (2 Cor. 4:17-18),[6] for God does not always shield us from our own fallible nature or the wrongs of others (2 Cor. 11:23-28).[7]

Flaw 2: Modern leaders can come to expect privilege, with a right to ease and comfort. King David's temptation with Bathsheba occurred after he dodged his kingly duty of leading his men into battle, staying behind because of feelings that he deserved this luxury. Theologian Joyce Baldwin observes, "While others spent themselves and risked their lives, he was 'killing time,' acting like one of the kings of the nations round about, and exercising a kind of 'right of a lord'" (to do whatever he pleased).[8] As we see from David's story, if leaders expect God to always make their work easier, a false sense of privilege and entitlement can blind leaders to their duty and even to temptation.

Flaw 3: Modern leaders can question God's participation if the work does not get easier. Prosperity thinking can thwart perseverance and persistence because a leader might conclude that if the route is not easy, God must not be in it. This thinking can leave leaders like Joan unprepared and confused by the onset of hardships. Criticizing his generation, Thomas à Kempis wrote,

Jesus hath . . . many desirous of comfort, but few of tribulation. . . . All desire to rejoice with him, few are willing to endure anything for him. Many follow Jesus unto the breaking of bread; but few to the drinking of the cup of his passion. . . . Many love Jesus so long as adversities do not happen. Many praise and bless him, so long as they receive comforts from him.[9]

All three flaws remind us that although God promises to bless his people (2 Cor. 4:18; 8:9; 9:10-11), there are also buffetings that accompany the mission (2 Cor. 4:17-18; 11:23-28). The modern inclination that God principally makes the work easier for the leader is not only unbiblical but also potentially debilitating.

MODERN PERIL 2: GOD'S PRESENCE IS A SIGN OF LEADERSHIP.

Another peril is that modern leaders will allude to the presence of God as a sign of validation for their ministry and/or vision. This manifests itself in several ways.

Flaw 1: Modern leaders may believe visions and dreams validate their leadership and will inspire followers. Supernatural revelation is a way that God can and does reveal his will (John 16:13), but many modern leaders overly apply and misapply this to buttress personal vision. Oral Roberts infamously declared that unless $8 million was raised, God would "call him home."[10] Whether Roberts felt God's warning would validate his plea for funds, inspire more giving, or was just a personal warning, to state it so publicly became self-serving. Modern leadership sometimes mutates into a view that because God has blessed and set apart the leader, followers should follow her or him (and by extension bless the leader too). Henri Nouwen warns pastors this is leadership based on "the temptation to be spectacular," a temptation the devil offered Jesus when he bid him to throw himself from the temple.[11]

> Modern leadership sometimes mutates into a view that because God has blessed and set apart the leader, followers should follow him or her (and by extension bless the leader too).

Flaw 2: Modern leaders can believe that because God's presence is so pervasive in their lives, God excuses them from corporate worship and prayer. Modern leaders will often feel that because they have so much personal time with God, they do not need congregational times of prayer, worship, and fasting. In a large and thriving church, leaders who were once actively involved in public worship will often be found backstage chatting during worship and prayer.[12]

God's presence is certainly needed for church leadership. But when leaders rely primarily on status and not fruit, they ignore Paul's advice:

If anyone wants to provide leadership in the church, good! But there are preconditions: A leader must be well-thought-of, committed to his wife, cool and collected, accessible, and hospitable. He must know what he's talking about, not be overfond of wine, not pushy but gentle, not thin-skinned, not money-hungry. (1 Tim. 3:1-3 *THE MESSAGE*)

MODERN PERIL 3: GOD CELEBRATES THE LEADER'S WORK
IN THE CHURCH'S MISSION.

Here again the modern leader's work often overshadows the *missio Dei*. This peril has at least two flaws.

Flaw 1: Modern leaders often think because God has blessed them in the past, God will bless them in the future. The modern leader has a strong sense of God's past blessings. Subsequently, whatever the modern leader can envision or recall, he or she feels that God's hand of blessing will be on it again. This error is similar to that of the New Testament Pharisees, who assumed that because God used a system of laws in the past, he would now bless the overly mechanical system into which it had evolved (Matt. 15:1-3).

> **In today's narcissistic culture, adoration for an individual does not necessarily translate into adoration for the God who is behind her or his talents.**

Flaw 2: Modern leaders can feel that when God blesses the leader, God gets the glory. Often the skill of a preacher or the talent of a musician can lead that accomplished person to think that all acclaim gives glory to God. However, in today's narcissistic culture, adoration for an individual does not necessarily translate into adoration for the God who is behind her or his talents. Not surprisingly, signage draped across websites and edifices often acclaims the quality of the performance and not the relevance of the encounter.

THREE ATTITUDES OF MILLENNIAL LEADERSHIP
REGARDING ⊖ (GOD)

	Modern Leadership	Millennial Leadership
⊖ **God**	1. God makes the work easier for the leader.	1. God strengthens the leader for the work.
	2. God's presence is a sign of leadership.	2. God's presence is a sign of the leader's need.
	3. God celebrates the leader's work in the church's mission.	3. God examines the leader's participation in the *missio Dei*.

Θ : God

MILLENNIAL ATTITUDE 1: GOD STRENGTHENS THE LEADER FOR THE WORK.

Unlike the modern leader who may hope the work gets easier, the millennial leader recognizes that the *missio Dei* will include cycles of tranquillity followed by quandary. Because of such patterns, the millennial leader knows to antici- pate hardship in order to surmount it. When trials and travesty come, millen- nial leaders are not surprised, angry, or offended; they recognize that this is part of life's cycle and rhythm. German pastor and martyr Dietrich Bonhoeffer observed, "The cross means sharing the

> Nouwen calls this the "wounded healer," who "is called to be the wounded healer, the one who must look after his own wounds but at the same time be prepared to heal the wounds of others."

suffering of Christ to the last and to the fullest...but he [we] would certainly break down under the burden, but for the support of him who bore these sins of all. The passion of Christ strengthens him to overcome."[13] Shortly, we will look at how millennial leaders tackle hardship with Christ's empowerment.

MILLENNIAL ATTITUDE 2: GOD'S PRESENCE IS A SIGN OF THE LEADER'S NEED.

The magnitude of the *missio Dei* requires God's presence because it is God's work in which we only participate. The scale and the source remind the millen- nial leader that he or she is inadequate for the task if not connected closely to God. When God blesses the millennial leader, he or she understands this not as a sign of preference but as a reminder of how much the leader needs to partner with God.

Precisely because of this acknowledgment of personal need, a millennial leader often embraces a new and heightened honesty. Nouwen calls this the "wounded healer," who "must look after his own wounds but at the same time be prepared to heal the wounds of others."[14]

Though they do not hide personal flaws, millennial leaders do not ignore them either, seeking God's power and presence to mend them. They find solidarity and solace in Bonhoeffer's image of Christ as "the Good Shepherd...[who] knows them all by name and loves them. He knows their distress and their weakness. He heals the wounded, gives drink to the thirsty, sets upright the falling and leads them gent- ly, not sternly, to pasture."[15]

MILLENNIAL ATTITUDE 3: GOD EXAMINES THE LEADER'S PARTICIPATION IN THE MISSIO DEI.

Millennial leaders have a strong wariness about self-weaknesses, temptations, flaws, and frailties; simultaneously, they sense the magnitude of the mission of God. When this is coupled with Jesus' parable of God as a task master (Matt.

25:14-30), an image of supervision, accountability, and liability emerges. Therefore, the millennial leader welcomes and expects God and others to judge her or his participation in the *missio Dei*. The millennial leader expects accountability from both Christian and secular realms.

One young leader told me, "If you are going to be a pastor today, you can't hide anything. God can forgive, but technology will make sure people don't forget.... The answer is building a good reputation and having respected people who hold you accountable, who can confront you and remind you of the consequences." And so the frailty and fallibility of human nature mean the millennial leader expects and sets in place an organism of answerability (which we will explore in the next section).

NURTURING THE THREE ATTITUDES REGARDING ☉ (GOD)

NURTURING MILLENNIAL ATTITUDE 1: GOD STRENGTHENS THE LEADER FOR THE WORK.

The millennial leader prepares and plans ahead for calamity by developing a support network where God can strengthen the spirit through word, worship, and other means.

> The voices, actions, and prayer partners that prepare the millennial leader for life's cycles come from others. Consequently, spiritual networks are not filled with yes-people and fawning flatterers, but robust relationships of peers who offer accountability and open honesty.

1.a. *Through God's word.* An appetite to understand, apply, and be empowered by God's story strengthens and cultivates the millennial leader (see Acts 2:42). For example, a creative and young church, Church of the Apostles in Seattle, chose the traditional-sounding name of apostles to emphasize that all attendees should be familiar with biblical stories of mission and hardships that characterized early apostles such as Paul (see table 2.1 for a few of Paul's hardships). Pastor Karen Ward emphasizes that there are danger, peril, and hardships in being sent away to tell others, but "Jesus... blessed and sent them to carry on in his way of living and to welcome others to do the same. The invitation still stands."[16]

1.b. *Through worship.* Worship, in its original Hebrew definition, means an intimate encounter with God.[17] As students of scriptural stories of triumph and travail, millennial leaders know that to survive, they must encounter God personally. They need fresh, lengthy, and anointed periods of time with God to maintain a supernatural bond and empowerment. They resonate with the psalmist, "So here I am in the place of worship, eyes open, drinking in your strength and glory" (Ps. 63:2 *THE MESSAGE*). Dan Kimball stated, "We desire to do things that happen and can be explained only by the Holy Spirit's involvement, not by our use of innovative ministry methodology."[18]

1.c. *Through others*. The voices, actions, and prayer partners that prepare the millennial leader for life's cycles come from others. Consequently, spiritual networks are not filled with yes-people and fawning flatterers, but robust relationships of peers who offer accountability and open honesty. Simon Hall, the leader of Revive, a young and growing congregation in Leeds, England, states, "We're moving toward membership of Revive having nothing to do with attending a particular meeting. Instead, it's about being accountable (through a small group, prayer triplet, soul friend, spiritual director, etc.) to five basic values of discipleship."[19]

NURTURING MILLENNIAL ATTITUDE 2: GOD'S PRESENCE IS A SIGN OF THE LEADER'S NEED.

2.a. *Regular times of fasting, journaling, and silence connect us with God.* In an increasingly hectic and multitasking world, millennial leaders are rediscovering the power of focusing on one thing and doing so at length. Churches such as St. Thomas's Church, England's largest and youngest Anglican congregation, expect all members to pray each day at three of the monastic hours.[20] Phyllis Tickle advocates more churches embrace fixed-hour prayers so that in contiguous time zones, "like relay runners passing a lighted torch, those who do the work of fixed-hour prayer do create thereby a continuous cascade of praise before the throne of God."[21]

> The commonly identified public religious activities are important to be sure, but the less commonly practiced activities like solitude and silence and meditation and fasting and submission to the will of others as appropriate are in fact more foundational for spiritual formation.

Experiment with varying spiritual disciplines to keep your connection to God fresh and frequent, including these:

1. prayer walks, meditation, and journaling;
2. an ordered rhythm of daily prayer (for example, fixed-hour prayer), perhaps at the monastic hours;[22]
3. prayer partners in the form of prayer triplets,[23] soul friend,[24] and so on; and
4. abstinence from pleasurable necessities (food, sex, and so on) for periods of presence with God.

Richard Foster notes that such actions

are many and varied: fasting and prayer, study and service, submission and solitude, confession and worship, meditation and silence, simplicity, frugality, secrecy, sacrifice, celebration, and the like. . . . All disciplines should be thought-fully and resolutely approached for the purpose of forming the life into Christlikeness, or they will have little or no effect in promoting this life.[25]

2.b. *Spiritual filling is an ongoing process; seek refilling.* Emerging leaders see themselves as vessels of God's love that constantly need to be refilled. While modern leaders may view spiritual experiences as defining moments (for exam-ple, entire sanctification[26] or the baptism of the Holy Spirit),[27] millennial lead-ers see the need for refilling and re-empowerment as trumping such turning points. Writer, Catholic priest, and former Protestant minister Thomas Smith said, "We are, by nature, leaky vessels. We need to continually be filled."[28] Millennial leaders return to the spiritual disciplines of 2.a (above) on a regular and frequent basis for refilling.

NURTURING MILLENNIAL ATTITUDE 3: GOD EXAMINES THE LEADER'S PARTICIPATION IN THE MISSIO DEI.

3.a. *Embrace prayer as a time of humility and openness before God.* The millen-nial leader may preface prayer with the attitude of the psalmist: "GOD, be gra-cious! / Put me together again—my sins have torn me to pieces" (Ps. 41:4 *THE MESSAGE*). To nurture such millennial leadership,
1. become sensitive to your failings and foibles, letting your prayer carry a tone of remorse that can lead to companionship.
2. include in your prayers a recounting of recent sins. But don't stop there. Continue on to repentance, and receive your forgiveness.
3. move on to prayer for the needs of others. Finish with prayer for yourself.

3.b. *Expect the scrutiny of God, his church, and his creation.* As James warns, "Don't be in any rush to become a teacher, my friends. Teaching is highly responsible work. Teachers are held to the strictest standards. And none of us is perfectly qualified" (James 3:1 *THE MESSAGE*). Therefore, to foster millennial leadership,
1. expect God to correct and adjust your course.
2. remember that though God may give the vision, human nature can color how we interpret it.
3. expect God to work through divine as well as human communica-tion to correct, adjust, and guide.

3.c. *Make knowing God's will your food.* The millennial leader hungers to know God's purposes and expectations. Knowing God's will is like having a spiritual diet, a provision that is more important than food. As regularly as you hunger for physical food, foster an appetite for times of prayer, silence, meditation, and spir-itual revelation. Jesus told his disciples, "The food that keeps me going is that I do the will of the One who sent me, finishing the work he started" (John 4:34 *THE MESSAGE*).

Θ : *God*

3.d. *Submit to honest and authentic accountability.* Sixty-two percent of my seminary students, mostly pastors, don't have an independent and impartial accountability group. When I break this down by age, the younger ones do. Those who have such accountability seem to feel safer, more self-assured, and less anxious. Though accountability can take many forms, here are three guidelines:

1. Accountability must be given by those closely acquainted with your strengths and weakness.
2. Accountability must be given by impartial peers. For pastors, this often means other pastors and impartial laypeople (that is, not people who directly report to the pastors or who benefit directly from their ministry).
3. Accountability must be ongoing. The best accountability is given by those who have an ongoing connection with your progress, regress, and aspirations.

Freely available and unrestricted scrutiny of leaders has become a trait of our interconnected world. While modern leaders could expect a degree of anonymity and secrecy, tomorrow's leaders are afforded no such luxury. In addition, the Christian leader's partnership in the *missio Dei* is scrutinized by God. The duality of such scrutiny could dissuade many Christians from taking up the task. Yet because the need is so great, the mission so vital, and the assistance (both divine and communal) so prevailing, millennial leadership risks the commission.

MOVING TOWARD MILLENNIAL LEADERSHIP: QUESTIONS FOR PERSONAL REFLECTION AND/OR GROUP DISCUSSION

The following questions are for personal reflection but can also be used in a group setting:

1. *For personal and group reflection:* create an organix leadership journal by
   - selecting two items from each box, and
   - writing in it what you will begin to do over the next thirty days to move toward millennial leadership in these two areas.

Θ	Nurturing Millennial Leadership
God	1. God strengthens the leader for the work.
	1.a. *Through God's word.*
	1.b. *Through worship.*

37

	1.c. *Through others*.
	2. God's presence is a sign of the leader's need.
	2.a. *Regular times of fasting, journaling, and silence connect us with God*.
	2.b. *Spiritual filling is an ongoing process; seek refilling*.
	3. God examines the leader's participation in the *missio Dei*.
	3.a. *Embrace prayer as a time of humility and openness before God*.
	3.b. *Expect the scrutiny of God, his church, and his creation*.
	3.c. *Make knowing God's will your food*.
	3.d. *Submit to honest and authentic accountability*.

2. *For group reflection:*

- Share your responses to the chart above with your group (omitting answers/plans that are overly personal).
- Take notes in your journal on the following:
    a. Does your group agree or disagree with your assessments and plans?
    b. What input did they give you regarding moving toward millennial leadership?
- Then rewrite your plans in your journal using their input.

3. *For personal and group reflection:*

- Revisit your notes in your journal every month for six months. Ask yourself:
    a. Are there areas where I am making progress? If so, describe them.
    b. Are there areas where I am still weak? What will I do to address this?
- At the end of six months reread the chapter and update your plans.

38

As a physician, I believed—and still do believe—that there must be some prescription or antidote to heal or at least improve almost any condition. . . . I sought out a specialist . . . [for] I suffered from a spiritual malady. . . . The name I kept encountering was that of Mother Teresa of Calcutta.

—Paul A. Wright, describing why he spent five years with Mother Teresa[1]

	Modern Leadership	Millennial Leadership
R̲x̲ **Prescription**	1. Healthy people emerge out of healthy churches.	1. The prescription for a healthy church is healthy people.
	2. Spiritual health results from a largely private effort.	2. The prescription for spiritual health results from a personal and communal effort.
	3. Volunteering in a large organization will make people healthy.	3. The prescription for volunteer health is a network of small groups.

LIFE TOGETHER

This was the second church Gordon had visited this month, and Ekklesia Church was a refreshing change from the previous week when Gordon and his family had visited Community Church. He had been impressed with the programs of the large, growing community church in a trendy suburb. That week he met with the pastor of Community Church to ask about joining.

"We don't emphasize membership," Pastor Steve responded. "We're about sharing the good news. And we need a lot of volunteers to do it." Gordon then told Steve about his ill-fated pastorate at Clarkston Church. "I couldn't last even three years," Gordon recalled. "My family and I were pretty beat up. I guess we just need a place to get healthy." For the next fifteen minutes Pastor Steve extolled the therapeutic power of volunteerism. "Get your mind off your own problems," Steve summarized. "When you see others are needier than you, you will feel better about yourself." The statement left Gordon cold. How could he now tell Steve that his wife of thirty-five years was preparing to file for a separation? Confusion, hopelessness, and unease came over Gordon, and he decided right then to try a different church.

The church they visited the following week was a small Anglican congregation that had been founded some eighteen months earlier. The worship was engaging, and Gordon liked how the pastor fielded questions from the congregation during his sermon. But Gordon needed counsel. And so, with trepidation after the previous week's office visit, he met with Joel, one of two planters of this congregation.

"I'm glad you came to Ekklesia Church. And getting involved is very important here," Joel began. "We're not talking membership, but community. We have a network of three small groups. That's where people get their lives together as we learn together about our life with Jesus."

"But I've got things people don't want to hear," responded Gordon.

"They've probably heard it all," Joel replied. "Just check out our newest group. It was started by three people from our first Zoe Group."

With some gentle nudging the next Sunday from Joel, Gordon and his wife, Helen, visited the new group and found it engaging. The first three visits were times of getting acquainted, but the fourth week the conversation got personal. Joel had been preaching on child rearing, and each week the Zoe Groups discussed the previous week's sermon. Will and Sally, who had started this group, shared that they had been separated for six months due to different opinions on child rearing. "I guess it was our Zoe Group that got us through it," concluded Sally. Over the next few weeks, Sally and Will shared their personal journey back to a healthy marriage. Perhaps because of Will's and Sally's openness, or perhaps because they needed to, Gordon and Helen slowly shared their marital struggles too.

Six months later, Gordon and Helen were still attending Ekklesia when Joel came to call. "We've been praying, and we feel you might be good candidates to join the launch team for a new Zoe Group," said Joel.

"But we've become close to our friends at our current group," Helen stated.

"Some of them are going, too, and if you don't want to go, that's OK," Joel said. "I was just inquiring."

A few weeks later Gordon and Helen joined three other members from their group to launch the new group. The new group comprised middle-aged adults. They chose marital problems and the remedies as their focus. One year later, this new group launched another Zoe Group for young parents. Though Gordon and Helen had every intention of staying with this group, they agreed to meet with Joel at his request. "We're going to link together your Zoe Group and the new one to help needy people in this community," began Joel. "Your group has been too small to do much by yourself. But with the two groups combined once a month, you will have sufficient volunteers. Someone needs to coordinate this ministry to the needy. Would you two do it?" Joel's suggestion startled them, but after a week of prayer, Gordon and Helen agreed.

Within the next two years Gordon and Helen managed the social needs ministry of an expanding network of Zoe Groups. Eventually, five groups were under their care when Joel requested another visit in their home. "I always get nervous when you visit us at home, Joel," began Helen. "It seems you've always got something new for us."

"You're right, Helen," Joel said. "I know at one time Gordon was a pastor in Clarkston. And you got pretty beat up. But it seems you've healed, and if you think it is the right time, there is a need for an interim pastor at Bethel Church. I'd like to recommend you, Gordon. It won't be easy. They've just endured division and scandal. But I felt led to contact you."

So much has happened, Gordon thought. He and Helen had patched up their marriage. He hadn't felt this healthy in years. But he was nearing retirement age, and the last pastorate had almost ended their marriage. Looking back on the healing that took place at Ekklesia Church, he sensed he now had the answers he lacked in Clarkston. "We'll do it," Gordon replied two weeks later.

"The first meeting won't be an easy one." Joel's response was ominous. "But I sense you're up for the task."

R̵ STANDS FOR "PRESCRIPTIONS"

An R with a slash through the right leg is a Latin abbreviation for "recipe," which has come to indicate a recipe or prescription for health.[2] In the new leadership world the Rx serves as a fitting descriptor for a millennial emphasis on first addressing the spiritual and physical health of leaders.

This chapter contrasts how prescriptions for helping hurting people vary between modern and millennial leadership approaches. On the one hand, many modern leaders approach healing and health from a top-down, organizational perspective. This usually means, get the organization healthy, and it will, in turn, foster healthy people.

On the other hand, the millennial perspective takes a more organic approach, believing that if you get people healthy, a healthy organization will result. Let's look more closely at these perspectives, and then consider solutions that can help today's leaders nurture a more holistic and person-centered approach to healthy leadership.

THREE SYMPTOMS OF MODERN LEADERSHIP REGARDING ℞ (PRESCRIPTION FOR HEALTH)

	Modern Leadership	Millennial Leadership
℞ Prescription	1. Healthy people emerge out of healthy churches.	1. The prescription for a healthy church is healthy people.
	2. Spiritual health results from a largely private effort.	2. The prescription for spiritual health results from a personal and communal effort.
	3. Volunteering in a large organization will make people healthy.	3. The prescription for volunteer health is a network of small groups.

MODERN MISCUE 1: HEALTHY PEOPLE EMERGE OUT OF HEALTHY CHURCHES.

The first miscue is to think that organizational health precedes individual health. The thinking is, *If I can get the church organizationally healthy, it will help people, and they, in turn, will get healthy.* But achieving organizational health is difficult, and when the organization comes first, volunteers may burn out in the process. This creates worn-out leaders, who then model this lack of

> "Many pastors heard these insightful mega-church leaders and simply copied their methods without reflecting on the principles behind the methods."
> —Ed Stetzer

health to others. "I don't want to be a pastor, a church leader, or anything," was the summation of one of my undergraduate students. "I've seen how the church burns out and spits out leaders. That's not for me."

But if an organic organization is the goal, church health should start with getting a church's foundational components healthy, and that means people. The fact that healthy organizations arise from healthy people has been blurred by two factors.

> "This one factor alone helped shape our strategy... [we] kept our focus on people."
> —Rick Warren

The first factor is the church health movement. Church health became a popular term in the 1990s when megachurch pastor Rick Warren said, "Church health is the key to church growth."[3] Though Warren emphasized that church health depends on certain principles, researcher Ed Stetzer summarized the fallout: "Many pastors heard these insightful megachurch leaders and simply copied their methods without reflecting on the principles behind the methods."[4] The unintended result was that pastors started focusing on programs that might create church health and not the health of the individual components (that is, people who compose the church).[5] For modern leaders, church health soon came to represent a healthy organizational structure that would then make people healthy. Warren, however, had no such intention. He emphasized that healthy people were the starting point and stated, "Many people look at the so-called 'megachurches' and assume those churches have always been big....Saddleback met for fifteen years before being able to build our first building. This one factor alone helped shape our strategy... [we] kept our focus on people."[6] In spite of Warren's protestations, church health was popularly perceived as emphasizing organizational health.

A second factor that has clouded an organic approach to church health has been a poor distinction between organization and organism. The church is an organization that must be led and managed. Theologian Emil Brunner even suggested that since earliest times, this is the primary way theologians have viewed the church.[7]

Scripturally, the church is also an interdependent and living organism (1 Cor. 12:12, 14, 20, 27) where each person has something to contribute (Rom. 12:4-8; Eph. 4:11-13) to the community's involvement in God's

> Modern leaders often fall back on an emphasis on organization over people. Their aspiration is to foster a healthy organization in hopes that it would then trickle down and foster healthy people.

mission (Matt. 28:18-20; Acts 1:8). Such Scriptures indicate that healthy components (that is, people) are necessary to form a healthy organization.[8]

Modern leaders tend to view the church as an organization that must be made healthy, but millennial leaders view the church as more of an organism to be fed and nurtured to health. Which is needed? Both are. To summarize this dilemma, "a common weakness among church leaders is a poor distinction between organization and church. Thus, what they are managing gets confused."[9]

For example, in one congregation a number of staff leaders left the church over conflict with the pastor. In response the pastor launched a program to build a new facility. Conflict ensued. One leader told me, "I think we thought that getting the church back to being healthy meant getting people's minds off of the staff departures. . . . It really backfired. We're unhealthy as a church. There is too much backbiting, suspicion, and conflict. At our core, we are not healthy, and no amount of building a new Sunday school wing will cover that."

When faced with a need to marshal the troops, modern leaders often fall back on an emphasis on organization over people. Their aspiration is to foster a healthy organization in hopes that it will trickle down and foster healthy people. The problem is that unhealthy components will never create a healthy organization, as Paul reminded the Corinthians:

> The way God designed our bodies is a model for understanding our lives together as a church: every part dependent on every other part, the parts we mention and the parts we don't, the parts we see and the parts we don't. If one part hurts, every other part is involved in the hurt, and in the healing. If one part flourishes, every other part enters into the exuberance. (1 Cor. 12:25-26 *THE MESSAGE*)

MODERN MISCUE 2: SPIRITUAL HEALTH RESULTS FROM A LARGELY PRIVATE EFFORT.

Another modern miscue is created because the heroic modern leader is not supposed to be fallible.[10] For a modern leader to acknowledge a fault may seem like either letting people down or destabilizing the leader's platform, and discretion requires health and holiness to remain private. Modern leadership expectations place the onus of the problem on the leader's self. A quest for spiritual help, especially with a delicate or controversial temptation, will usually go unaddressed until public humiliation results. "I carried a secret many years," recalled one pastor after he was found out. "I didn't feel I had the support to share my weaknesses and get help," he told me. "They wanted a perfect pastor, and there is no such thing. My penitence is the public embarrassment of my family, my friends, and my Lord. . . . There should be a mechanism to prevent this."

Chapter 5, "Recycle," details the different ways millennial leaders react to the fallibility of leaders and use mechanisms to create and maintain health.

MODERN MISCUE 3: VOLUNTEERING IN A LARGE ORGANIZATION WILL MAKE PEOPLE HEALTHY.

Another fallacy is that if individuals get involved in church work, they will soon become healthy. In the name of getting people healthy, modern leaders often encourage hurting people to volunteer. "My thinking was that I needed to persuade people into doing something at the church. Then they would get around healthy people, and in turn they would get better," recalled one of my students. Instead he recounted, "The unhealthy people got more unhealthy and started infecting the healthy ones too. Our whole church got sicker as a result. They got too focused about their work and didn't really connect with people about their spiritual issues." When work is the focus, and not the health of the worker, unhealthy relationships, unhealthy work, and unhealthy cycles result. Disastrous effects include group exits, scandals, and quarrels.[11]

A massive study at one of America's most influential churches, Willow Creek Church in South Barrington, Illinois, found that volunteerism helped very little in creating healthy people. The researchers of the REVEAL study called this a "stunning discovery."[12] Willow Creek's founding pastor Bill Hybels lamented, "We made a mistake. What we should have done when people crossed the line of faith and become Christians. . . . We should have gotten people, taught people, how to read their Bible between services, how to do the spiritual practices much more aggressively on their own."[13]

How does a church tell if it is putting people first or the organization first? Short of just asking volunteers (as the Willow Creek study appropriately did), figure 3.1 offers a simple comparison. The left column describes a top-down approach to creating health while the right column contrasts the millennial approach. Modern leaders often try to persuade hurting people to focus on the left column (where the organization comes first).

Figure 3.1: A comparison of organization-first and people-first volunteerism

The organization might come first if . . .		People probably come first if . . .
Volunteers are given only brief skill and talent assessment.	Assessment	Volunteers are given personal interviews with in-depth need and health assessment.
Willingness trumps suitability.	Recruitment	Suitability and stability trump willingness.
Training is the primary goal, e.g., Leadership training school is emphasized.	Goals	Volunteer health is the primary goal, e.g., 12-step programs

The goal of newcomer courses is volunteerism.		The goal of newcomer courses is holiness and health.
If a leader fails, provide more training.		If a leader fails, reevaluate suitability.
The level of leadership attained is evaluated.	Evaluation	Happiness and satisfaction with the volunteer experience are evaluated.

THREE ATTITUDES OF MILLENNIAL LEADERSHIP REGARDING R̴ (PRESCRIPTION FOR HEALTH)

	Modern Leadership	Millennial Leadership
R̴ **Prescription**	1. Healthy people emerge out of healthy churches.	1. The prescription for a healthy church is healthy people.
	2. Spiritual health results from a largely private effort.	2. The prescription for spiritual health results from a personal and communal effort.
	3. Volunteering in a large organization will make people healthy.	3. The prescription for volunteer health is a network of small groups.

MILLENNIAL ATTITUDE 1: THE PRESCRIPTION FOR A HEALTHY CHURCH IS HEALTHY PEOPLE.

The millennial leader stresses that God places people first and organizations second. The millennial leader would never think of building a new church facility (or some other visionary goal) to make hurting people "forget their own problems" and volunteer their way to health.

One emerging leader who made the transition from modern to millennial perspectives on volunteerism described his change this way:

> When I was a pastor, if you had come to me and said, "I'm having trouble with my prayer life," I would have asked you what books you had read.... Now I would also ask, "What are your prayer practices, and who are the people who taught you to pray, and how did they pray?"... I now understand Christian formation to involve... knowledge, experience, and a small group.[14]

One Willow Creek leader summarized the congregation's response to the REVEAL report this way: "In other words, spiritual growth doesn't happen best by becoming dependent on elaborate church programs but through the age-old spiritual practices of prayer, Bible reading, and relationships. And, ironically, these basic disciplines do not require multi-million dollar facilities and hundreds of staff to manage."[15]

MILLENNIAL ATTITUDE 2: THE PRESCRIPTION FOR SPIRITUAL HEALTH RESULTS FROM A PERSONAL AND COMMUNAL EFFORT.

Spiritual health begins with self-discipline and tenacity. Commenting on the study, Bill Hybels stated, "We should have started telling people and teaching people that they have to take responsibility to become 'self feeders.'"[16] Millennial leaders often maintain this spiritual focus through the collective accountability of small groups.[17] There are three important contributions that small groups can make to the health of individuals.

> **Small groups foster not only leadership development and confidentiality but also bonds of friendship that are not easily broken.**

Communal training for leadership. "Leadership grows out of the relationships formed in small groups," stated John Marsh, a leader in one of England's largest and most youthful congregations. He went on to say,

> Leadership is about first being accountable to others in a small group and their group leader. You can't hide anything [in a small group]. People overcome their weaknesses and temptations there. And [get] accountability.... Then they can grow into leadership with the small group's support.... When people are healthy, they will make good decisions, and the church will be healthy.[18]

While modern leadership might put an emerging leader into a large volunteer crowd to get lost, millennial leadership integrates him or her into the life of a small group to foster connections and training.

Communal confidentiality. Correction can take place semiprivately and be tailored to the situation in small circles of like-minded individuals. Hurting people are not left to wrestle with their weaknesses alone. A small group of fellow Christians creates an intimate environment to discuss and address failings that might be inappropriate for larger gatherings.[19]

Communal stickiness. In the millennial world, small groups foster not only leadership development and confidentiality but also bonds of friendship that are not easily broken. Larry Osborne calls this "stickiness" because small groups create a "glue" between people.[19] Osborne's church fosters this by creating small-group discussions from the previous week's sermon. This creates a link between the message the lead pastor is sharing at the Sunday worship celebration and the small group.[21] Osborne also discovered that sticky groups create an organic evangelism

> Thom Rainer discovered that new Christians who connect with a small group are five times more likely to be active in the church five years later than those who attend only worship services.

with natural follow-up and assimilation.[22] New Christians who connect with a small group are five times more likely to be active in the church five years later than those who attend only worship services.[23] Viewing the number of people involved in small groups as a more helpful number than counting the number of attendees at a worship event has become a trend in emerging churches.

Millennial leaders often value their small-group system more than they value a great worship celebration. Leaders of Mars Hill Church in Granville, Michigan, a church known for the oratory skill of its former pastor Rob Bell, cite the church's small-group network as its number one asset.[24] Even in a church known for the preaching skill of its pastor, most congregants found the expansive small-group network as the church's most satisfying and health-producing attribute.[25] To create such health, churches are multiplying all sorts of small groups, such as 12-step groups, sermon-based groups, geographically located groups, and so on.

MILLENNIAL ATTITUDE 3: THE PRESCRIPTION FOR VOLUNTEER HEALTH IS A NETWORK OF SMALL GROUPS.

Many times people who want to volunteer never do so because of two concerns: they feel ill equipped, or they are afraid of leadership burnout. Let's look at each of these, and see how clear structures of small groups can lead to increased volunteerism.

Ill equipped. Emerging leaders often feel they have little potential and even less qualification for leadership. Fuller Seminary's professor of leadership, Robert Clinton, concluded that emerging leaders need to be given their first leadership tasks in small groups. Clinton states, "Ministry tasks involve getting experience, attaining knowledge, or doing things that will bring out character and giftedness. Often the 'little-much' principle stated in Luke 16:10 is operating. Can you be faithful in little things?...Can you learn to influence a small group because of who you are?"[26] Clinton goes on to tell that it was in a small group he discovered many of his gifts for ministry.[27] Further, one of the five keys to mentoring is to do so in "small group settings."[28]

Burnout. Potential for leadership burnout or fatigue also dissuades volunteerism. This malady often arises from lack of rest. "If you take that committee position," summarized one senior saint, "you'll still be on it years from now." Yet the Scriptures are replete with God's command to rest. God rested (Gen. 2:1-3) and commanded his followers to do the same (Exod. 20:8-11). Helmut Thielicke said, "We are not bound to go on slaving like mad and succumb to the frenzy of an exaggerated sense of duty and work our heads off (preferably even in the name of God...). On the contrary, we are called upon to stop, to interpose pauses in the round of our work."[29] To counter this problem, millennial leaders have rhythms of work and rest through a Groups-MissionalNets-Cultures model.

NURTURING THE THREE ATTITUDES REGARDING ℞ (PRESCRIPTION FOR HEALTH)

NURTURING MILLENNIAL ATTITUDE 1: THE PRESCRIPTION FOR A HEALTHY CHURCH IS HEALTHY PEOPLE.

Millennial churches put in place careful and clear routes to volunteerism that begin with assessment and mentoring. This assessment is usually accomplished by accountability and ministry experimentation in a small group.[30] When researchers studied the founding of Methodism, they discovered that John Wesley's emphasis on small groups was a key element. Wesley's small groups were "small-group spiritual direction. You're praying, you're singing, you're getting spiritual advice, and you bring your questions."[31]

> One researcher describes Wesley's small groups: "You could call it small-group spiritual direction. You're praying, you're singing, you're getting spiritual advice, and you bring your questions."

1.a. *Small-group leaders assess the needs and health of emerging leaders.* Spending time in a small group, one-on-one, and in an ongoing mentoring role provides the opportunity to recognize the potentials and pitfalls of emerging leaders. Thus, the leader of a small group need not be a Bible scholar, an organizer, or a captain. Small-group leaders are primarily delegators, encouragers, and counselors. In Wesley's time it was from a small group, not from the pulpit, that seekers would find someone to guide them along on their spiritual journey.[32]

1.b. *Small-group leaders foster spiritual direction and service via the small group.* Give emerging leaders opportunities to experiment with leadership. Note how Jesus gave the disciples such opportunities in Luke 9:1-6; 10:1-16. Give them permission to fail, and then correct their course. Note how Jesus handled the inability of his disciples to cast out the demons in Matthew 17:20-21 and Mark 9:29. Remember, Fuller Seminary's Robert Clinton states that his personal leadership journey began by experimenting with leadership in small groups.[33]

> **Missionalize describes an atmosphere that fosters a passion for reconnecting people with God (the *missio Dei*).**

1.c. *Small-group leaders help emerging leaders establish fitting goals.* Left on their own, some potential leaders may adopt goals that are self-seeking, unsuitable, or misdirected. Small-group mentors can help clarify the mission of God (*missio Dei*) to the emerging leader and help this novice leader understand how one can participate. To keep a focus on Christ's mission even while using a 12-step small-group program, Shepherds' Training, a ministry of Church of the Saviour in Washington, D.C., begins each meeting with

> a litany in which participants claim Jesus Christ as the "higher power." Every group meeting begins with a reading from the Bible instead of from the AA Big Book. In addition, members commit themselves to pray for one another, to engage in prayer and Bible study 15 minutes a day, to tithe to the group and to earnestly seek God's call in their lives.[34]

The result is that personal goals begin to reflect Christ's goals.

1.d. *Small-group leaders offer emerging leaders honest evaluation.* Mentoring via a small group also includes an authentic appraisal of the emerging leader's gifts and calling. While the small group as a whole may do this, the leader's duties include being a compassionate evaluator. And because the small group is an ongoing community, evaluation can be conducted over an extended period of time.

NURTURING MILLENNIAL ATTITUDE 2: THE PRESCRIPTION FOR SPIRITUAL HEALTH RESULTS FROM A PERSONAL AND COMMUNAL EFFORT.

A small group also has an important role in fostering communal mission and intimacy along with the leader's role in mentoring. The three words *UP-IN-OUT* describe how to missionalize a small group by balancing community and accountability. The term *missionalize* describes an atmosphere that fosters a passion for reconnecting people with God (the *missio Dei*).

2.a. *Locate all of your small groups.* Though we've discussed small groups, it is time to pinpoint them more specifically. Many churches do not think they have small groups when in reality they have dozens. And because leaders don't think they have small groups, they don't missionalize them.

Though there are many ways to define small groups, the best way is to follow organizational theory and define them in the broadest general terms, which means any small group of three to more than twelve people "formally or informally meeting approximately one or more times a month within the church fellowship network."[35] They are "people centered and characterized by intimacy and interpersonal involvement."[36]

> Gordon Cosby, longtime pastor of Church of the Saviour in Washington, D.C., states that "smallness is important to intimacy, and needed if we are to really get to know the people, to feel our way into their pain and allow them to feel their way into our pain."

From this definition small groups could include Sunday school classes, Bible study groups, leadership committees, sports teams, worship teams, and so on.[37] Gibbs and Bolger, in studying millennial congregations, discovered that a recurring opinion is that "small groups are the *essential* meeting of the church."[38] Asbury Seminary's George G. Hunter III even declared, "Today a healthy church is not a church with small groups, but a church *of* small groups."[39]

2.b. *Create healthy people by embracing UP-IN-(OUT) discipleship in all small groups.* UP reminds all small groups that every gathering should have an interlude of connection with God through prayer, Bible study, quiet time, meditation, and so on. This can be an eye-opening and effective requirement for leadership committees. Require leadership committees to undertake regular heavenward worship and prayer, and you will be surprised how often this creates a supernatural bond that leads to less bickering, new unity, and more progress.

IN means that every small-group meeting should include a time of building up one another. This can be sharing prayer requests, communicating personal stories/testimonies, listening and encouraging one another, and so forth. Gordon Cosby, longtime pastor of Church of the Saviour in Washington, D.C., states that "smallness is important to intimacy, and needed if we are to really get to know the people, to feel our way into their pain and allow them to feel their way into our pain."[40] When leadership committees are required to recognize they are a small group and undertake this, they become healthier. They are no longer interested only in organizational duties, but now realize that their meetings can be a time of mutual encouragement and ministry. There is something rewarding in seeing a church administrative board sharing prayer requests and laying hands on one another in prayer before they take up the tasks of organizing the church.

2.c. *Missionalize your small groups by practicing (UP-IN)-OUT discipleship.*

OUT is the third element of a healthy small group and reminds us that every small group, team, committee, class, and gathering should be working together to share the good news to others on their spiritual journeys. The Greek word *euangelion* (good news; see Matt. 24:14)[41] is sometimes translated as "evangelism." But too often evangelism is associated only with the point of conversion and not the process that leads up to conversion or the process that occurs after conversion. To be true to the New Testament meaning, evangelism should mean good news no matter where it arrives on a person's journey.[42] For a hungry person to be given food in the name of Christ is good news to that person. When a person experiences conversion and suddenly has power over temptations one did not have before, this is good news also. And when a person discovers one's God-given leadership "gifts" (as Robert Clinton described),[43] this too is evangelism, or God's unfolding good news. Although small groups are often good at the UP and IN parts of good news, they are usually not as good at going OUT-side the church community to minister to the needs of others. But such ministry is required if, as Billy Graham said, we are to take regeneration in one hand and a cup of cold water in the other.[44] John Stott, writing for the Lausanne Committee for World Evangelism, stressed that going OUT to others while ministering IN-ward to the needs of existing Christians was analogous to "the relationship between two wings on a bird or two oars in a boat...being inseparable."[45]

> To be true to the New Testament meaning, evangelism should mean good news no matter where it arrives on a person's journey. For a hungry person to be given food in the name of Christ is good news to that person.

Figure 3.2 illustrates how the UP-IN-OUT elements function together to create a healthy small group.

Figure 3.2. The small group as a triangle of three purposes: UP-IN-OUT[46]

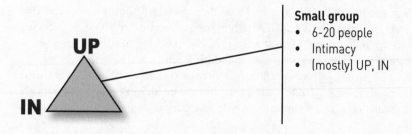

UP

IN

Small group
- 6-20 people
- Intimacy
- (mostly) UP, IN

: *Prescription*

NURTURING MILLENNIAL ATTITUDE 3: THE PRESCRIPTION FOR VOLUNTEER HEALTH IS A NETWORK OF SMALL GROUPS.

There must be clear organizational structure to help emerging leaders move forward on their faith journeys. The spiritual traveler must understand the next stage of leadership, what it looks like and what is required. But in most modern churches this structure is foggy at best. To continue missionalizing small groups, some millennial churches embrace the Groups-MissionalNets-Cultures church structure.[47]

1. *Groups* are small groups that we defined by the more inclusive definition as any formal or informal small group of three to more than twelve people meeting one or more times a month within the church fellowship network. They are characterized by intimacy[48] and are good at fostering IN (building up one another) and UP (connecting with God).

2. *MissionalNets* are gatherings of two to five small groups. This MissionalNet creates the feel of an "extended family" with approximately 20 to 150 people that usually meets one or more times a month. Although a MissionalNet does not have the intimacy of a small group, it is the most efficient way for small groups to join together and accomplish social outreach. For example, if a small group were to schedule a social action project, such as cleaning up a vacant lot in a neighborhood on a Saturday morning, out of the six to twenty regular small-group attendees, only four to six might actually show up. This could be a disappointment for the small-group members and might even feel like a failure. This often occurs because people are so busy today. However, if two to five small groups are "netted together," then the minimum turnout for social action usually occurs. MissionalNets thus link two to five small groups to create the critical mass needed for OUT-reach to occur. See figure 3.3 for how MissionalNets fill a missing element in the outreach strategies of small groups.

3. *Cultures* are defined by Paul Hiebert as an "integrated system of learned patterns of behavior, ideas and products characteristic of a society."[49] By this definition, there are today tens of thousands of cultures.[50] Ethnicities, affinity groups, socioeconomic groups, and age groups are cultures. Also note that the word *cultures* is plural, not singular, because the Groups-MissionalNets-Cultures approach means that churches that reach out to more than two cultures at the same time will have the best chance of longevity. Health occurs because

as one culture may be waning in the neighborhood (for example, ethnicity or generational), another culture is usually emerging. Healthy churches will usually reach out to several cultures at the same time.[51]

Volunteer mobilization benefits in two ways from the Groups-MissionalNets-Cultures approach.

3.a. *The Groups-MissionalNets-Cultures approach creates healthy people by clearly defining routes into accountability and leadership*. A healthy small-group structure means that someone is in charge of that small group and that the leader is accountable to someone above him or her. With a MissionalNet, there is a net leader who oversees two to five small groups. Giving oversight to too many groups may swamp the overseer.

Surprisingly, such direct and uncomplicated supervision is one of the most neglected aspects of contemporary small-group leadership. Having someone to whom the small-group leader is accountable can minimize the chances that the small group becomes divisive. This potential for division is a primary reason cited for not having small groups. But by not having small groups, many churches forfeit the best environment for spiritual direction.[52] Remember, Jesus used the small group of the twelve disciples to foster a learning environment that would one day propel the disciples into worldwide ministry.

3.b. *The Groups-MissionalNets-Cultures approach shares the good news with people outside a church via MissionalNets*. As we saw above, MissionalNets create the needed critical mass of volunteers for social action to be accomplished. For example, when England experienced the great floods of 2007, the MissionalNets of the Philadelphia Church in Sheffield mobilized for action. One net leader called his four small-group leaders and told them to meet in an hour with as many small-group members as possible to shore up a breaking levee. "The church staff didn't even know they were doing it," recalled one of the church's leaders. "If they had called us, we wouldn't have been able to mobilize anything near as fast as they could. The cluster [their name for a MissionalNet] leader was nearer to the need, and by mobilizing his net of four small groups, they had a sufficient turnout to sandbag the breach."

Bob Hopkins, the English pastor who helped create the MissionalNet idea in England, observes that these nets create an extended family environment, as do house churches. However, millennial leaders do not like to use the term *house church* because of a house church's "'react against institution' mentality."[53]

In figure 3.3 MissionalNets create a network of small groups mobilized for mission, which creates a more proactive rather than reactive approach to creating an extended family, extended health, and extended missional impact.

Figure 3.3. Groups-MissionalNets-Cultures structure

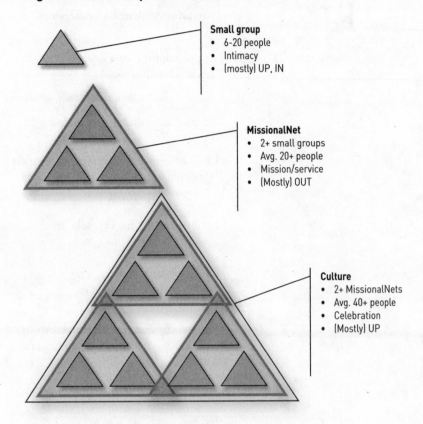

Small group
- 6-20 people
- Intimacy
- (mostly) UP, IN

MissionalNet
- 2+ small groups
- Avg. 20+ people
- Mission/service
- (Mostly) OUT

Culture
- 2+ MissionalNets
- Avg. 40+ people
- Celebration
- (Mostly) UP

MOVING TOWARD MILLENNIAL LEADERSHIP: QUESTIONS FOR PERSONAL REFLECTION AND/OR GROUP DISCUSSION

The following questions are for personal reflection but can also be used in a group setting:[54]

1. *For personal and group reflection:* create an organix leadership journal by

- selecting two items from each box, and
- writing in it what you will begin to do over the next thirty days to move toward millennial leadership in these two areas.

R_x	**Nurturing Millennial Leadership**

Prescription	1. The prescription for a healthy church is healthy people.
	
	  1.a. *Small-group leaders assess the needs and health of emerging leaders.*
	
	  1.b. *Small-group leaders foster spiritual direction and service via the small group.*
	
	  1.c. *Small-group leaders help emerging leaders establish fitting goals.*
	
	  1.d. *Small-group leaders offer emerging leaders honest evaluation.*

	2. The prescription for spiritual health results from a personal and communal effort.
	
	  2.a. *Locate all of your small groups.*
	
	  2.b. *Create healthy people by embracing UP-IN-(OUT) discipleship in all small groups.*
	
	  2.c. *Missionalize your small groups by practicing (UP-IN)-OUT discipleship.*

	3. The prescription for volunteer health is a network of small groups. 3.a. *The Groups-MissionalNets Cultures approach creates healthy people by clearly defining routes into accountability and leadership.*

℞ : *Prescription*

> 3.b. *The Groups-MissionalNets-Cultures approach shares the good news with people outside a church via Missional Nets.*

2. *For group reflection:*

- Share your responses to the chart above with your group (omitting answers/plans that are overly personal).
- Take notes in your journal on the following:
  a. Does your group agree or disagree with your assessments and plans?
  b. What input did they give you regarding moving toward millennial leadership?
- Then rewrite your plans in your journal using their input.

3. *For personal and group reflection:*

- Revisit your notes in your journal every month for six months. Ask yourself:
  a. Are there areas where I am making progress? If so, describe them.
  b. Are there areas where I am still weak? What will I do to address this?
- At the end of six months reread the chapter and update your plans.

CHAPTER FOUR

Each time history repeats itself, the price goes up.

—*Graffiti*[1]

	Modern Leadership	Millennial Leadership
Graffiti	1. Modern leadership avoids risk.	1. Graffiti leadership embraces risk.
	2. Modern leadership is concerned about white male privilege.	2. Graffiti leadership practices and repeats reconciliation.
	3. Modern leadership grows museum churches.	3. Graffiti leadership grows mosaic churches.

A TRUE ART

Joan leaned back in her chair and thought, *This is more like it . . . and better!* After a stormy eighteen months, she had left Aldersgate Church, landing in a small urban church, Smith Street Church. The congregation of eighty attendees was one-third the size of Aldersgate, but almost twice the size of Clarkston Church when she began to lead it to growth. "This is familiar territory," she began as we started a new consultation in this church with a storied history. "This church was a stopping point on the Underground Railroad," she continued. "They have a distinguished history, helping slaves escape to freedom in the 1800s. That's why I'm here, Bob. This is the place where I sense God wants to start racial reconciliation in this city."

Reconciliation was certainly needed. The city had experienced the good and the bad of racial tensions. While churches like Smith Street Church had spirited slaves to freedom, this city was also the site of one of the last lynchings in America. "Strange fruit from this city," I mused. "Strange fruit once. New fruit now," Joan replied.

Joan realized that despite its storied history, the largely white Smith Street Church now had a "we-them" attitude toward the black neighborhood. To start to address this, she began a book study for the church's leaders, choosing a book by Soong-Chan Rah titled *The New Evangelicalism: Freeing the Church from Western Cultural Captivity*.[2] Hoping to begin with a less controversial topic (at least for Smith Street Church) of white churches and their relationship to Asian American communities, she planned to slowly move the leaders to eventually address the tensions between the Smith Street Church and the African American community. She was little prepared for the reaction.

"I agree with the concept of the book," stated Larry at the following month's board meeting. "But the tone's way off."

"That's right," added George. "It's like he's got a chip on his shoulder. And that puts me off to what he is saying."

"Perhaps we should study a book on women ministers instead," Shelly offered. "I've just finished a great book titled *The Stained-Glass Ceiling: Churches and Their Women Pastors*." Shelly was an energetic single mother and business owner, and her suggestion garnered the support of the rest of the board. Glenn, one of the few African Americans in the church and a well-liked business owner, agreed, saying, "This could be a good starting place."

"That's your choice then," summarized Joan. "We'll discuss the first three chapters at our next meeting."

Shelly left elated, but soon reality came crashing down. At next month's meeting the board voted to discontinue reading *The Stained-Glass Ceiling* too. "The problem is overblown, and the author just wants to make you feel guilty," summed up George. "The book makes matters worse," continued Larry. "We should read a book on worship, like *Reaching Out Without Dumbing Down: A Theology of Worship for This Urgent Time*.[3] Worship is what people in this community want. I've seen their services on TV, and that's what we're missing." With that, the books were changed again. Before long, Shelly changed churches. Glenn sat quietly that night, either not wishing to make matters worse or having no hope things would change. Regardless of what he was thinking, two months later Glenn was gone too.

G IS FOR "GRAFFITI"

One of the most influential art forms in American history[4] first appeared in its current form on public walls in the late 1960s.[5] Graffiti is an improvised, colorful, and risky art that is layered on public buildings, bridges, railway cars, and subways. A product of urban artists who often eschew training, it is a fitting metaphor for another characteristic of millennial leadership. While modern leadership often disciplines itself to keep colors and lines in their place, millennial leaders create a leadership collage of colors, symbols, and statements. (Paradoxically, the style known as modern art, including the works of Matisse, Picasso, and others, shunned the orderliness of previous periods of art and acted as a precursor to millennial thinking. This demonstrates the broad strokes and limitations underscored by the term *modern*.)

Here are some attributes of graffiti artists:[6]
- take risks
- improvise
- led by spirit and passion
- break human convention for the sake of improvement
- create collage of colors, styles, messages, and meanings that make the world take notice
- add their style to others' art
- retain individuality using personal symbols and icons

Graffiti often contains recurring elements, including[7]
- name or epithet
- a philosophy line
- synergy created by blending multiple shapes, styles, and colors
- arrows that create a sense of busting out[8] (such as the arrow that is added to the *G* of this chapter)

Therefore, we employ a graffiti *G* with an arrow busting out to remind us of the improvisational, risky, and outward-focused collage of millennial leadership. Millennial leadership is not for the fainthearted or the small-minded.

THREE PERILS OF MODERN LEADERSHIP REGARDING *G* (GRAFFITI)

	Modern Leadership	Millennial Leadership
G Graffiti	1. Modern leadership avoids risk.	1. Graffiti leadership embraces risk.
	2. Modern leadership is concerned about white male privilege.	2. Graffiti leadership practices and repeats reconciliation.
	3. Modern leadership grows museum churches.	3. Graffiti leadership grows mosaic churches.

MODERN PERIL 1: MODERN LEADERSHIP AVOIDS RISK.

The modern world is risk aversive, seeking to create a stable environment of minimized risk. Michel Crouhy, Dan Galai, and Robert Mark in *The Essentials of Risk Management* argue that a key characteristic of modern leadership is the leader's ability to transfer or lessen risk.[9] Whether in the stock market, which regulators seek to make less volatile, or in our cities, which municipalities seek to gentrify, the modern goal is less chaos, not more.

But this may be out of sync with reality. When millennial leaders look back on the last century, they see the ravages of Stalin, Lenin, Hitler, Mao, Pol Pot, and others as signs of a world more conflicted than cohesive. In a world where cultures, traditions, and bigotry collide with ever-increasing damage, millennial leaders see transferring or lessening risk as not just unattainable, but unrealistic.

MODERN PERIL 2: MODERN LEADERSHIP IS CONCERNED ABOUT WHITE MALE PRIVILEGE.

Modern leaders endeavor to eliminate bias and create equality for the sake of less risk and increased stability. These are laudable objectives. The modern leader becomes concerned when he or she witnesses bias or bigotry that threatens this harmony. And though modern leaders themselves will attempt not to be biased or bigoted, let us look at how residue remains.

2.a. *White male privilege remains a reality.* To understand this statement, let's define *white male privilege*.

> "The pastorate is a men's club. But almost every other area of church life is dominated by women."
> —David Murrow

Male privilege. Though many modern leaders will bristle at the thought that women have not attained equality, males continue to dominate secular and church leadership. Harvard University's Barbara Kellerman points out that

> 2% of Fortune 500 companies are headed by women (2009), 6% of the 100 top tech companies are headed by women (2010), 15% of members of Fortune 500 boards are women (2009), 16.8% of members of the U.S. Congress are women (2010)....This does not of course mean there is no improvement whatsoever. Rather it is to point out how abysmally low the numbers remain.[10]

The church fares little better. According to the American Religious Identification Survey,[11] men overwhelmingly hold leadership positions in churches, while women make up the majority of the congregants. Some traditions that once allowed women pastors have backtracked on that decision.[12] And the Roman Catholic Church continues to prohibit women from being deacons, much less priests or bishops.[13] David Murrow, author of *Why Men Hate Going to Church*, states, "The pastorate is a men's club. But almost every other area of church life is dominated by women."[14]

White privilege. Sociologists have long known that the dominant group in a society, because of its sheer size, will receive preferred treatment in that society.[15] Such preferred treatment is sometimes called "unwarranted favor" or "privilege." When the dominant group is Caucasian, such as in North American society, a phenomenon called "white privilege" results. Researchers have learned that once a group is "privileged," that group then defines what is normal in a society. And people without privilege are subconsciously branded "abnormal" or irregular.[16] Normal people receive mostly trouble-free assistance as they go about their daily lives. But those who are perceived as irregular receive regular doses of heightened suspicion, added evaluation, and questionable genuineness. This makes daily life harder for non-privileged people. Robert Jensen summarizes, "The dirty secret that we white people carry around with us every day in a world of white privilege, [is that] some of what we have is unearned."[17]

> "The dirty secret that we white people carry around with us every day in a world of white privilege, [is that] some of what we have is unearned."
> —Robert Jensen

The Apostle Paul was once the recipient of similar privilege. Figure 4.1 is a comparison of his relationship with privilege before and after his conversion.

Figure 4.1. The Apostle Paul and privilege

Before Conversion	After Conversion
Paul emphasizes that he was "circumcised on the eighth day, of the people of Israel, of the tribe of Benjamin, NIV). a Hebrew of Hebrews; in regard to the law, a Pharisee; as for zeal, persecuting the church; as for legalistic righteousness, ... faultless" (Phil. 3:5-6 NIV).	Paul states, "There is neither Jew nor Gentile, neither slave nor free, nor is there male and female, for you are all one in Christ Jesus" (Gal. 3:28
Paul "began to destroy the church. Going from house to house, he dragged off men and women and put them in prison" (Acts 8:3 NIV).	Paul states, "For we were all baptized by one Spirit so as to form one body—whether Jews or Gentiles, slave or free—and we were all given the one Spirit to drink" (1 Cor. 12:13 NIV).

Paul states, "I am a Pharisee, descended from Pharisees" (Acts 23:6).	Paul summarizes, "Here there is no Gentile or Jew, circumcised or uncircumcised, barbarian, Scythian, slave or free, but Christ is all, and is in all" (Col. 3:11 NIV).

This comparison reminds us that New Testament Christians were familiar with bias and unearned privilege. And Paul, the recipient of such privilege, was likewise fervent in its emphasis that such distinctions should not continue in the new faith community.

2.b. *White male privilege is largely unperceived by those who benefit from it.* To this statement, a modern leader might say, "But affirmative action gives women and people of color benefits that they have not earned, just because of their race or gender." This is correct. But when the majority of one's life is filled with lack of privilege, promoting underprivileged people can become a positive action to move toward balance.

At the same time the modern leader often does not recognize privileges that the non-privileged are denied. Sociologists have long known that "privilege is rarely seen by the holder of the privilege."[18] The modern leader honestly says, "I am not bigoted or biased, for I have some of the best people of color and women working for me." But often without realizing it, the modern leader may benefit from unearned favor because of one's gender and/or ethnicity. Thus, the ongoing lack of a level playing field, coupled with the dominant culture's myopia about its privileges, makes the non-privileged justly angry.

> Anger, not tolerance, in a young black woman had shifted the gears of racial inequality in America. And it was anger, not tolerance, that drove Jesus' reaction in John 2:14-17.

2.c. *Being "concerned" about white male privilege is not an adequate response.* A modern mind thinks, *Bias and bigotry have been problems in the past, but now that the non-privileged have a level playing field, they will advance.* The modern leader's concern results in actions that promote tolerance.

But is tolerance enough? If as Harvard professor Barbara Kellerman says, "The modern women's movement is almost a half century old, but so far, as women leaders are concerned, we have precious little to show for it,"[19] then fifty years of tolerance have yielded little change. When Philip Klinkner and Rogers Smith studied two hundred years of racial equality in America, they concluded, "Few would deny that America's unsteady march toward racial equality remains remote from that grand destination."[20]

Thus, we return to the question, is tolerance really enough? White culture in 1960s Alabama was tolerant "enough" to let African Americans ride in the backs of buses until Rosa Parks got angry and refused to be reseated. Before his conversion to Christianity, Black Panther Eldridge Cleaver observed that at that moment, "Somewhere in the universe a gear in the machinery had shifted."[21] Anger, not tolerance, in a young black woman had shifted the gears of racial inequality in America. Similarly, it was anger, not tolerance, that drove Jesus' reaction when

> in the temple courts he found people selling cattle, sheep and doves, and others sitting at tables exchanging money. So he made a whip out of cords, and drove all from the temple courts, both sheep and cattle; he scattered the coins of the money changers and overturned their tables. To those who sold doves he said, "Get these out of here! Stop turning my Father's house into a market!" His disciples remembered that it is written: "Zeal for your house will consume me." (John 2:14-17 NIV)

Merely practicing racial and gender tolerance, while laudable, may be too little to reverse such deep-seated prejudices and privileges. Millennial leaders are more sensitive to the failure of a tolerance strategy and see anger as justified and obligatory.

MODERN PERIL 3: MODERN LEADERSHIP GROWS MUSEUM CHURCHES.

3.a. *The church is a museum.* The modern church often appears to the outside observer as a museum, preserving masterpieces of song, prose, and art (and some amateurish imitations) from previous cultures for the curious, studious, or bored. The church as museum has arisen because the church has dual duties. The church must be the guardian of theology and tradition, but it is also the mechanism through which God translates his good news to emerging cultures. When a church errs on the side of guardianship, the result can be a museum church: cataloging artifacts

> **The modern church often appears to the outside observer as a museum, preserving masterpieces of song, prose, and art (and some amateurish imitations) for the curious, studious, or bored.**

and traditions. But this is also an inadequate metaphor for the true church.[22] The church's work is twofold, and one is searching for new expressions of eternal truth.

3.b. *The church separates cultural artistic expressions by genre.* Churches today often multiply their worship services and venues to connect to multiple cultures. On Sundays a church may have a "traditional" worship service at 8:30 a.m., a "contemporary" worship service at 10:30 a.m., and a celebration for people under age thirty-five at 6:00 p.m. Such tactics allow churches to reach out to multiple generations and should be lauded.[23]

But a problem arises when these multicultural congregations do not gather together their cultural segments and foster authentic intercultural fellowship. Different cultural segments within the same church still fellowship primarily within their own time slot and venue, with little cross-cultural bonding. In business, such partitioning is recognized as a blunder and is labeled the "silo effect"[24] because each silo contains unconnected with often redundant communities and processes.[25] A millennial generation raised in such disconnected communities of faith sees the fallacy of this approach. Millennials seek true multiculturalism: maintaining some separation, but even more unification.

THREE ATTITUDES OF MILLENNIAL LEADERSHIP REGARDING 𝒢 (GRAFFITI)

	Modern Leadership	Millennial Leadership
𝒢 Graffiti	1. Modern leadership avoids risk.	1. Graffiti leadership embraces risk.
	2. Modern leadership is concerned about white male privilege.	2. Graffiti leadership practices and repeats reconciliation.
	3. Modern leadership grows museum churches.	3. Graffiti leadership grows mosaic churches.

MILLENNIAL ATTITUDE 1: GRAFFITI LEADERSHIP EMBRACES RISK.

In response to these modern perils, the millennial leader seeks a more elastic and organic approach. While the modern leader tries to create stability and minimize risk, the millennial leader recognizes that chaos is a by-product of the human condition (Rom. 3:23; 5:12). According to organizational theorist Mary Jo Hatch, the millennial leader "embraces complexity and uncertainty and their contradictory demands."[26]

When researcher Lois Barrett and her colleagues studied churches that were effectively reaching young non-churchgoers, they found that a recurring pattern was "taking risks as a contrast community."[27] This is a church that is

> learning to take risk for the sake of the gospel. It understands itself as different from the world because of its participation in the life, death, and resurrection of

its Lord. It is raising questions, often threatening ones, about the church's cultural captivity and it is grappling with the ethical and structural implications of its missional vocation.[28]

A moving example of risk taking comes from the story of John Perkins, a black man who left Mississippi after his brother was shot by a police officer. After an encounter with Christ, he returned to Mississippi to work with children during the turbulent civil rights struggles of the 1950s. Eventually, Perkins founded a Christian ministry that included student tutoring, co-ops to share food, child care, nutrition programs, medical facilities, and Bible studies. This was risky behavior in 1950s Mississippi. The millennial leader understands such risk because as Lewis Drummond observes, "In postmodern terms, we might say that Jesus came to bring equal access and opportunity to those in substandard living conditions, to give voice and identity to those other than the dominant social elite, and to alleviate the ravages of capitalistic imperialism and colonialist economic aggression."[29]

Figure 4.2 contrasts risk-aversive actions I have observed in modern churches seeking to minimize their risk (left column) with examples of risk taking in millennial congregations (right column):

Figure 4.2. Risk aversion and risk taking in churches

Risk Aversion (Modern Reactions)		Risk Taking[30] (Millennial Reactions)
Set up group homes for immigrants in the inner city.	Immigration	Welcome immigrants to live in homes of congregants.
Fund a homeless shelter with other churches.	Homelessness	Let homeless people live on the church property.
Support indigenous worship venues in substandard facilities away from the church location.	Worship Venues	Move the church's entire worship gathering into a neighborhood blighted with crime and poverty.

Live an affluent lifestyle to inspire the poor.	Affluence	Live a simpler and less affluent lifestyle in solidarity with the poor and to better meet their needs.
Send young leaders away to receive training.	Leadership Development	Give young leaders significant responsi- bilities locally.
Send surrogates with your money and cast- off items to the poor.	Poverty	Share with the poor face-to-face your time, life, knowledge, and possessions.
Take financial risks to enhance church reputation.	Finances	Take financial risks "for the sake of compassion."[31]

Lois Barrett concluded, "These congregations seem to be living by a set of rules different from that of dominant culture. Their priorities are different. They act against 'common sense.' They are trying to conform to Jesus Christ rather than to the surrounding society."[32] Such risk taking for the sake of the *missio Dei* is akin to the risks a graffiti artist takes for one's craft.

MILLENNIAL ATTITUDE 2: GRAFFITI LEADERSHIP PRACTICES AND REPEATS RECONCILIATION.

As we saw above, a result of white male privilege is that those who are denied this privilege can get frustrated and justifiably angry. This can carry over into the tone of their writings. The criticism leveled against Soong-Chan Rah's book in the story that opened this chapter is taken directly from a meeting I observed. The participants took issue not with one of Rah's prem-

> The problem is not the anger of those frozen out of the white, male dominant culture, but that modern leaders don't recognize that this anger is warranted.

ises (that modern evangelicalism is blind and captive to a white privilege) but with what they perceived as Rah's anger.

Modern leaders do not understand fully the plight of those less privileged because modern leaders usually have never experienced such bias, personally or continually. The problem is not the anger of those frozen out of the white, male dominant culture, but that modern leaders don't recognize that this anger is warranted. Thus, while bias concerns modern leadership, change won't occur (as we saw in Rosa Park's case and Eldridge Cleaver's commentary) until modern leaders get angry too.

2.a. *Anger by the non-privileged is understandable.* Why? Edward Gilbreath, a black journalist, comments on a revealing e-mail exchange with a friend about her feelings working for an evangelical Christian company:

> She's actually a gentle, peace-loving black person . . . expressing her fatigue over the running-in-place stagnancy she believed was passing for racial unity among evangelicals. . . . My friend's e-mail sticks in my head. Despite all the visible advances in racial relations, something is still broken. . . . My young friend who wrote that e-mail added: "The white Christians I encounter often display a shocking provincialism—a real naiveté about the world around them. Frankly, it's as if they are stunned to find out that their cultural, political, and religious frame of reference is not the only one.[33]

Though largely unperceived by white males who are trying to be more fair and equal, those on the daily receiving end of this bias get understandably fatigued, frustrated, and angry.

2.b. *Anger is necessary or things won't change.* We saw in Barbara Kellerman's research that fifty years of a quest for gender equality has resulted in little change. Thus, millennial leaders sense that change won't come until the dominant class gets angry too. Writing about the spark that ignited the civil rights movement, Jo Ann Robinson said, "I think people were fed up, they had reached the point that they knew there was no return. That they had to do it or die. And that's what kept it going."[34] White male privilege won't go away until a righteous anger spreads among those who are white, male, and privileged.

2.c. *The church should be a haven, free of intolerance and bias.* Jesus' prayer for the church was unity, stating, "I pray also for those who will believe in me through their message, that all of them may be one" (John 17:20-21 NIV). The church must do a better job of reconciling different cultures if it is to be an example (and force for) unity in an increasingly divided world. Regardless of a church's theological stance on female leadership, bias and unfair partiality based on gender should also not characterize a church. Paul, by birth a member of the privileged class, spoke to a heavily patriarchal and segregated audience and still stressed the importance of an unbiased, unprivileged Christian community. He asked the Corinthians to look at their own history to verify this:

Take a good look, friends, at who you were when you got called into this life. I don't see many of "the brightest and the best" among you, not many influential, not many from high-society families. Isn't it obvious that God deliberately chose men and women that the culture overlooks and exploits and abuses, chose these "nobodies" to expose the hollow pretensions of the "somebodies"? (1 Cor. 1:26-28 *THE MESSAGE*)

Because the millennial leader believes that the dominant culture, such as a white male culture in North America, can never truly understand minority cultures, the millennial leader sees that the only person the white person can change to make things better is the white person himself or herself. No amount of empathy will keep a white male culture from acting in a way that comes off as superior, better, and privileged until that dominant culture is angered by its sin.

2.d. *The church must be the torchbearer of reconciliation.* Mere anger is not enough. Anger must result in tangible change. Rosa Parks's anger at a bus driver's attempt to reseat her would not have been notable, or enough, if it had not resulted in change. And what is that change? The change that is needed mirrors the change that God seeks. In God's mission (the *missio Dei*) God seeks to reconcile or bring back together and resolve differences that separate God and God's offspring. Paul, once biased and bigoted toward Christians, described this as the "ministry of reconciliation," stating:

> From now on we regard no one from a worldly point of view.... Therefore, if anyone is in Christ, the new creation has come: The old has gone, the new is here! All this is from God, who reconciled us to himself through Christ and gave us the ministry of reconciliation: that God was reconciling the world to himself in Christ, not counting men's sins against them. And he has committed to us the message of reconciliation. We are therefore Christ's ambassadors, as though God were making his appeal through us. We implore you on Christ's behalf: Be reconciled to God. (2 Cor. 5:16-20 NIV)

John M. Perkins, whose story we encountered earlier in this chapter, came to believe that in order for the church to be the torchbearer of reconciliation, it must practice three Rs: "relocation, redistribution and reconciliation":[35]

1. Relocation means incarnational evangelism: sharing the good news while living among the poor, worshiping among them, and taking the poor into your life. Ron Sider, the director of Evangelicals for Social Action, labels this koinonia ministry, for "koinonia means fellowship with someone or participation in something.... I am thoroughly convinced, however, that the overwhelming majority of Western churches no longer understand or experience biblical koinonia to any significant degree."[36]

2. Redistribution denotes an intentional sharing of resources, talents, knowledge, and time with the needy. Perkins urges the church to create people and policies that "break the cycle of wealth and poverty."[37]

3. Reconciliation means living daily and consistently the message that "there is neither Jew nor Gentile, neither slave nor free, nor is there male and female, for you are all one in Christ Jesus" (Gal. 3:28 NIV).

Martin Luther King Jr. often said his goal was not to overthrow white society, but "to awaken a sense of shame within the oppressor and challenge his false sense of superiority.... The end is reconciliation; the end is redemption; the end is the creation of the beloved community."[38] In the same way that graffiti artists break convention for the sake of change, millennial leaders call attention to white male privilege and call for righteous anger to see such privileges end.

MILLENNIAL ATTITUDE 3: GRAFFITI LEADERSHIP GROWS MOSAIC CHURCHES.

Millennial leadership recognizes the need for cultural sensitivity, awareness, and autonomy. Though there is a healthy respect for different traditions, there is also a concern that the body of Christ not be splintered into smaller and less holistic factions. Millennial leaders are recognizing that there are two types of church planting,[39] and they are increasingly using internal instead of external church plants.

> **Many millennial leaders have seen their parents' churches use a "church planting excuse" to push out a different culture.**

3.a. *External church plants.* When modern leaders think of church planting, they usually think about launching a new and autonomous congregation to reach a new culture. However, many millennial leaders have seen their parents' churches use a "church planting excuse" to push out a different culture. Whether it is a generational culture or an ethnic culture, these forced plants often don't survive. The millennial leader often wonders, why can't the church just get along and stay together as a spiritual network?

> **More cultural sharing will take place if multiple ethnicities meet in the same building and share the same budget and so on than will take place if an emerging culture is forced to move down the street to an independent church plant.**

3.b. *Internal church plants (or network churches).*[40] This is an increasingly popular strategy that plants new subcongregations but keeps them part of one inclusive and multicultural congregation. Called "network churches,"[41] these can be multiple-site and multiple-venue churches, and as such, they are examples of internal church planting.

Here are advantages of internal church plants:

- *Sharing finances*. In the business world this is called an "economy of scale," which means that a network of subcongregations will have more financial resources together than if each were an independent organization. For example, if emergency funds are needed by one subcongregation, the network can provide those funds more readily and smoothly because they are all part of one organizational system.
- *Sharing facilities*. Internal church plants that employ a multivenue approach foster a sharing of facilities, technology, and physical resources. This can help fulfill John M. Perkins's goal of "redistribution."
- *Sharing staff*. Network churches benefit from sharing support staff, allowing subcongregations to avoid reduplicating their workforces.
- *Sharing culture*. This is a strategic advantage. More cultural sharing will take place if multiple ethnicities meet in the same building and share the same budget and so on than will take place if an emerging culture is forced to move down the street to an independent church plant.

> The end result is the mosaic church, where the glue of being one united organization unites different cultural expressions. A true image of a mosaic is created.

But disadvantages of *internal* church plants must be kept in mind:

- *Divisiveness*. This is often cited as a main concern. But if a subcongregation exits the church, it is divided anyway. Division can be addressed by having different preachers at different venues/times share the same message and by holding regular unity events.
- *Marginalized cultures*. Often the largest cultures will try, sometimes unintentionally and sometimes intentionally, to dominate the smaller culture. Yet this should not deter a congregation from practicing a ministry that reconciles different cultures in the same church. One way to address this is to require proportional representation on decision-making committees.

If these caveats can be addressed, the end result is the mosaic church, where the glue of being one united organization unites different cultural expressions. A true image of a mosaic is created, where different colors and shades create a unified picture when viewed from a distance, but up close reveals a collage of different cultures working in unity and harmony. Graffiti is full of colorful layering and icons that, when combined, produce a new multifaceted, yet integrated image. This is the church.

NURTURING THE THREE ATTITUDES
REGARDING 𝒢 (GRAFFITI)

NURTURING MILLENNIAL ATTITUDE 1: GRAFFITI LEADERSHIP EMBRACES RISK.

1.a. *Take risks for the sake of the good news.* Risk taking is a part of the Christian journey. Theologian Walter Brueggemann emphasized that in the Old Testament, Israel was "in every phase of this history profoundly in jeopardy" and "could never eliminate the risk."[42] Anthony Robinson and Robert Wall describe how in the New Testament, Paul undertook "the risk of engagement" by preaching in Athens and other hostile environs where "he did venture out on the edges, out to the margins, as Acts so often does."[43] And when Lois Barrett and her colleagues studied churches that were making a difference in their community, they found that a recurring pattern was taking a "risk for the sake of the gospel...raising questions, often threatening ones, about the church's cultural captivity and...grappling with the ethical and structural implications" of outreach.[44]

1.b. *Contrast with the usual way of doing things.* This is a second aspect of millennial leadership, for the church is a community that should contrast with the usual manner of doing things. The people of God must live a life, to the best of their ability, that is beyond what others have come to expect. It is to live a life filled with actions of love, forgiveness, and reconciliation. Such actions create a community that is in contrast with and dissimilar to how the world usually goes about such things. This creates a pattern for the world to follow toward its hoped for reconciliation between humans and God.

> When a white pastor of a megachurch washed the feet of a young black mother who had been displaced by the church's parking lot expansion...the pastor's actions reminded church leaders that regardless of how efficient or insistent, church actions must not make the plight of the disadvantaged more arduous.

1.c. *Undertake such actions publicly.* Contrast must be open and overt. Paul reminded his hearers, "You know that I have not hesitated to preach anything that would be helpful to you but have taught you publicly and from house to house" (Acts 20:20 NIV).

But risk taking by its very nature can lead to failure. Randy Komisar, author of *The Monk and the Riddle: The Art of Creating a Life While Making a Living*, suggests three questions to ask before undertaking risks:[45]

1. What is the risk to me personally, my family, and those who depend on me? You have dependents, and they are often brought unwillingly into your risk. Evaluate and discuss risk

73

with those who depend on you and/or will be affected by your risk taking.

2. What risks are you already taking? A church, like any person or organization, can become overcommitted to good causes. Evaluate whether you can take on new risk without compromising relevant actions you have already taken.

3. How does the risk affect your long-term goals? Some risk is fashionable, some is urgent, and some is strategic. The key is to ask how risk will affect your long-term strategic goals and not be swayed into taking on risk simply because it is trendy or compelling.

Once a person and/or a congregation has evaluated Christlike risk taking through these three questions, risk can become a powerful manner to exhibit Christ's good news.

NURTURING MILLENNIAL ATTITUDE 2: GRAFFITI LEADERSHIP PRACTICES AND REPEATS RECONCILIATION.

Action is useless unless it springs from an attitude of spiritual reconciliation. To foster such attitudes, repetitive actions such as liturgical acts of worship and physical actions in the community can foster a lifestyle of reconciliation (2 Cor. 5:18).

2.a. *Liturgical acts of reconciliation* can include, but are not limited to

• *foot washing.* I come from a tradition that practices foot washing,[46] but I never really appreciated it. It seemed to be bred from tradition, not from need (at least in today's world of foot powders and cotton socks). But when a white pastor of a megachurch washed the feet of a young African American mother who had been displaced by the church's parking lot expansion, I saw the attitudes of the congregants of the megachurch start to change. The pastor's actions reminded the church leaders that regardless of how efficient or insistent, church actions must not make the plight of the disadvantaged more arduous. Leon Morris describes Jesus' action of washing feet (John 13) as "a parable in action, setting out that great principle of lowly service which brings cleansing and which finds its supreme embodiment in the cross, setting out also the necessity for the disciple to take the Lord's way, not his own."[47]

• *prayers from the needy, creating 50/50 prayer.* In many churches, the vast majority of public prayers are directed at the needs of existing church members. In Jesus' prayers there is no such lopsidedness (John 11:41; 17:1-26; Luke 23:34).[48] One solution is 50/50 prayer,[49] where 50 percent of a congregation's prayers are directed toward congregational needs and 50 percent of the prayers are directed toward the needs of non-churchgoing people. To foster this, every church can add to its prayer lists the needs of people from outside its membership. Prayers *from* the needy also mean that we gather prayer requests from those who don't go to church to pray for them discreetly (see the note for guidelines for praying discreetly).[50]

• *ceremonies of reconciliation*. Within our worship ceremonies should be prayers, Scriptures, rituals, and acts that emphasize reconciliation of humans to God and humans to one another. The Bible states, "While we were God's enemies, we were reconciled to him through the death of his Son" (Rom. 5:10 NIV), and thus "all this is from God, who reconciled us to himself through Christ, and has given us the ministry of reconciliation" (2 Cor. 5:18). Let this ministry of reconciliation transform and reclaim your worship structure. For example, Taizé worship has become a popular trend in some American churches. Derived from worship in a Catholic monastery in Taizé, France, it includes simple Bible passages sung in unison, often combined with chants from the Eastern Orthodox Church. Yet according to its founder, its purpose is not to be a new worship style, but to be a reminder to the worshiper through liturgical acts of reconciliation about the needs of the poor.[51] If you look closely at the Taizé liturgy, you will find (and can recapture) its ministry of reconciliation to the needy. Other examples of liturgies of reconciliation may be found in the notes at the end of this book.[52]

> John M. Perkins urges Christians to be people who "plead the case of the poor, defending the weak, helping the helpless.... We must as Christians seek justice by coming up with means of redistributing good and wealth to those in need."

2.b. *Public acts of reconciliation* can include, but are not limited to

• *events of reconciliation*. Many churches have annual outdoor socials, meals, picnics, block parties, and so on. And many of these are designed to be evangelistic outreach to the community by promoting fellowship with community residents. However, this fellowship will never get beyond superficial interaction unless inner reconciliation takes place before, during, and after the event. Such reconciliation can be a public witness with speakers, musicians, testimonies, and so forth sharing examples and illustrations of racial and social reconciliation. Such events should also be created in consultation with the community. One church hosted a yearly block party and garage sale. However, when community residents were asked their impressions, they told us the prices were too high and the music was too old (it was gospel quartet music). In response, the church invited a young Christian rap group, changed the garage sale to a "give what you want" sale, and invited local speakers to share what the community could do to foster racial reconciliation. Several speakers mentioned that more events like that were needed. The church became a center for reconciliation in the community.[53]

- *sacrifice that reflects reconciliation*. An African American church purchased a boiler for a nearby struggling Hispanic congregation. When the pastor of the Hispanic church offered his thanks, the African American pastor replied, "We did it because we should know what it feels like to be treated differently. And sadly, there's been times we've treated you differently. We've been wrong. This action reminds us, and the community, that Christ gives a ministry of reconciliation." Such sacrificial actions should exemplify to the watching world that the church is living out its ministry of reconciliation.

2.c. *Personal acts of reconciliation* can include, but are not limited to

- *actions of reconciliation*. Actions of reconciliation take many congregational forms, but individual Christians should practice them too. For example, businesspeople can behave toward everyone the same, homeowners can open their lives to the needy, and neighbors can reach out to assist emerging new cultures. In all of these actions risk and sacrifice are needed, but as we saw above, such risk taking is a prerequisite for reconciliation. John M. Perkins urges Christians to be people who "plead the case of the poor, defending the weak, helping the helpless.... We must as Christians seek justice by coming up with means of redistributing goods and wealth to those in need."[54]

- *an understanding of their anger*. A healthy and godly anger leads to action against the maltreatment meted out against God's creation. Anger that leads to sin is not the objective, but anger that leads to godly change that advances reconciliation is. Thus, while some anger can be overwrought and unwarranted, the reconciling millennial leader recognizes that anger can be godly and lead to action that tears down artificial walls of separation.

- *prayer for personal reconciliation*. The task of reconciliation is too great for humans to complete unaided. That is why the *missio Dei*, God's mission to reunite with God's offspring, is God's mission in which we only participate. But God has given the Holy Spirit as the counselor, guide, and power to complete superhuman tasks such as the *missio Dei* (John 14:26; 16:5-15). Thus, God requires that we petition for such aid (James 5:14-16). Robust prayer is a prerequisite to robust reconciliation. As Paul states,

> Dominating cultures like to hire people of alternative cultures who see things from the view of the dominant culture. Thus, the dominant culture never really hears an authentic voice from a dissonant culture.

Don't fret or worry. Instead of worrying, pray. Let petitions and praises shape your worries into prayers, letting God know your concerns. Before you know it, a sense of God's wholeness, everything coming together for good, will come and settle you down. It's wonderful what happens when Christ displaces worry at the center of your life. (Phil. 4:6-7 *THE MESSAGE*)

2.d. *Regular attention to voices that challenge you.* Seminaries as well as churches can practice tokenism in the selection of potential new faculty. "Tokenism furthers the existing power structures and the systems of privilege (but now with a few colorful additions), while true diversity looks toward a future beyond Western, white cultural captivity."[55] John Drury states, "Let us beware that a candidate must 'fit in' to the extent that they will have no discernible effect on us and our way of thinking. Collegiality is great; group-think isn't."[56]

Churches and seminaries prefer to hire voices from an emerging culture that agree with the dominant culture. In other words, dominating cultures like to hire people of alternative cultures who see things from the view of the dominant culture. If a dominant culture never really hears an authentic voice from a dissonant culture, change cannot occur.

The first step toward hearing dissonant voices is understanding levels of adaption:

1. *Consonant adaption* occurs when the emerging culture adapts almost completely to the dominant culture.
2. *Selective adaption* occurs when the emerging culture adapts to some parts of a dominant culture, but rejects other elements.[57]
3. *Dissonant adaption* happens when the emerging culture fights to preserve its culture in the face of a dominant culture's influence. As a result, gaps form between cultures.[58]

These dissonant voices are the ones to which you should listen and to which Drury was referring. Authenticity and reconciliation, even while still preserving anonymity and multiculturalism, happen only by exploring the gap with those who feel it.

NURTURING MILLENNIAL ATTITUDE 3: GRAFFITI LEADERSHIP GROWS MOSAIC CHURCHES.

3.a. *Balance autonomy and partnership to grow a mosaic church.* Ethnomusicologists know that indigenous people prefer to worship in their heart music, especially when they are from emerging cultures.[59] *Heart music* is defined by Brian Schrag and Paul Neeley as "the musical system that a person learns as a child or youth that most fully expresses his or her emotions."[60] To help people worship in heart music forms, churches should accommodate autonomy by allowing different cultures to offer different worship times and styles rather than trying to make everyone fit into one blended style. Blending does not help one express "his or her emotions" as well as does heart music.

Style blending is often use to foster unity and offset the silo effect mentioned earlier where each culture has little to do with the other. But blending often results in less evangelism because Sunday morning continues to be the time when most unchurched people will visit a church. And most unchurched people will best relate to the message and the music if that message/music is in the language to which they are accustomed. Missiologists emphasize, and I agree, that those who prefer a blended style of music are actually a culture themselves, more affluent, more traveled, and less in tune with emerging cultures.[61] Churches that are going to reach and include emerging cultures must provide a variety of worship expressions so they can connect with a variety of cultures in heart music and heart language. Figure 4.3 explains the interplay of this synergy and diversity.

Figure 4.3. Growing a mosaic church with diversity and partnership

Both Columns Are Needed in a Mosaic Church		
	Diversity through Subcongregations	Partnership through Subcongregations
Facilities	Each culture has rooms and worship venues that reflect its heart music and language via art, colors, styles, icons, etc., that represent its culture.	Though there are culturally distinct rooms, cultures share much of the facility (kitchens, training rooms, restrooms, hallways, playgrounds, prayer rooms, etc.). Sharing facilities results in more efficient use and more financial stability.
Finances	Each cultural group has a budget that is a sub-budget of the overall church budget.	Because there is an overall church budget overseen by an integrated board, if one cultural group has a

		large financial need, the board can vote to take money from the whole to help the one.
Boards and Committees	Each cultural group has committees as needed for its different styles of ministry.	Yet there are common integrated committees (balanced with representatives from all subcongregations) that make major decisions for the overall organization.[62]
Organizational Behavior	Subcongregations are equal and culturally different subcongregations that unite together as one organization for the sake of unity, strength, longevity, and impact.[63]	The overall congregation recognizes it is a "congregation of congregations,"[64] and thus the overall organization is there to serve equally the various parts.
Results	Strength in diversity. The congregation can share resources and create unity between different cultures by working together in the same church.	Unity in diversity. The partnership of subcongregations in a church fosters and testifies to Christ's ministry of reconciliation to a watching world.

3.b. *Unify different cultures within a mosaic[65] church.* North America has been called the great "melting pot,"[66] but some sociologists have argued that such imagery is not only inaccurate but also disturbing. It smacks of cultural imperialism to hope that people with long and illustrious heritages will be melted into a cultural gray-green goo of indistinct colors.[67] Instead, psychologist Andrew Greeley suggested that the image of a "stew pot" serves up a more hopeful picture.[68] In a stew pot each ingredient remains physically distinct while adding its own unique flavor to the whole.

But in a modern world with microwave ovens and dining out, people may find it harder to picture a stew pot. Not surprisingly, the metaphor of a mosaic church has emerged.[69] There has been some criticism that the imagery of a mosaic church does not carry the impact of a stew pot "because pieces of a mosaic barely touch each other and do not interact."[70] In a mosaic, however, each tile retains its color while glued together by grout. Perhaps the glue can be thought of as the Holy Spirit. And so, a mosaic has the characteristics of figure 4.4, as fitting descriptors of the church that millennial leaders seek to foster.

Figure 4.4. Contrasting the melting pot and the mosaic church

Modern Melting Pot Church		Millennial Mosaic Church
Adaption: the emerging culture should assimilate fully into the dominant culture with as little change in the dominant culture as possible.	Goal	Unity in diversity: the church should preserve the good in each culture, which means celebrating God's diversity in art, history, and narrative.
Colonialization: the dominant culture is superior, and other cultures must be made over in its image.	Ethos	Globalization: each culture has value.
Because negative elements of an emerging culture cannot be easily sifted out, prohibit all cultural elements from that emerging culture. Favor one style of worship, teaching, etc., over others, arguing for its supremacy. Leadership should comprise the most assimilated members.	Leadership Actions	Cultural characteristics that support the good news are retained, but attributes that go against the good news are "sifted" out.[71] Favor all worship styles, arguing for equality. Leadership should comprise the most culturally sensitive and diverse members.

Graffiti art, with its risk, improvisation, and color, serves as a fitting metaphor for leadership actions that will nurture tomorrow's multifaceted congregation. The risk and synergy are worth it if they move the church to the beloved community that Christ envisioned when he prayed to God:

> I'm praying not only for them
> But also for those who will believe in me
> Because of them and their witness about
>   me.
> The goal is for all of them to become one
>   heart and mind—
> Just as you, Father, are in me and I in you,
> So they might be one heart and mind with
>   us. (John 17:20-21 *THE MESSAGE*)

MOVING TOWARD MILLENNIAL LEADERSHIP: QUESTIONS FOR PERSONAL REFLECTION AND/OR GROUP DISCUSSION

The following questions are for personal reflection but can also be used in a group setting:

1. *For personal and group reflection:* create an organix leadership journal by

  • selecting two items from each box, and
  • writing in each box what you will begin to do over the next thirty days to move toward millennial leadership in these two areas.

G	Nurturing Millennial Leadership
Graffiti	1. Graffiti leadership embraces risk. 1.a. *Take risks for the sake of the good news.* 1.b. *Contrast with the usual way of doing things.* 1.c. *Undertake such actions publicly.*

81

2. Graffiti leadership practices and repeats reconciliation.

> 2.a. *Liturgical acts of reconciliation*
>
> 2.b. *Public acts of reconciliation*
>
> 2.c. *Personal acts of reconciliation*
>
> 2.d. *Regular attention to voices that challenge you*

3. Graffiti leadership grows mosaic churches.

> 3.a. *Balance autonomy and partnership to grow a mosaic church.*
>
> 3.b. *Unify different cultures within a mosaic church.*

2. For group reflection:

- Share your responses to the chart above with your group (omitting answers/plans that are overly personal).
- Take notes in your journal on the following:
    a. Does your group agree or disagree with your assessments and plans?
    b. What input did they give you regarding moving toward millennial leadership?
- Then rewrite your plans in your journal using their input.

3. For personal and group reflection:

- Revisit your notes in your journal every month for six months. Ask yourself:
    a. Are there areas where I am making progress? If so, describe them.
    b. Are there areas where I am still weak? What will I do to address this?
- At the end of six months reread the chapter and update your plans.

Recycling is a good thing to do. It makes people feel good to do it. The thing I want to emphasize is the vast difference between recycling for the purpose of feeling good and recycling for the purpose of solving a problem.

—Barry Commoner, biologist and eco-activist[1]

	Modern Leadership	Millennial Leadership
Recycle	1. Repurpose defective people as a warning to others.	1. Recycle defective people to honor their creation in the image of God.
	2. Repurpose resources globally.	2. Recycle resources glocally.
	3. Repurpose worship.	3. Recycle worship.

RECYCLING DAY

Microphones to record the deliberations were arranged between each of the thirteen chairs that circled the table. As Gordon entered the room, he noticed Denny, gaunt and haggard and nervously fiddling with his papers. To Denny's right sat Leon, and to his left, Larry, associate pastors of Bethel Church. Both Leon and Larry were skilled pastors, competent to lead almost any church. But they had forsaken their own plans to join Denny, who as senior pastor was revitalizing Bethel Church, a once again proud church in the inner city. Yet today their fate was tied to Denny's immorality.

Seeing Gordon enter, Leon wondered out loud to his friend, "Where does it go from here?" Gordon wondered the same thing. But he sensed God had called him to Bethel Church, and he was prepared to undertake whatever was necessary. The door flew open again and in hurriedly walked nine local pastors. Gordon knew most of them, for they were some of the most well-known pastors in the community. Reverend Morris, an older gentleman, brought the meeting to order. Morris's church had once been the most flourishing and cavalier church in town. But in the last seven years, Bethel Church had replaced it in prominence. "The first order of business is who is going to preach at Bethel Church this Sunday. Denny can't do it, and I don't think it's fair to make Leon or Larry do it," began Reverend Morris. A robust discussion ensued as various pastors recommended themselves or their assistants to fill the pulpit at Bethel Church, which numbered almost 450 in attendance. Without a denominational affiliation to fall back on, Denny's immoral conduct had left Bethel Church at the mercy of other non-denominational churches in the community.

As the discussion escalated, Gordon felt neglected and somewhat happily so. Then Leon leaned over to Gordon and said, "Joel said you were here to help us. Well, you better start soon before they completely dismantle Bethel Church."

"I've made mistakes too," began Gordon. Either because he had been so quiet or because this was revelatory, he quieted the crowd. "I know what it is like to feel you don't have friends inside or outside the church. But I've talked to Pastor Joel, and we both sense God is going to use Denny again. Maybe not today, maybe not next year... but sometime. And Bethel is an autonomous church. So, let's help them, and at the same time honor their independence. I'm ready to assume leadership and help make it so."

"What will you do?" replied Reverend Morris. Suddenly, Gordon forgot all of his premeeting plans. Falling back on his most recent experiences at Ekklesia, he stated, "I'd start with a small group." An audible chuckle came from those gathered. "I don't mean just any kind of small group, but a group that could include Leon and Larry and some of you," Gordon continued. "We also would include some lay leaders from Bethel. Members of this group would be chosen because of their experience, their character, and their ability to work together."

"And you would chair this team?" Reverend Morris asked.

"If that meets your approval," Gordon responded.

After an afternoon that stretched into the evening, the assembled pastors agreed to support Gordon's plan. In addition, they agreed to create a similar group to provide accountability and restoration to Denny. A well-known psychologist was asked to join Denny's accountability group as well. As Gordon left the meeting that night, he unexpectedly felt overcome with doubt about his abilities. But then he thought back to his Zoe Group at Ekklesia, which had helped him through many troubled times. A sense of peace passed over Gordon as he walked back to his car. The power of community and accountability reassured him. "Hey, Gordon," came the voice of Leon from behind him. "How does it feel to return to the pastorate?" Gordon was uneasy for a minute, but then sensed a peace coming over him. He took comfort that God had brought him back to where he was intended to be, and he was thankful that he had not made the journey alone.

△ IS FOR "RECYCLE"

The dark side of today's innovation and change is that they can be carried out at the expense of non-sustainable resources. Researchers warn of a future when cumulative effects of air, soil, and marine depletion coupled with shrinking resources such as oil and gas will destabilize future existence.[2] As the reins of leadership are being passed to millennial leaders, such gloomy forecasts have not gone unnoticed. Scholar and organic farmer Sharon Astyk laments, "I want my family to have the comfort of a simple, clean, healthy life, but everywhere I turn there are more toxic chemicals in the air and food."[3]

In this world of unsustainable natural resources and uncontrollable non-recyclables, both modern and millennial leaders recognize that the church must do its part. Books are being published on the importance of ecologically sound church facilities, and congregations are being encouraged to adopt ecologically wise practices.[4]

Yet for millennial leaders this fervor goes deeper. It goes to the very core of their leadership. Their practice of recycling is more than just programs, for it forms a philosophy that undergirds how millennial leaders relate to people and planning. Bill McKibben speaks for a generation when he exclaims, "The momentum...can't be turned off quickly enough to prevent hideous damage. But, we will keep fighting in that hope that we can limit that damage."[5] To help readers understand this passion, figure 5.1 contrasts two words that appear interchangeable but really describe two very different approaches to the future.

Figure 5.1. A comparison of *repurposing* and *recycling*

Repurpose		Recycle
Rescue material that is no longer useful, redeploying it for a new purpose.	Material	Rescue material that is still useful, redeploying it for the original purpose.
Rework material for a new purpose.	Strategy	Return material to its original purpose.

A new purpose is created.	Outcome	The original purpose is served.
It can be useful at times, but often squanders the original purpose and applicability.	Caveats	It may not be useful if the original purpose is no longer valid.
It is practiced by modern leadership.	Leadership Style	It is practiced by millennial leadership.

Repurposing can be a valid action if the original purpose can no longer be served (as noted in figure 5.1). But millennial leaders see repurposing as a last resort, for it creates more things in a saturated society. Repurposing only multiplies and reduplicates materials and purposes.

Instead, millennial leaders often embrace recycling as the preferred route, for it returns the material to its original purpose. Such recycling is also often more successful, for it is more organic to original intent and material.

Why do modern leaders focus on repurposing?[6]

THREE PERILS OF MODERN LEADERSHIP REGARDING ♲ (REPURPOSING)

	Modern Leadership	Millennial Leadership
Recycle	1. Repurpose defective people as a warning to others.	1. Recycle defective people to honor their creation in the image of God.
	2. Repurpose resources globally.	2. Recycle resources glocally.
	3. Repurpose worship.	3. Recycle worship.

△ : *Recycle*

MODERN PERIL 1: REPURPOSE DEFECTIVE PEOPLE AS A WARNING TO OTHERS.

As noted in chapter 1, flaws and failings are part of the human journey. Yet when these weaknesses arise, the modern leader often takes a different approach from millennial leaders. The reaction of the modern leader is especially obvious when a moral, ethical, or managerial failure is involved. Let's look at some common aspects of the modern reaction.

1.a. *Embarrass defective people as a warning to others.* The quintessential example of this strategy is Nathaniel Hawthorne's heroine in *The Scarlet Letter*, who is publicly branded for her improprieties as a warning to others. In the church this often takes place when an errant leader is castigated publicly and repeatedly. I have overheard modern leaders privately hope that such public embarrassment will make other potentially errant leaders think twice. Though public disclosure is required, a repeated and drawn-out public rebuke as a warning to others has two drawbacks:

1. Modern leaders may hide their weaknesses and avoid getting help because they fear the toll of public scolding on their self-worth and their families. Paul understood how such castigation can be debilitating and emphasized forgiveness, too, stating, "The punishment inflicted on him by the majority is sufficient. Now instead, you ought to forgive and comfort him, so that he will not be overwhelmed by excessive sorrow" (2 Cor. 2:6-7 NIV).

2. Leaders may not aspire to leadership positions because they fear the public humiliation that results from even minor infractions. An end result is that those leaders who are called into the ministry and who need help in overcoming weaknesses may avoid help or calling.

The modern leader's approach is thus really based not on helping the hurting leader but on warning tomorrow's leaders. The hurting leader is largely neglected in this modern tactic.

1.b. *Plunder powerless people as a warning to others.* While public exposure of a leader's weaknesses should be anticipated (Num. 32:23), so should help (2 Cor. 2:5-11). But powerlessness and exposure often lead to unanticipated pillage. As this chapter's opening and true story illustrates, other leaders may swoop down to divvy up the spoil from a fallen leader's ministry. This pillaging of the leader's power and influence is often lauded as "necessary for the sake of the flock (congregants)." As the story implies, it may be more to ransack another's leadership assets. Regardless of the motivation, such plundering often occurs.

1.c. *Forbid their return as a warning to others.* The final straw in the modern leader's arsenal is to bar the leader from reentering previous leadership duties. In the story that began this chapter, the insinuation of Reverend Morris was "You better find some other line of work, [because] you'll never be back in the ministry." This quotation was taken from an actual case study. It is the ultimate warning, which some would argue belittles God's redemptive power and purposes (cf. Matt. 19:26).[7] Still, its intention seems to be to send a message to other leaders that failings will result in banishment from their chosen, and often called, vocation. Subsequently, unmitigated punishment fills leaders with fear.

Yet in some cases a person should be barred from environments and activities that foster failings. Fuller Seminary's Archibald Hart states, "A small percentage of pastors, an estimated 10%, who succumb to sexual temptation are clear-cut sexual seducers. They are predators who use the ministry as an opportunity to get to women."[8] Hart urges that such individuals should never be placed in ministry roles or environments that could foster this behavior again. However, the modern strategy to embarrass, plunder, and forbid does not distinguish between types and degrees of weaknesses.

MODERN PERIL 2: REPURPOSE RESOURCES GLOBALLY.

Another seemingly innocuous tactic of modern leadership is to repurpose assets, such as buildings, monies, and programs. Again, there is nothing wrong with this approach, but repurposing can squander original intent and substance. As an example, let's look at two of the most common assets that modern leaders repurpose.

2.a. *Repurpose buildings*. When churches encounter trouble, they are often tempted to avoid spiritual and interpersonal conflict and instead shed assets. One congregation, struggling over dissatisfaction with a lead pastor, began the process of selling and/or renting the church facility to deal with dwindling numbers. The real problem was an interpersonal one, but the church avoided it by seeking to discard assets. In many churches, buildings have been repurposed because church leaders found it easier to do than addressing conflict.

Modern leaders often see nothing wrong with repurposing churches as personal residences, antique malls, and professional buildings while other churches sit vacant. But many communities lack a centrally located and functional facility to house a faith community. Plus, there may be damage to the esteem of the cause of Christ, as once stately church buildings sit abandoned or repurposed for commercial aims.

2.b. *Repurpose finances*. In a similar vein, when a church closes, the modern tactic is to send financial assets back to the denomination or give them to non-local charitable work. Although laudable, this tactic is similar to repurposing the church building, for it takes finances out of the neighborhood and sends them to a distant locale. Money and facilities that are so needed within the local community are repurposed elsewhere. While repurposing salvages assets, it often does so at the expense of original intent.[9] One senior saint in a Detroit congregation said, "My family has stood behind this church for over eighty years, and now it's gone. I still live here. And there are people here who still need Jesus. . . . Where did the hard work go? Where did the money go?" The church's assets had been sold and given back to the judicatory, and a drugstore chain occupied the church's former site.

The above actions are not unethical or illogical, just in the viewpoint of many millennial leaders not the most effective strategy. Millennial leaders prefer a more organic approach that connects local assets to the local mission context for which they were originally purposed.

MODERN PERIL 3: REPURPOSE WORSHIP.

Though there are many examples of repurposing by modern leadership, the repurposing of worship is a final conspicuous example. Such repurposing often occurs when a church ends a traditional worship celebration, repurposing the time and talents of congregants to serve a different (usually younger) constituency. This is often carried out by one of two tactics:

> **Blended worship has just about enough of everything to make just about everybody mad.**

1. *Option 1: Out with the old.* Modern leaders often abruptly terminate the traditional worship celebration and create something new. Though older members may protest that they have lost a style of worship that is relevant to them, these leaders will say, "They should learn to enjoy the modern way of doing things," or they are "out of touch," "old-fashioned," and "their music is irrelevant." They are actually saying that the traditional style is irrelevant to them. Yet for older members who have some of their best memories attached to such symbols, hymns, and liturgy, the traditional style is very relevant. And so, the "out with the old" approach damages the older generation's connections with one another and with God.[10] We shall see shortly that millennial leaders have a more inclusive solution.

2. *Option 2: Blending.*[11] This tactic occurs when different styles are intermingled in a single worship celebration. While a viable option for a congregation of one hundred or fewer attendees, such blending rarely satisfies people from different cultures. Usually, blended worship has just about enough of everything to make just about everybody mad. This conflict arises because many people come to church to connect with God. And when artistic styles change abruptly, congregants' focus and meditation may be unexpectedly interrupted. "It's like you are constantly changing stations on the car radio," was the reply from one senior saint. "I can't concentrate when you jump between classical music and country." I knew how she felt. Neither could I.

89

For all of its popularity, repurposing usually fails to reconnect people, places, and worship to their original intent. Repurposing creates a new purpose for damaged or well-worn items. But let's look at recycling and see how it better fulfills the original intent, ability, and purpose of people, places, and worship.

THREE ATTITUDES OF MILLENNIAL LEADERSHIP REGARDING ♲ (RECYCLING)

	Modern Leadership	Millennial Leadership
♲ **Recycle**	1. Repurpose defective people as a warning to others.	1. Recycle defective people to honor their creation in the image of God.
	2. Repurpose resources globally.	2. Recycle resources glocally.
	3. Repurpose worship.	3. Recycle worship.

MILLENNIAL ATTITUDE 1: RECYCLE DEFECTIVE PEOPLE TO HONOR THEIR CREATION IN THE IMAGE OF GOD.

While modern leaders may castigate and humiliate to prevent a return to sinning, millennial leaders understand humanity's fallen nature and need of grace. Millennial leaders are not surprised when leaders fall, so they put structures in place to recycle damaged leaders to their purpose, if possible, that God intended. "We grew up watching our parents' churches implode because of sin in leaders' lives," stated one young staff pastor. "We're not like boomers who think nothing will ever go wrong. We know it will, so we plan for it.... We don't make it easy. We just don't eliminate the idea of a return."

We discovered in the introduction that God invites humans to participate in the *missio Dei*, God's grand mission to reconnect with his offspring. And God bestows supernatural gifts on humans to help bring about this mission (Rom. 12:4-8; 1 Cor. 12:12-27). When a leader is recycled to the purpose that God intended and with the gifts that God previously bestowed, the millennial leader senses this honors God's intent and redemptive power.[12]

△ : *Recycle*

MILLENNIAL ATTITUDE 2: RECYCLE RESOURCES GLOCALLY.

Millennial leaders have a strong sense of returning things to their original purpose. To them, doing this seems more efficient and logical than repurposing them for another objective. A fitting example is the way they regard assets such as facilities and finances. To millennial leaders, a church's buildings and finances were given to anchor local ministry.

> **To millennial leaders, a church's buildings and finances were given to anchor local ministry.**

Millennial leaders identify with the writer who famously intoned, "The light that shines the farthest, shines brightest at home."[13] The writer was emphasizing that people in the neighborhood should not be overlooked in a church's grand scheme to make a global impact. Those who live nearest the church have a heightened expectation of help from that church. This is the church's foremost responsibility.

In response, millennial leaders seek to balance local needs and global needs. The term *glocal*, a combination of the words *global* and *local*, has emerged as a description of this balance.[14] Therefore, the millennial leader often avoids repurposing in favor of an organic recycling strategy that seeks to keep facilities and finances in a local community. The results are that local sacrifices for facilities and finances continue to benefit local constituents.

MILLENNIAL ATTITUDE 3: RECYCLE WORSHIP.

If a goal of recycling is to return to the original purpose, then millennial churches are discovering the power of recycling traditional worship celebrations. And they are doing so through two tactics.

> **Those who live nearest the church have a heightened expectation of help from that church.**

3.a. *Preserving traditional worship celebrations.* Many young churches, such as St. Thomas's Church in Sheffield, England, are discovering the value in preserving and subsidizing a traditional worship celebration for older attendees (or simply for those who prefer a more traditional style). In Sheffield they call this celebration "the mother church," for it has birthed eight contemporary worship celebrations across town, each appealing to a different culture.[15] And because older congregants who prefer such traditional celebrations may be waning in finances and energy, younger churches like St. Tom's are finding it essential to support and subsidize them.

3.b. *Creating unity by preserving traditional elements to create an ancient-future mix.* In addition to preserving traditional worship celebrations, millennial leaders often like to retain some traditional elements in their contemporary

91

worship to remind younger attendees of their heritage. This is different from the blended celebration that modern leaders try to foster. Millennial leaders do not create an awkward blend between two different styles. Instead, for the sake of unity, they often carefully weave in traditional elements in their contemporary worship to remind them of the traditional congregation that birthed them. Sometimes called "ancient-future" worship, this celebration is focused on helping younger members gain a respect for their forebears and their traditions.[16]

Millennial recycling tactics create three results. First, recycling traditional worship expressions to their original purpose retains ministry to older members of the church. Second, this nurtures a mosaic of generations in one church. Third, ancient-future elements allow millennial leaders to emphasize an appreciation and respect for their forebears and their traditions.

NURTURING THE THREE ATTITUDES REGARDING ♲ (RECYCLING)

NURTURING MILLENNIAL ATTITUDE 1: RECYCLE DEFECTIVE PEOPLE TO HONOR THEIR CREATION IN THE IMAGE OF GOD.

The area of recycling defective leaders is controversial and precarious. And this short treatise is only an overview (fuller examination can be found through the citations in the endnotes). However, in a comparison of various approaches to recycling fallen leaders, the following millennial principles emerge:

1.a. *Emphasize the good before contrasting it with the bad.* The millennial leader begins by reminding the fallen leader of the good that God has created. The sin is not overlooked, but the good that God has brought about in the leader's life forms the foundation for recycling the leader (if possible) to his or her original purpose. This initial focusing on the good also helps to contrast how far the leader has fallen. Scriptures may help prepare the repentant leader to move to 1.b and include these:

> You walked away from your first love—why? What's going on with you, anyway? Do you have any idea how far you've fallen? A Lucifer fall!
>
> Turn back! Recover your dear early love. No time to waste, for I'm well on my way to removing your light from the golden circle. (Rev. 2:4-5 *THE MESSAGE*)
>
> Think of the gift you once had in your hands, the Message you heard with your ears—grasp it again and turn back to God.

△ : *Recycle*

If you pull the covers back over your head and sleep on, oblivious to God, I'll return when you least expect it, break into your life like a thief in the night. (Rev. 3:3 *THE MESSAGE*)

The above Scriptures remind us that starting with the good does not mean the sin is overlooked, ignored, or lessened. Sin is sin. But starting with the good and then addressing the sin creates a contrast that emphasizes the magnitude of the problem.

1.b. *Acknowledge and address the sin.* Both the sin and the sinner must be dealt with directly. Sin is the responsibility of the sinner, as James reminds us: "The temptation to give in to evil comes from us and only us. We have no one to blame but the leering, seducing flare-up of our own lust. Lust gets pregnant, and has a baby: sin! Sin grows up to adulthood, and becomes a real killer" (1:15 *THE MESSAGE*). And admitting and addressing the sin require forthright action (Col. 3:5-6; 1 John 1:9). But unlike modern leaders who might repurpose fallen leaders to a new occupation or life, the millennial leader will try, if at all possible, to recycle the leader to his or her original purpose—but only once the sin is sufficiently addressed and its power over the leader broken.

1.c. *Chart a route for return.*[17] If defective leaders acknowledge their flaws, address them, and conquer their pull, the millennial leader comes alongside to travel with such leaders. More than just a travel companion, the millennial leader also becomes a guide back to wholeness and holiness. Here are some important time frames within the restoration processes:

1. *A period of withdrawal for personal/professional evaluation and repentance.* Fuller Seminary's Archibald Hart pleads "for a period of withdrawal from ministry and for that person to undergo evaluation to understand why it happened."[18]
2. *A period for those wronged to forgive.* This stage will be lengthy as well as necessary for congregations, families, and colleagues. One restorer who eventually needed restoring emphasizes, "The only way to be restored is by submitting to the scrutiny of trustworthy individuals who at some point in the healing process can say that they are willing to vouch for the fact that the restored individual has regained his or her integrity."[19]
3. *Recycling to occur (but may not be wise in the local context).* Lewis Smedes recounts a comment of a denominational leader who wisely advised, "We will forgive you, but you can never work here again."[20] Balancing this return to ministry with sensitivity to those who were wronged requires diligence, prayer, and often relocation.
4. *An ongoing period of accountability.* Because millennial leaders recognize how penetrating human fallibility may be, they recognize that once addressed, sin can still recur. Ongoing accountability

among peers and professionals helps leaders openly and support-ively address inclinations before they again become sin. Gordon MacDonald suggests twenty-six questions that groups can use to foster accountability.[21] Much earlier, John Wesley suggested four probing questions for the small accountability bands of the Wesleyan movement. Today Wesley's questions still provide a helpful gauge:[22]

    a. What known sins have you committed since the last meeting?

    b. What temptations have you met with?

    c. How were you delivered?

    d. What have you thought, said, or done that may or may not be sin?

5. *Scars to result and remain.* Though all those involved may hope that spiritual blemishes and scars will not remain, they will. Jacob's limp was a reminder of his selfish nature (Gen. 32). And though God continued to use King David to lead his people (1 Kings 1–2), David lamented, "My sin is ever before me" (Ps. 51:3).

1.d. *Watch over personal temptations.* The millennial leader who helps navigate this process must in turn watch her or his own temptations. Paul warns, "Brothers and sisters, if someone is caught in a sin, you who live by the Spirit should restore that person gently. But watch yourselves, or you also may be tempted" (Gal. 6:1 NIV). Yet when dealt with in a diligent, honest, and forthright manner, a recycled leader can say with David:

> Generous in love—God, give grace!
>   Huge in mercy—wipe out my bad record.
> Scrub away my guilt,
>   soak out my sins in your laundry.
> I know how bad I've been;
>   my sins are staring me down.
>
> You're the One I've violated, and you've seen
>   it all, seen the full extent of my evil.
> You have all the facts before you;
>   whatever you decide about me is fair.
> I've been out of step with you for a long time,
>   in the wrong since before I was born.
> What you're after is truth from the inside out.
>   Enter me, then; conceive a new, true life. (Ps. 51:1-6 THE MESSAGE)

This complex and difficult recycling of defective leaders returns them to their original purpose and call. Rather than repurposing them to some other objective for which they may not have been divinely called or equipped, recycling leaders (when appropriate) can create effective, pliable, and spiritually sensitive leaders who meet tomorrow's church needs.

NURTURING MILLENNIAL ATTITUDE 2: RECYCLE RESOURCES GLOCALLY.

2.a. *Recycle facilities.* Rather than view church buildings as potential antique malls, professional buildings, and so forth, the millennial leader sees a local asset for spiritual renewal and influence. Millennial leadership thus opts for organic solutions that ensure assets remain within and serve the local community. The following are two examples:

1. *Giving or selling a building cheaply to a nearby congregation.* One white church rebuffed a denominational request to return its building and instead sold it inexpensively to a growing African American congregation nearby. The district superintendent told me unofficially that she was happy with their decision: "Even though our denominational policy says they should return the building to the denomination, we all would rather see a nearby growing church benefit. After all, that money was given locally to help people here."

> If a traditional celebration is waning in effectiveness, millennial leaders often search for ways to support it to make it viable again, even on a smaller scale.

2. *Sharing a building with another congregation.* One congregation, after it was no longer capable of keeping up the church, decided to rent it inexpensively to a nearby congregation. "We've paid off the mortgage," one layman recounted. "So there were no expenses except for upkeep and utilities. We decided to keep the church open, and let the Hispanic congregation rent it as long as they could keep it up and pay utilities." "Why didn't you just sell it to them?" I asked. "They couldn't get the loan, so I guess we're the bank now," the layman replied. The gracious act of this older church gave a young Hispanic congregation the opportunity to build their credit history and eventually purchase the building.

2.b. *Recycle finances.* Millennial leaders often recycle finances by recycling a significant amount into the community, resulting in a significant amount of local monies that stay in struggling communities and within the control of local residents. One congregation gave away the proceeds from the sale of their facility to fund a new local day care. Another church sold a parsonage and funded a Habitat for Humanity project. These actions helped members with long legacies in both congregations see the fruit of their sacrifice and hard work still in action within the community.

NURTURING MILLENNIAL ATTITUDE 3: RECYCLE WORSHIP.

3.a. *Preserve traditional worship celebrations to create stability for older congregants.* While millennial leaders may launch new worship celebrations, they also often retain, even subsidize, traditional worship celebrations. For example, if a traditional celebration is waning in effectiveness, millennial leaders often search for ways to support it to make it viable again, even on a smaller scale. "Why would I want to end the worship service my grandparents liked?" responded one young man. "They're not here, but somebody's grandparent is." Millennial leaders try to create stability for older saints in their increasingly uncertain world. A few examples of the increasing insecurities that older congregants face include these:

1. their health life;
2. their financial life, living on fixed incomes as inflation and the cost of living increase; and
3. their personal life as children and friends move away.

Millennial leaders recognize that ending a traditional worship celebration can cause more instability for older saints. A predictable liturgy filled with memorable hymns can provide a measure of stability in the lives of older congregants. Thus, millennial leaders often work diligently to subsidize traditional worship celebrations even while adding other, more contemporary options.

3.b. *Embrace ancient-future elements to honor traditional worship and build unity.* Millennial leaders see value in creating unity by not just preserving traditional worship celebrations but also by honoring their history and their icons. To foster cross-cultural appreciation, millennial leaders embrace ancient-future worship, combining traditional elements such as the Apostles' Creed, *lectio divina*,[23] and religious icons with electronic music and arts. Millennial leaders do not expect traditionalists to embrace these fusions, but they hope that younger generations will begin to appreciate the power and effectiveness of traditional elements.

3.c. *Recapture the original purpose of worship: a culturally relevant encounter.* The purpose of worship, according to the Hebrew word *shachah*, is a close encounter with a king that fosters reverence, respect, and praise.[24] Thus, the purpose of worship in the church is to create such an encounter between humans and God. Millennial leaders emphasize that encounter—not a concert or a show—is the purpose of worship. Thus, millennial leaders seek to create worship that above all else fosters an encounter with the living God because such an encounter is a way that God reconnects with God's creation (that is, the *missio Dei*).[25] Millennial leaders recognize that a purpose for celebration is not needed, only a recycling to make the purpose (that is, worship) relevant again.

MOVING TOWARD MILLENNIAL LEADERSHIP: QUESTIONS FOR PERSONAL REFLECTION AND/OR GROUP DISCUSSION

The following questions are for personal reflection but can also be used in a group setting:

1. *For personal and group reflection:* create an Organix leadership journal by
   - selecting two items from each box, and
   - writing in it what you will begin to do over the next thirty days to move toward millennial leadership in these two areas.

⟳	Nurturing Millennial Leadership
Recycle	1. Recycle defective people to honor their creation in the image of God. 1.a. *Emphasize the good before contrasting it with the bad.* 1.b. *Acknowledge and address the sin.* 1.c. *Chart a route for return.* 1.d. *Watch over personal temptations.*
	2. Recycle resources glocally. 2.a. *Recycle facilities.* 2.b. *Recycle finances.*
	3. Recycle worship. 3.a. *Preserve traditional worship celebrations to create stability for older congregants.*

	3.b. *Embrace ancient-future elements to honor traditional worship and build unity.* 3.c. *Recapture the original purpose of worship: a culturally relevant encounter.*

2. *For group reflection:*

- Share your responses to the chart above with your group (omitting answers/plans that are overly personal).
- Take notes in your journal on the following:
    a. Does your group agree or disagree with your assessments and plans?
    b. What input did they give you regarding moving toward millennial leadership?
- Then rewrite your plans in your journal using their input.

3. *For personal and group reflection:*

- Revisit your notes in your journal every month for six months. Ask yourself:
    a. Are there areas where I am making progress? If so, describe them.
    b. Are there areas where I am still weak? What will I do to address this?
- At the end of six months reread the chapter and update your plans.

Humans like to know about the good, the bad, and the ugly side of people, places, and situations, as well as to share this information with others, often as quickly as possible.

—Lon Safko and David Brake, The Social Media Bible[1]

	Modern Leadership	Millennial Leadership
N Networks	1. Modern leaders rely on historical networks.	1. Networks of relationships are just as important as organizational networks.
	2. Modern leaders seek to control networks.	2. Networks should be accessible.
	3. Modern leaders create network restrictions.	3. Network restrictions may be personal, but are necessary.

BRIDGES OF GOD

This was Joel's first job in a United Methodist church. Seven years in the Anglican Church, including four at Ekklesia Church, had been rewarding. But ever since he met Joan in an online discussion room, he was captivated by her vision for racial reconciliation. Though they were from different denominations, Joan often reminded Joel that John Wesley had been a lifelong Anglican. Joel felt a connection to Joan's vision. In fact, she articulated it more forcefully than anyone he knew within his own denomination. For younger pastors like Joel, informal networks of like-minded people trumped historical and denominational connections.

But now Joel was embarking on a new and uncharted adventure. Joan wanted to hire Joel to reach students at a traditionally African American college nearby. Since almost all college students have a computer, Joel reasoned online small groups might be the best way to connect busy college students to one another, to the church, and to their Lord. After proposing this to the church council, the moderator named Frank was the first to state his displeasure. "I can't believe you can have real community just by typing stuff online," stated Frank. "This is a waste of our money. How did you come up with this crazy plan, Joan?"

"I came up with this plan because it was over the Internet that I got to know and appreciate Joel," Joan replied. "Frank, Smith Street Church has doubled since I've been here. And it is because we've added new ways to connect God's mission to people of different cultures. Online may be a good way to connect with the college culture. Give it a try." And with that a vote was taken empowering Joan to hire Joel as the connections pastor. Within six weeks Joel would have two connection groups of non-churchgoing college students regularly meeting online for fellowship, Bible study, and prayer.

Things seemed to be going well, so Joan was surprised to receive a midday visit from Frank. "I want you to see this, Joan," began Frank. He then showed Joan pictures that a church volunteer had taken of Joel's computer screen. The images of pornography were unsettling to Joan, and she looked quickly away. Later that day she confronted Joel. "Is this true, Joel?" she asked.

"I'm really sorry," Joel replied in an almost inaudible voice. "I came across this site once, and I returned a few more times. Eventually, I got hooked. I'm really sorry, Joan."

"You didn't just let me down, Joel, but your wife, your church family, and dozens of college students as well. You and I first connected over the Internet. You connect each week with dozens of college kids on it too. It can be a web for good or for bad. Each follower of Christ has to understand his or her weaknesses and have discernment—"

"I guess that's my problem," interrupted Joel. "I spend so much time on the web with students. And I am always just a click away from pornography. But I can't just go offline. We've got too many students who depend on my facilitation of their online groups."

"Perhaps it is time for an Internet sabbatical," replied Joan. "I know it might hurt our online groups to have you absent for some time. But it is worth it to get the old Joel back." Within a few months Joel transferred to another church where he began leading onsite small groups. Though Joan was happy for him and the progress he was making there, she missed his youthful exuberance. She found it hard to get excited over a candidate in his sixties applying for the connections pastor job. But he came highly recommended, so she felt obligated to conduct an interview.

"Well, what have you been doing, Gordon?" began Joan. Gordon replied, "I've been interim pastor for two years at an independent church downstate, Bethel Church. Things are pretty well sorted out there, and because I enjoyed teaching online courses for a local community college, Joel thought I might like this job."

"You know Joel?" was Joan's startled reply.

"Sure, he was my pastor at Ekklesia Church," said Gordon. "He got me back into the ministry. And he knows how much I like teaching online. For years it was a big part of my job as a fund-raiser for our denomination. I guess I communicate well through written words." After two weeks of deliberation and several more meetings, Gordon was hired.

"It was a lifesaver for me," recalled Gordon later. "I helped Bethel Church back to health, and a small team did it. But after two years I needed a different kind of team. Helen and I needed a team where we could receive ministry. When Joel told us about the connections pastor job here, and how part of our role would be for both Helen and me to meet online with leaders each week, we knew it was a good fit. We now have seven online connections groups. Some people might think you can't get close to one another online, but for Helen and me, the fellowship has been as real and genuine as any face-to-face group we've attended."

N IS FOR "NETWORKS"

In April 1963 a Pentagon scientist named J. C. R. Licklider argued the time had come for a universal computer network to speed scientific collaboration.[2] Not surprisingly, over the next few years an internet of computers began to take form. Today it gains speed, complexity, and scope every hour, and the Internet has become the universal network that connects disparate people across disproportionate distances.

But like communication technologies such as the quill, the printing press, the telegraph, and the landline telephone that went before it, there is a life cycle after which this current network will become obsolete. Therefore, to maintain this chapter's relevance, we will study not only the Internet but also *networkings*, those networks of connections between people that define life, communicate ideas, and create community.

Some networks to which the principles of this chapter apply include the following:

- social networks of friends, relatives, acquaintances, and neighbors[3]
- cultural networks based on ethnic, socioeconomic, generational, or affinity connections[4]
- face-to-face (or offline) networks[5]
- electronic online networks[6]

This chapter discusses these connections (or networks) and how best to use them in a fast and furious millennial culture. As such, this chapter is less concerned with impermanent tools (for example, websites, text messaging, Twitter, and so on) and more concerned with how Christians can use the increasing speed and reach of networked communication. First, let's look at how modern leaders relate to these networks and then contrast this with how those who have grown up in today's electronic mesh[7] use them.

THREE MISCUES OF MODERN LEADERSHIP REGARDING NETWORKS

	Modern Leadership	Millennial Leadership
N **Networks**	1. Modern leaders rely on historical networks.	1. Networks of relationships are just as important as organizational networks.
	2. Modern leaders seek to control networks.	2. Networks should be accessible.
	3. Modern leaders create network restrictions.	3. Network restrictions may be personal, but are necessary.

MODERN MISCUE 1: MODERN LEADERS RELY ON HISTORICAL NETWORKS.

Modern leaders understand the power and complexity of networks, whether they are interpersonal, electronic, or organizational. But leaders raised in the twentieth century can be overwhelmed by the speed at which new networks emerge and their expanding power. Even though the modern leader has been raised in a realm of experimentation, creativity, and science, the rapidity of network expansion has led many modern leaders to prefer historical networks with which they have familiarity. As a result, the modern leader often prefers time-honored interpersonal networks, such as ministerial colleagues and denominational structures. There is nothing wrong with this approach, but it limits the flexibility of the modern leader to communicate and engage others across emerging networks.

Public school and Sunday school teachers in the mid-nineteenth century resisted using the blackboard because of unfamiliarity and newness. They eventually accepted it because they realized that children remembered better when they could see the words.[8] As technology progressed, other forms of media, including photographs, film, and video,[9] were greeted with the same controversy only to be eventually accepted because of their practicality (but not without some restrictions). Electronic technologies at first befuddled David Morgan's Duke University colleagues:

> I recall about a decade ago my university's lead cheerleader for such media standing before a roomful of faculty, holding aloft a few CDs and announcing with aplomb: "Here are Plato, Aristotle, and Ovid. Can you believe it? Everything they had to say, right here in my hand." I didn't believe it, nor did most of my colleagues.... The administrator's faith in technology was typically American; but so was the faculty's skepticism.[10]

Today, new online networks have grown in ease, scope, and complexity such that they even foster online kinship. Rather than go to the local ministry association or a district superintendent for ideas, a local pastor can join a like-minded online community to probe new ideas, receive feedback, and learn about new strategies.

> "'Here are Plato, Aristotle, and Ovid. Can you believe it? Everything they had to say, right here in my hand.' I didn't believe it, nor did most of my colleagues."

Many modern leaders question whether these online communities are truly a community. Howard Rheingold, one of the first researchers to study online communities, describes them as such:

> [An online community is] a group of people who may or may not meet one another face-to-face, and who exchange words and ideas through the mediation of computer bulletin boards and networks...[with] social aggregations that emerge from the Net when enough people carry on public discussions long enough, with sufficient human feeling, to form webs of personal relationships in cyberspace.[11]

Reviewing Rheingold's work, fellow researchers Heidi Campbell and Patricia Calderon conclude: "While these new forms of community did not fit into traditional notions of face-to-face, geographically bound communities, the members themselves felt that the connection and affinity they experienced in these groups fully justified their designation as a form of community."[12]

In other words, if online users feel a sense of community is being formed in their online networks, regardless of the modern leader's interest or experience, a community has been formed. The church must be ready to nurture and shepherd the spiritual experiences that grow in such communities.

MODERN MISCUE 2: MODERN LEADERS SEEK TO CONTROL NETWORKS.

The modern leader has lived most of life in a realm of *command and control*. Command and control are necessary in crisis situations, such as warfare or fire-fighting.[13] For baby boomers born after World War II, the command and control way of leadership became a popular leadership style in business[14] and the church.[15]

Modern leaders of this generation believe the way to succeed is to control through power, rewards, and punishments. Some researchers trace this to the slow-cycle growth of the agricultural economy in the 1900s.[16] For example, a horse could be broken and ridden only after some difficulty. Then the horse would provide valuable use for many years. Eventually, the horse might have a colt, and the colt would also go through the entire command and control process. Usually, several years passed between these cycles. Slow cycles that grew out of an agricultural economy began to affect business principles, where the agricultural approach of command and control began to be applied to the business world. Like a horse, "the worker must be trimmed to fit the job," Frederick Taylor famously intoned.[17] Subsequently, modern leaders bristle at the thought of losing control. When wrestling with the freedom found in emerging networks, the modern leader tends to try to exert control through ownership. In the ever-democratizing world of electronic communication, control through ownership is increasingly difficult.

> **When wrestling with the freedom found in emerging networks, the modern leader tends to try to exert control.**

Modern leaders attempt to take possession of networks that shape them. Modern leaders do this through some of the following tactics of command and control:

1. *Fee-based networks*. These are customary at electronic connection points, such as with wi-fi and Bluetooth. Businesses see an opportunity for controlling access by charging a fee and thus reinforcing a modern notion of ownership.

2. *Restricted network access*. Modern leaders see network access not only as a way to increase revenue but also as a way to restrict access to those times and places the modern leader deems fitting. Former Silicon Valley executive Rusty Rueff noted, "Movie theatres have long tried to control mobile phone signal in their movie theatres. They say it is because it disturbs people. Really, they don't want teens text-messaging their friends that the movie is dreadful."[18] From the days of passing notes in church to text messaging a friend far removed from the church sanctuary, church leaders have also tried to limit the location and occasion of electronic communication.

3. *Ownership of tools that access networks.* In the modern world, big and powerful conglomerates are trying to control large sections of emerging networks. Companies such as AT&T and Microsoft try to control and limit access to the Internet in a similar fashion to how AT&T tried to control the telegraph and telephone in years past. In an interview with National Public Radio, researcher Tim Wu stated,

> "Movie theatres have long tried to control mobile phone signal in their movie theatres. They say it is because it disturbs people. Really, they don't want teens text-messaging their friends that the movie is dreadful."

There is a repeat pattern we see with America's information monopolists. A new invention is created by a disruptive inventor and it goes through a period of openness, entrepreneurial activity, a kind of a boom, and eventually, and typically, some great strongman arises who integrates the entire industry into a lasting monopoly. This repeats itself for the radio industry, the early telephone industry, the film industry, and today it may be repeating itself in the Internet industry.[19]

Millennial leaders, who have grown up in the expanding world of communication networks, view these networks as public property. And to restrict access or monopolize them seems tyrannical. Modern leaders may recall similar unfair restrictions. At one time, restaurants and businesses charged a fee to use the restrooms. Such access to something that is naturally needed should seem as illogical to the modern leader as charging a fee for network access.

MODERN MISCUE 3: MODERN LEADERS CREATE NETWORK RESTRICTIONS.

New millennial networks can be a force for good or for ill. One student wrote me that "the negative content, tools and tricks that can be found online are growing...pornography, gruesome horror movies, gruesome and graphic videogames—websites now allow any user to upload or see anything." A hard-fought battle with cyber addiction almost derailed the student's spiritual and academic journey. Sometimes with justification a modern leader will decry the uncensored expansion of communication. Modern leadership tries to constrain new networks by some of the following tactics:

1. Creating alternative, yet narrow networks. In the early part of the millennium, Facebook has been a popular website for social networking. But because of potentially inappropriate pictures, messages, and links, many churches have tried to create an alternative and expurgated Facebook-type website.[20]

2. Labeling networks sinful instead of branding the sin. One church pastor banned Facebook for all church staff members, stating, "I've been in extended counseling with couples with marital problems because of Facebook for the last year and a half. What happens is someone from yesterday surfaces, it leads to conversations, and there have been physical meet-ups. The temptation is just too great."[21]

These constraint strategies follow in the failed attempts of Christian revival movements to control inner attitudes by monitoring outer behaviors such as dancing, movie going, card playing, and so on. The control of inner temptation is not served well merely by outward domination and monitoring. In a quickly expanding world of new networks, millennial leaders prefer to train the disciple in the skill of spiritual constraint.

THREE ATTITUDES OF MILLENNIAL LEADERSHIP REGARDING NETWORK

	Modern Leadership	Millennial Leadership
N Networks	1. Modern leaders rely on historical networks.	1. Networks of relationships are just as important as organizational networks.
	2. Modern leaders seek to control networks.	2. Networks should be accessible.
	3. Modern leaders create network restrictions.	3. Network restrictions may be personal, but are necessary.

MILLENNIAL ATTITUDE 1: NETWORKS OF RELATIONSHIPS ARE JUST AS IMPORTANT AS ORGANIZATIONAL NETWORKS.

Millennial leaders have grown up with a world of ever-increasing ease and speed of communication. Their networks are not restricted by place, distance, or time. They are able to choose relationships based on interests and not just proximity. One millennial leader might have several communal networks of shared interests. And while some of these networks wane in popularity, others increase in use. Consider one waning network and two emerging networks that are replacing it.

1.a. *The fall of text-based communal networks.* Text-based communication is a difficult way for an individual to communicate because of the dexterity needed for keyboard skills, coupled with the loss of facial expressions and body language. In a previous era, medieval priests added pictures while copying manuscripts to help visualize the text-based message.[22] Even today small emoticons such as :-) for a smile and ;-) for a wink attempt to substitute for the complexity of facial expression. Though a laudable attempt, the time required to paint small pictures and the lack of intricacy of emoticons have led to the fall of text-based communication and the rise of visual communication.

1.b. *The move to spoken- and action-based communal networks.* Emerging networks are becoming increasingly based on video and three-dimensional (3D) elements. Rusty Rueff, who worked as an executive for online gaming giant EA (Electronic Arts), cited a chart demonstrating how text-based communication (for example, via static Web pages and instant messaging) is being replaced by videos and 3D. Even instant mood/messaging services such as Twitter have plateaued in popularity, for their text-based communication fails to translate the wealth of information of a video. Chris Anderson and Michael Wolff in their *Wired Magazine* article, "The Web Is Dead: Long Live the Internet," noted how Web-based traffic and even peer-to-peer traffic on the Internet is decreasing, while online video traffic is increasing.[23] The authors point out that at the end of the first decade of the new millennium, text-based websites and messaging were being discarded in favor of vocal- and visual-based communication through video and 3D.

> Even instant mood/messaging services such as Twitter have plateaued in popularity, for their text-based communication fails to translate the wealth of information of a video.

The three-dimensional format creates an interesting new milieu for social communities. In 3D games such as *Second Life* participants are able to take on new characters that they might never undertake in real life. *Second Life* has been described as "a free 3D virtual world where users socialize, connect and chat on every topic imaginable, including spiritual themes."[24]

Such "second lives" can be for good or for ill. Not surprisingly, online 3D worlds like *Second Life* allow the user to opt out of more risqué levels. These games have also allowed Christians to form hundreds of online churches.[25] A benefit of these online communities, according to Russ Gunsalus, is that "people who might be too shy or timid to visit a real church and ask their questions, can go to church in *Second Life*, ask their questions, and have their questions answered . . . all with the anonymity of an avatar."[26]

Online worlds provide avenues for more communication across broader and faster networks (though not without sensual caveats as noted above). Still, in the millennial world it is not uncommon for a maturing Christian to be called to be a missionary in a virtual world while remaining physically at home. "Millions of people are active in these virtual worlds," urges Gunsalus, "and it is important to have a Christian presence there too."[28]

MILLENNIAL ATTITUDE 2: NETWORKS SHOULD BE ACCESSIBLE.

Rusty Rueff, who serves as an advisor to the president at Purdue University, recently showed a picture of a classroom at that university. The classroom had stadium seating (that is, the seats are higher at the back of the room) with more than thirty rows of students. I knew the classroom well. I had taken a biology course there more than thirty years ago.

> "They want to be educated by, hear their news from, and get their product reviews by people they know and trust."

I remember bending over my notes, hastily scribbling on my yellow notepad insights that I hoped would finally result in an A. Now as I looked at the picture of this contemporary student throng, I noticed that every student was sitting up straight, yet intently looking down. Of the almost one hundred students assembled, every one was sitting behind a laptop computer. "Think of when this will happen in your church," Rueff said. "What do you do in church? Is there a place for those who want to communicate with laptops? Or would an usher ask them to put their computer away?"[29]

2.a. *Immediate, even critical feedback.* In a millennial world where unfettered networking is routine, millennial church leaders are starting to accommodate instant feedback. Some young churches have an "ask-assertive environment"[30] where those who disagree are encouraged to state their differences of opinion, even during the sermon. Millennial congregations such as Solomon's Porch in Minneapolis regularly invite questions or challenges from the audience during the sermon.[31] Even millennial megachurches such as Mars Hill Church in Granville, Michigan, sometimes welcome an audience member on the stage to ask the preacher questions during the sermon (since the congregation is too vast for everyone to shout out a query).[32] Lon Safko, author of *The Social Media Bible*, calls this "A Fundamental Shift in Power. . . . No longer does the consumer trust corporate messages. . . . They want to be educated by, hear their news from, and get their product reviews by people they know and trust."[33]

In addition to critical feedback, immediate feedback is expected. At recent conferences I keynoted, participants were given a keypad so they could rate the presentation and/or their understanding of the content in real time.[34] Even now, increasingly smaller smartphones allow electronic feedback as presentations unfold. Though modern leaders might initially resist such quick and honest feedback in the church, the day is not far off when immediate, even critical feedback will be visually displayed in our churches in much the same manner that words are displayed to a song.

2.b. *Fact checking and further research.* Allowing laptops and smartphones into churches may at first seem disruptive, but it will enhance understanding as it allows checking of facts and further research. Going back to the story of my biology ordeals at Purdue University, I remember balancing a three-inch-thick (or so it seemed) textbook on one knee while holding in my left hand a large diagram of the human organs. Amid this balancing act, I tried desperately to write what the professor was stating. Today, multiple items sit neatly on computer desktops where only a click of a mouse is required to separate sources or conduct further research.

MILLENNIAL ATTITUDE 3: NETWORK RESTRICTIONS MAY BE PERSONAL, BUT ARE NECESSARY.

The breadth and reach of today's networks can make them not only consuming but also alluring. While the modern tack is to restrict access, the millennial approach is to foster spiritual and personal discernment. Consider two phases that millennial leaders use to sift out the negative elements of their networks while holding on to the good:

3.a. *Open discussions about the good and the bad.* To separate the good and the bad of networks requires discussion among friends. The goal of two researchers was "not to tell readers what to think about the media, but to encourage conversation about living faithfully."[35] Some modern leaders, like the pastor in New Jersey who forbade his leaders to use Facebook, might want to return to an age of banning networks. But millennial leaders realize that in the new open-source world, this is not possible. Melissa Rogers, director of the Center for Religion and Public Affairs, sums up this dynamic tension: "I recognize the need to resist the temptations of this media age. But I would never go back to the old days."[36] The millennial leader lives in a new, more dynamic, and possibly decadent system of intertwined networks, and thus authentic debate (and not artificial suppression) initiates the discernment discussions among friends.

3.b. *Open sifting of the good from the bad.* Richard Niebuhr, in his seminal book *Christ and Culture*, suggested that every culture has elements that run counter to the message of Christ, which, therefore, must be rejected.[37] But he also suggested that there are good elements that must be preserved.[38] A barrage of network information both good and bad has made millennial leaders painfully aware of this. The simple image of sifting is a fitting metaphor for the process of sifting out the negative elements from the good.[39] Such sifting took place at one weekly worship service in England for young people that attracted crowds from the downtown club scene. One of the church leaders described the scenario.

> The new Christians were coming to the worship services dressed in the scanty and rather sensuous clothing that they typically wore to the clubs. The young leaders of this celebration, and it was a very healthy thing, had to debate among themselves what should and shouldn't be worn at their church services, even at church services held in a club with techno-pop music. The discussion was very healthy, and led to them making some hard but good decisions.

Due to a network barrage of different cultures and behaviors, tomorrow's leaders are sifting to discern the fortes and flaws of their millennial culture.

NURTURING THE THREE ATTITUDES REGARDING NETWORKS

NURTURING MILLENNIAL ATTITUDE 1: NETWORKS OF RELATIONSHIPS ARE JUST AS IMPORTANT AS ORGANIZATIONAL NETWORKS.

1.a. *Online networks supplement but do not replace traditional face-to-face networks.* Researchers studying online communities found two interesting facts:

1. *Most Christians involved in online communities also have robust offline friendships.* Some have feared that online Christian communities will cause participants to withdraw into cyberspace and away from face-to-face or offline fellowship. But "for many believers, Christian community involves both online *and* offline friendships and affiliations."[40]
2. *Online communities help connect people between their face-to-face encounters.* Another online researcher, Duke University's David Morgan, found that most people use online communities to connect with people between their face-to-face encounters. "It is helpful to realize," states Morgan, "that most [people use] the Web for task-specific purposes to bolster off-line social relations and not as a replacement of them."[41]

Therefore, most people today use both online networks and traditional face-to-face networks to create community. Thus tomorrow's church leader must be careful not to abandon either offline or online networks. The actual result could be less communication, not more.

1.b. *Use social networks as bridges of God to discuss faith.* Sociologists have long known that faith flows best across networks of friends, relatives, acquaintances, and neighbors.[42] Donald McGavran coined the term the *bridges of God*[43] to describe how discussions of faith naturally cross these networks. McGavran wrote, "Though Christians are surrounded by fellow citizens, the Christian faith flows best from relative to relative or close friend to close friend. This was true whatever the nationality or language. It was as true in the heartland of America as in Uganda or the High Andes."[44] Therefore, since these social networks are the bridges of God over which the *missio Dei* has historically traveled, Christians should view these bridges as primary routes over which to discuss faith.

Today the ability of computer software to quickly map such social networks has made millennial leaders greatly aware of their scope. Figure 6.1 shows how an actual faith network was depicted in 1995 (top).[45] The lower image (2011) shows how computer mapping software can illustrate the breadth of these social networks on popular websites such as Facebook. In the social network image, names radiate out from the edge of the circle. Connecting lines in the middle show connections between people (names are excluded for anonymity).

Figure 6.1. Visualizing social networks

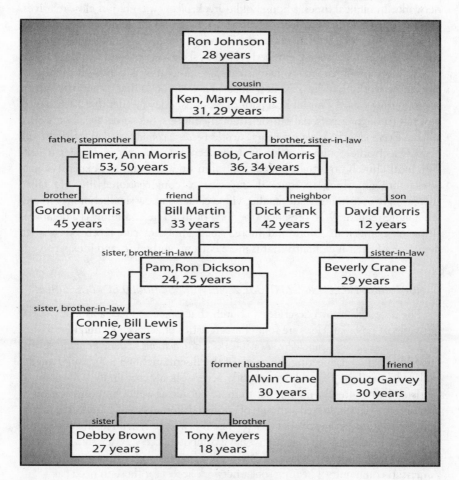

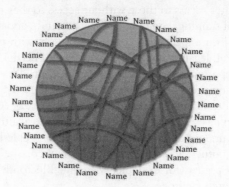

Social webs are also evident in Bible times where they are called "household" networks. In biblical times, a household (Greek, *oikos*) was not just close relatives, but extended families and coworkers who lived, worked, and networked often under the same roof.[46] Michael Green observes, "The [*oikos*] family, understood in this broad way as consisting of blood relations, slaves, clients and friends, was one of the bastions of Graeco-Roman society."[47] And it was across these Greco-Roman networks that the good news first spread, a process that came to be known as *oikos evangelism*.[48] This biblical pattern reminds today's leader that faith travels best not through impersonal on-the-street encounters, but across social networks.

1.c. *Every church should use new networks because communication is cheaper and easier*. Electronic communication is daily becoming cheaper and easier to use. The local church on a tight budget can often find new and less expensive networks through which to share its message of congregational life and faith. Increasingly user-friendly and smaller video cameras allow small churches to create a more realistic Web presence (for good or ill). The end result is a democratizing of evangelism. More and more, small churches can reach out with a depiction of their life of faith that is more current, authentic, and inexpensive.[49]

NURTURING MILLENNIAL ATTITUDE 2: NETWORKS SHOULD BE ACCESSIBLE.

The *accessible church* describes a church that is accessible via as many social networks as possible. Here are four characteristics of accessible churches:

2.a. *The accessible church creates networks that reach out to those in need*. As discussed in chapter 1, meeting the needs of the disenfranchised is a priority among millennial leaders. Expanding network access should be limited not just to Christians who attend a church but to those outside as well. One congregation in Edmonton, Alberta, started a church plant in an Internet café.[50] Unexpectedly, the free Internet access they offered met the needs of a large Asian American community in the neighborhood that did not have computer access. As a result, this accessible church in an Internet café created an ongoing network with a growing Asian American community. Creating social network access for those in need can

- provide computer access to those without access so they can hunt for jobs, find vocational training, communicate with friends, and so on.
- help a person locate local agencies that can assist with professional needs (such as medical, legal, emotional, or educational needs).
- provide an opportunity for those inside and outside a church to work together and link their personal social networks.

2.b. *The accessible church offers free-based access to knowledge*. Christianity is not only a faith based on meeting the needs of others but also a faith based on acquiring knowledge and understanding. Therefore, to help people better understand the Christian faith-journey, access to knowledge should occur. This may mean

- offering access points (for example, wi-fi and Bluetooth) without cost in and nearby church facilities.

- loaning computers free of charge to congregants and non-churchgoers. For example, an online university student benefited greatly from a computer loaned to her by a nearby church.

2.c. *The accessible church fosters instantaneous feedback and research at teaching venues, including during the sermon.* Because Christianity is an experience- and knowledge-based faith, access to information can foster a better understanding about God. This can take place through many avenues, including the following:

- The accessible church can offer Internet access at teaching times, such as during sermons, Sunday school, committee meetings, and so on. Many modern leaders bristle at the thought of laptops and smartphones being used during church, but so did professors several years ago (only to lose the battle). At one time sound systems, video projectors, guitars, and even pipe organs were banned from many churches. Though they may cause discomfort at first, new ways of communication and exploration will emerge, first among these cutting-edge millennial congregations, and eventually among everyone else. When speaker Stan Toler speaks to younger audiences, he often uses instant messaging so attendees can ask their questions via a smartphone while he is still speaking. He then displays their questions on the screen and answers them during his lecture.[51]

- The accessible church can connect congregants to electronic libraries, databases, and religious information. Martin E. Marty describes how he conducts research: "I am two hours by bus or $25 by cab from our university library. I cannot picture life in my emeritus situation without the Internet at hand."[52] Congregants and community members may want access to a church's resources, such as sermon citations/notes, meeting minutes, denominational resources/histories, and so forth. Providing access for those within and without the congregation can create openness, interest, and companionship.

2.d. *The accessible church provides online communities to augment its offline fellowship.* Online communities "felt the connection and affinity they experienced in these groups fully justified their designations as a form of community."[53] Online communities often enhance offline friendships. So, consider the following ways churches can use online networks to enhance offline relationships:

- A church offering a 12-step program can create an online group in which participants can dialogue between meetings.

- Groups, committees, Sunday school classes, and small groups can create, share, and edit documents via Web-based word processors, such as Google Docs. These online documents allow collaborative work (such as designing a Bible study) prior to face-to-face meetings.

- Online communities can allow those who have special needs or limited time/resources to still feel like full participants in the community. In the same way that Robert Schuller continued a lifelong ministry to drive-in worshipers because a physically challenged woman's husband requested it,[54] online communities can engage people who might be challenged in their ability to physically connect with a church. When one university faculty member suggested online students post their pictures with their homework, a student protested, "I like that people don't judge me by appearances. I like the anonymity that the online interface allows."

Readers having little experience with online communities may wonder about their cohesiveness, value, and permanency. Consider six positive attributes of online Christian communities (figure 6.2):

Figure 6.2. Six positive attributes of online Christian communities[55]

Attribute	How Online Communities Provide This
1. Relationships	Ability to provide space and support for personal relationships.
2. Care	Ability to give and receive support, such as sharing prayer requests and encouragement to one another.
3. Value	Ability for members to contribute to the group and invest in communal conversations.
4. Intimate communication	Ability to create a safe place for transparency and to encourage accountability.
5. Twenty-four-hour connection	Accessibility of twenty-four-hour-a-day communication that transcends normal space-time limitations. This makes finding and connecting with other like minds easier.
6. Shared faith	Environment where participants can share a common search for meaning and purpose in light of a distinct interpretation of life and reality.

NURTURING MILLENNIAL ATTITUDE 3: NETWORK RESTRICTIONS MAY BE PERSONAL, BUT ARE NECESSARY.

An online community's twenty-four-hour and immediate accessibility can create "a safe place for transparency and...encourage accountability."[56] This accountability is not only convenient but necessary because networks have tremendous ability to empower and to corrupt. Colin McAlister of Aberdeen University wrote, "On first appearances the church and modern media might not be ideal bed-fellows since the former represents the spiritual, the moral and the eternal, and the latter represents the present, the trivial and the narcissistic. Yet one thing remains paramount, modern media is a permanent fixture in the world we live in."[57] Because of the Web's permanence and power, the millennial leader must adhere to personal restrictions based on spiritual discernment. Below are three elements involved in fostering spiritual discernment:

3.a. *Restrict yourself to those networks for which you are gifted and called.* The first restriction is to limit access to those networks God has called and equipped you to use. Although certain networks may be attractive, they may be beyond a leader's or a church's ability. Colin McAlister tells of his embarrassment over late night TV shows produced by churches lacking the talent to effectively use the new media networks. McAlister recalls, "I remember being highly amused by...real ministers and priests [who] paraded the facets of Christianity on our screens...much of which should never have seen the light of day." He concludes, "Too often the church becomes involved in trends that divert it from its main objective because adaptations are needed and are carried out badly."[58] According to the Scriptures, churches are a blend of people with different giftings (1 Cor. 12:4-7). Sometimes those giftings give a church the ability to use a certain network. But the same giftings may mean that a church is not gifted (or called) to make use of another network.

3.b. *Avoid perverse elements of networks.* Networks comprise all elements of life, including sensuality, voyeurism, and perversity. Avoidance of immorality might be difficult, but it must be sought. Some might argue that sensual elements are so omnipresent that there is no use trying to avoid them. St. Augustine tells of a voyeur with such an outlook.[59] Alypius was a student of St. Augustine, whom he introduced to the Christian life. Alypius, though, had a lifelong love of bloody gladiator games. Friends invited him to the arena, and Alypius went, saying, "You may drag me there bodily, but do you imagine that you can make me watch the show and give my mind to it? I shall be there, but it will be as if I were not present."[60] Alypius was attempting to enjoy his network of friends, but not be influenced by their blood sport get-togethers. Yet Alypius could not resist the bloody spectacle, and when turning his eyes to watch a gladiator die, "his soul was stabbed with a wound more deadly than any which the gladiator, whom he was so anxious to see, had received."[61]

What makes Augustine's story ring true today is that emotional and spiritual damage can result from even limited access to the wrong parts of these networks. The only option may be avoidance. Online filters allow seamier elements of the Web to be restricted, such as those in *Second Life*. Even among social networks, some friendships should be avoided. Here are two principles for avoiding the more perverse elements of a network:

1. Avoid people in your network who will lead you off course.
   a. "The righteous choose their friends carefully, but the way of the wicked leads them astray" (Prov. 12:26 NIV).
   b. "Go from the presence of a foolish man, when you do not perceive in him the lips of knowledge" (Prov. 14:7 NKJV™).
   c. "But we command you, brethren, in the name of our Lord Jesus Christ, that you withdraw from every brother who walks disorderly and not according to the tradition which he received from us" (2 Thess. 3:6 NKJV™).
   d. "Do not be deceived: 'Evil company corrupts good habits.' Awake to righteousness, and do not sin; for some do not have the knowledge of God" (1 Cor. 15:33-34 NKJV™).
2. Choose friends in your network who will give you authentic and wise advice:
   a. "Without counsel, plans go awry, but in the multitude of counselors they are established" (Prov. 15:22 NKJV™).
   b. "Listen to counsel and receive instruction, that you may be wise in your latter days" (Prov. 19:20 NKJV™).
   c. "Cease listening to instruction, my son, and you will stray from the words of knowledge" (Prov. 19:27 NKJV™).

3.c. *Take network sabbaticals.* Some people enjoy worship celebrations because they get away from electronic annoyances. Yet with the relentless march onward of technology, such retreat, though needed, may be difficult. Therefore, the Christian leader should practice times of network sabbaticals. A network sabbatical is a resting (and relenting) from network participation. Melissa Rogers, professor at Wake Forest School of Divinity, tells why she practices such sabbaticals: "In many ways, this new media age is a dream come true for those of us with addictions to the national news. The downside is that managing those addictions is especially difficult.... I've learned that I need to observe an Internet-free Sabbath."[62] Author William Powers, who has further popularized the idea of an Internet Sabbath in his book *Hamlet's BlackBerry*, tells how he restored sanity to his family by each weekend unplugging all of their electronic communication devices including phones, TV, and Internet.[63]

This sabbatical rest should not be from electronic networks only; it should include social networks too. The idea of spiritual disciplines such as solitude and meditation are historically regarded as opportunities to withdraw from human networks and connect in a more focused way with God. Philip Yancey wonders, "What would a church look like that created space for quietness, that bucked the celebrity trend and unplugged from surrounding media?"[64] Isaiah 58:13-14 reminds us what such a church might experience:

> If you watch your step on the Sabbath
> and don't use my holy day for personal advantage,
> If you treat the Sabbath as a day of joy,
> God's holy day as a celebration,
> If you honor it by refusing "business as usual,"
> making money, running here and there—
> Then you'll be free to enjoy God!
> Oh, I'll make you ride high and soar above it all. (*THE MESSAGE*)

THE *MISSIO DEI* REMAINS

The *missio Dei* will outlast all evolving technologies. God's mission to reunite with his offspring and to enlist our partnership in doing so has outlasted pen, ink, vellum, and the printing press. Still, the ability to misuse emerging networks has led to suspicion about their use. Although cries of danger must not dissuade the church from taking risks as a contrast community, caution and discernment must prevail.

The strident voices that bemoan the rise of new networks may be of little consequence. Despite our protestations, new communication networks will emerge, as an editorial from *Christianity Today* reminds us:

> The Benedictine abbot Johannes Trithemius published a book entitled *In Praise of Scribes*, in which he defended the use of pen, ink, and vellum. "Printed books will never be the equivalent of handwritten codices," he argued. Ironically, Trithemius took his book to a printer in Mainz and had it published for wider distribution.[65]

MOVING TOWARD MILLENNIAL LEADERSHIP: QUESTIONS FOR PERSONAL REFLECTION AND/OR GROUP DISCUSSION

The following questions are for personal reflection but can also be used in a group setting:

1. *For personal and group reflection:* create an organix leadership journal by

   • selecting two items from each box, and
   • writing in it what you will begin to do over the next thirty days to move toward millennial leadership in these two areas.

N	Nurturing Millennial Leadership
Network	1. Networks of relationships are just as important as organizational networks. 1.a. *Online networks supplement but do not replace traditional face-to-face networks.* 1.b. *Use social networks as bridges of God to discuss faith.* 1.c. *Every church should use new networks because communication is cheaper and easier.* 2. Networks should be accessible. 2.a. *The accessible church creates networks that reach out to those in need.* 2.b. *The accessible church offers free-based access to knowledge.* 2.c. *The accessible church fosters instantaneous feedback and research at teaching venues, including during the sermon.* 2.d. *The accessible church provides online communities to augment its offline fellowship.* 3. Network restrictions may be personal, but are necessary. 3.a. *Restrict yourself to those networks for which you are gifted and called.* 3.b. *Avoid perverse elements of networks.* 3.c. *Take network sabbaticals.*

2. *For group reflection:*

- Share your responses to the chart above with your group (omitting answers/plans that are overly personal).
- Take notes in your journal on the following:
  a. Does your group agree or disagree with your assessments and plans?
  b. What input did they give you regarding moving toward millennial leadership?
- Then rewrite your plans in your journal using their input.

3. *For personal and group reflection:*

- Revisit your notes in your journal every month for six months. Ask yourself:
  a. Are there areas where I am making progress? If so, describe them.
  b. Are there areas where I am still weak? What will I do to address this?
- At the end of six months reread the chapter and update your plans.

CHAPTER SEVEN

*The Word became flesh and blood, and moved into
the neighborhood.*

—*John 1:14 (THE MESSAGE)*

	Modern Leadership	Millennial Leadership
Incarnation	1. Send others.	1. Go in person.
	2. Teaching is one-sided and directive.	2. Teach and be taught.
	3. Gathering is an attractional event.	3. Gathering is a supernatural encounter.

THROWING AWAY GOOD MONEY

Joel relished leading the onsite small-group network at University Church. This had been his first experience in a large church, and he found some things easier, but other tasks more daunting. He noticed that in this large church there seemed to be less empathy for the poor than he had observed at the much smaller Ekklesia Church. "I can see a passion in our small groups for helping the poor, but they just don't see themselves doing it," Joel lamented in one of our meetings. "There is something about a large church that makes people want to send others and not go themselves."

Though Joel's ministry at University Church had revitalized its small groups, he was disappointed with the lack of impact they were making in the nearby urban area of Fallsgate. Joel insisted that each small group reach UP in worship, reach INward to minister to one another, and reach OUT to help the needy. It was this last area that was the hardest for Joel to accomplish.

"Let's meet this Saturday in the Fallsgate neighborhood," suggested Joel to the group he attended. "Terry's friend owns a home there, and it needs repainting."

"Wouldn't it be better to send professional painters to do it?" Murray asked. "They could do it faster and better."

"But that's not the point," Joel retorted. "We need to get to know the people in that neighborhood personally. We can't know their needs if we don't meet them face-to-face." With that the group decided to reconvene next Saturday morning to paint the home.

That Saturday evening I connected with Joel for an update. "How'd it go?" I asked. Joel responded, "Not good." It seemed only four people showed up out of fourteen group members, and one spent most of the day getting supplies. When sunset arrived, they had painted only one side of the house and half the front. "I'm afraid we can't get anyone back for a few weeks, and it looks atrocious," stated Joel. "I'm worried the community will think we don't follow through with things."

"What makes you feel that way?" I interrupted.

"It was because of what Bill said," replied Joel. "Bill lives next door, and he said that painting that house was the least of the neighborhood's problems. Bill told us that the woman across the street has three kids and her boyfriend beat her up last week. She's afraid of him, but has nowhere to go. And she can't afford to move out because she has a minimum-wage job. Bill asked me why a church as big as ours wasn't doing something."

"What did you tell him?" I asked.

"I told him if she needed money to move to a new home, the church would provide it. But Bill said she needed something more than money. She needed people to count on to help her break a cycle of poverty and abuse. 'You can't throw money at us down here and expect anything to change,' was Bill's reply."

"What did you say then?" I asked.

"I couldn't say a thing," Joel said.

The conversation with Bill had been revelatory for Joel. "I learned from Bill that we need to ask them about their needs. No longer are we just going to throw money indiscriminately at a need," recalled Joel. "Plus, we've combined four small groups, and together they adopt a family and meet all of their needs for a year. If they need tutoring, we help. If they need a place to stay, we help. If they need a better job, we help. We just aren't there with a handout. We are there with a shoulder to bear their pain."

Over the next year, two clusters of small groups moved their meetings to the Fallsgate neighborhood. After a few months, the two clusters started a Sunday afternoon worship celebration for Fallsgate residents. "It [the worship] shows people what we are about: the mission of God. We're not about just doing good deeds. We're connecting people back to God," said Joel. "I guess you'd say our small groups are not just sending their money or their time to Fallsgate, but they are sending God's message that all are welcome to come back home."

ĪĪ IS FOR "INCARNATION"

Latin: in- (into) + carn- (flesh) + ation (to become, to transform)[1]

Incarnation describes how God sent his Son, Jesus, to earth in the flesh and in person (John 1:14; Col. 2:9) in lieu of sending a surrogate (such as an angel) or just speaking through a prophet as he had done in Old Testament times. Scholar N. T. Wright says that this incarnation "implies that God wants to make his presence felt around the place, and he may well want to do so especially where people are trying to run things their own way and making a mess of it."[2]

The incarnation is an important subject, for it reminds us that God is a "missionary God,"[3] coming to humanity to restore fellowship between himself and his offspring. Though there are many attributes to God's incarnation, we shall focus on four aspects:

1. God himself went to earth. He did not send a surrogate.

> The Word became flesh and blood,
>   and moved into the neighborhood.
> We saw the glory with our own eyes,
>   the one-of-a-kind glory,
>   like Father, like Son. (John 1:14
>   THE MESSAGE)

2. God in the form of Jesus came to explain himself to us in a personal manner, with face-to-face dialogue.

> Jesus said, "I am the Road, also the Truth, also the Life. No one gets to the Father apart from me. If you really knew me, you would know my Father as well. From now on, you do know him. You've even seen him!" (John 14:6-7 THE MESSAGE)

3. God wishes the result of this encounter to be a reconnection of people to God.

> All this comes from the God who settled the relationship between us and him, and then called us to settle our relationships with each other. God put the world square with himself through the Messiah, giving the world a fresh start by offering forgiveness of sins. (2 Cor. 5:18-19 THE MESSAGE)

4. God wishes his followers to participate in his mission and tell others about his offer of reconciliation.

God has given us the task of telling everyone what he is doing. We're Christ's representatives. God uses us to persuade men and women to drop their differences and enter into God's work of making things right between them. We're speaking for Christ himself now: Become friends with God; he's already a friend with you. (2 Cor. 5:20 *THE MESSAGE*)

The following sections compare how modern and millennial leaders differ in their approaches to telling others about God's mission.

THREE PERILS OF MODERN LEADERSHIP REGARDING INCARNATION

	Modern Leadership	Millennial Leadership
I **Incarnation**	1. Send others.	1. Go in person.
	2. Teaching is one-sided and directive.	2. Teach and be taught.
	3. Gathering is an attractional event.	3. Gathering is a supernatural encounter.

MODERN MISCUE 1: SEND OTHERS.

Modern leadership has been characterized by a leader's tendency to send others in lieu of going himself or herself.[4] This is a trait of what philosophers sometimes call "the modern era." The modern era began around the time of the printing press (ca. mid-1500s AD) when getting a formal education emerged as the way to get ahead in life. Universities first arose at this time in Sorbonne, France, and Oxford, England. From that day until recently, getting ahead in life meant following the modern axiom that "you get an education, and you will get ahead."

Dissatisfaction with modernism's emphasis on formal education began to rise sometime around 1920. World War I had been an eye-opener. It was a war conducted among the world's most educated nations. And yet these nations used their educational prowess to build better weapons of mass destruction (for example, mustard gas).

Over time, a new, postmodern outlook criticized formal education as the best way to make the world a better place.[5] This new outlook emphasized that it was through experience and personal encounter with others and their culture that true learning took place. Though there are different varieties of postmodernism, most hold that personal encounter and experimentation are better teachers than mediation through the experience of a teacher.[6]

A few specific aspects of leadership illustrate how postmodernism has influenced the church for good[7] and for ill.[8] Figure 7.1 compares the different approaches that modernism and postmodernism take to education, status, and the supernatural.

Figure 7.1. A brief overview of modernism and postmodernism[9]

	Modernism (The Modern Era) ca. 1500–1970	Postmodernism (The Postmodern Era) ca. 1920–today
You learn by	reading about things.	experiencing things yourself.
Research is conducted by	others more trained and skilled than you.	you yourself as you go and learn.
Status is characterized by	excellence and quality.	genuineness and simplicity.
You encounter the supernatural	through common sense and reason.	through unexplainable encounter.
Do you question basic truths?	You do not question basic truths because knowledgeable people smarter than you believe them.	You question even basic truths that knowledgeable people have taught you.
Began	with the resurgence of learning after the so-called Dark Ages (ca. 1500).	with the failure of education to make the world a safer place after World War I (ca. 1920).

Modernism concluded that other, more educated people should be sent to help those in need. This emphasis on professionalism even influenced the church, where sending professional missionaries and aid workers and pastors was the preferred method of helping the needy. While these actions were born from sincerity, they created disconnectivity between the haves and the have-nots. Consider these charitable actions practiced by the modern church:

> **Sending professional missionaries and aid workers to connect with other cultures allowed the church back home to stay safe and secure away from teeming masses and their scarcities.**

- Churches sent money to support "experts" and "professionals" who would then help the needy.
- Periodicals such as *National Geographic* and *Life* became the way people back home experienced other cultures by proxy.
- Clothing drives, coat/mitten appeals, and canned goods campaigns were devised to send cast-off items to the needy.
- Churches planted autonomous churches among needy others. But because these independent churches had only limited ties to the mother church, many church plants failed because the indigenous culture did not have enough money to support them.

The results of sending others were both good and bad. Although much good work was funded and directed by trained experts, the church back home became disconnected. Sending professional missionaries and aid workers to connect with other cultures allowed the church back home to stay safe and secure away from teeming masses and their scarcities. The give-and-take of communicating Christ to a new culture was left to others until recently when those cultures came to the doorsteps of America's churches.

MODERN MISCUE 2: TEACHING IS ONE-SIDED AND DIRECTIVE.

Because modernism puts so much emphasis on scholars and their knowledge, teaching becomes top-down and one-sided. The students are not expected to know much until they have entered higher levels of education. The same is true in the church. The following are notable examples:

- Sermons, lectures, Bible studies, and small-group discussions are one-sided. Discussion is neither encouraged nor planned.
- Proper education gives a person the right to disagree. Only properly trained and designated lay teachers, lay preachers, pastors-in-training, and so on usually speak up or interject challenges.
- Ushers, coleaders, cohosts, and others keep watch over the meetings, ensuring that there are no disturbances, disagreements, and/or challenges.
- Leaders use catch phrases that remind hearers that leaders are the experts and their ideas should not be challenged, such as:

"When I was in seminary, I learned..."

"The original Greek says..."

"I've come to learn over the years..."

While learning does takes place, a one-sided and directive environment creates the following caveats:

- Hearers may not fully understand what is being taught because extended discussion and questioning are not encouraged.
- Congregants come to rely on trained leaders as the experts and expect them to do most of the work.
- Academic-oriented curriculum can create a caste system in our churches where those with more training are more highly regarded and their opinion carries more weight than local frontline workers who have more practical experience.
- People with genuine questions can feel overlooked and ignored in their quest for knowledge. The subtle insinuation is that if you want your questions answered, go to seminary where you will get answers. The result is that many people enter seminary (which is, after all, a professional program) not for training, but for answers to basic questions that the church back home should have provided.

MODERN MISCUE 3: GATHERING IS AN ATTRACTIONAL EVENT.

As a result of one-sided and directive teaching, the professional clergy become the ones who decide how people can best encounter God. And because these professional pastors spend most of their week working on administrative duties, they can often attempt to administrate and overregulate spiritual encounter.

Subsequently, modern churches often try to have the "best worship service in town" because if they do, people will encounter God. I speak from experience. I tried during most of my early ministerial career (ca. 1981–85) to organize the perfect worship service, but I never attained it. And the church that I helped plant didn't grow either. Instead, we experienced a slow loss of talented leaders, who grew tired of my relentless quest for the perfect worship service. I now know such perfection is impossible and absurd to seek. Failures in that church plant, coupled with my consulting work for many churches that have grown in a more organic manner, have helped me see the differences.

Here are some telltale signs that a church may be trying to attract an audience by excellence and exactness:

- The pastor convenes a Monday meeting to discuss the things that went wrong on Sunday and how to fix them. I did this for years, much to the exasperation of the church leaders. I never did create an errorless worship encounter, and no human ever will. Instead, I created an environment where volunteers and staff were more interested in pleasing the pastor than they were in pleasing God.

127

- More time is spent each week on the physical planning of the worship celebration than with the essentials of spiritual preparation.
- The church advertises itself
    - in superlative terms, such as "the best Sunday school in town," or "Our worship is like nothing you've ever experienced."
    - in terms that make it seem the church is smarter than or superior to you, such as, "It's a new year, why don't you do something new: go to church."[10]

Bob Kauflin in *Worship Matters: Leading Others to Encounter the Greatness of God* sums up this dilemma:

> We arrogantly think our church's worship is better than the church down the street. We over-rehearse and get impatient when others make mistakes. We minimize spiritual preparation and devote ourselves entirely to musical issues. We evaluate failure or success solely on right tempos, in-tune vocals, and well-executed plans. We take pride in our polished performance rather than being humbled by God's mercy.[11]

Attractional churches can thus err on the side of seeking excellence over seeking encounter. But there is nothing wrong with seeking excellence and quality. I have attended many churches that foster encounter with an accompanying excellence. The problem arises when excellence is stressed more than encounter in preparation, evaluation, and execution. Seeking to do things well is a biblical admonition (Phil. 4:8). Yet when excellence becomes the goal, the focus and the tool by which leadership is measured, this is unbiblical (1 Cor. 2:1). Our goal instead should be to encounter, and millennial leaders foster this.

Three Attitudes of Millennial Leadership Regarding Incarnation

	Modern Leadership	Millennial Leadership
I Incarnation	1. Send others.	1. Go in person.
	2. Teaching is one-sided and directive.	2. Teach and be taught.
	3. Gathering is an attractional event.	3. Gathering is a supernatural encounter.

I : *Incarnation*

MILLENNIAL ATTITUDE 1: GO IN PERSON.

I am continually surprised that young people today spend their spring vacations so much differently than I did forty years ago. I was part of a burgeoning boomer generation, and despite all of our protestations about peace, love, and unity, we still spent our spring vacations partying in Fort Lauderdale. We might march for peace one week, hold a sit-in the next week to protest unfair treatment of African Americans, and spend an exorbitant amount of money staying in a beachfront hotel overlooking the warm Atlantic the following week.

Although some students today undoubtedly follow in my unruly footsteps, I am surprised that many of our university students opt instead for mission trips to Haiti, South America, and Mexico. Pat Hannon, a leader connected with the university's short-term missions program, stated,

> This emerging generation of leaders is not content to merely talk about serving or to praise how others have served. They are eager to jump in and get their hands dirty by serving needs in the world around them. . . . Whatever the weaknesses are of the upcoming generation, we should celebrate the reality that they expect faith and action to be connected.[12]

Such attitudes are being mirrored in new and flexible church experiments. Shane Claiborne is a colleague and one of the founders of Potter Street Community in Philadelphia.[13] In solidarity with the poor this church bought what they called an "intentional community house"[14] in an urban area, expanded to a few houses, then decided to return to one house. They are now launching a new Apprenticeship House.[15] And Ron Sider has stated his respect for a movement in the Church of the Nazarene to create Samaritan churches that seek to empower the needy.[16] These churches are fulfilling what John M. Perkins advocated and we studied in chapter 4: wealthy churches should move into areas of urban blight and reconcile with them through a strategy of relocation.[17]

MILLENNIAL ATTITUDE 2: TEACH AND BE TAUGHT.

Professors and teachers have long known that students learn best through a two-way dialogue and discussion.[18] Not surprisingly, this was one of Jesus' primary methods of discourse. In Scripture we see Jesus teaching and taking questions. He did not seem perturbed by the sometime audacity of the questioner. In Mark alone Jesus often asked questions to foster more discussion (2:9, 25; 3:4, 23, 33-35; 4:13, 30, 40, and so on).

To cultivate more learning, here are some ways that churches are fostering more dialogue:

- Churches are using electronic networks to stimulate feedback and questions during presentations and teaching, as noted in the previous chapter.

- Churches are going out of the sanctuary into the community to dialogue with others. This puts the listener at ease by providing her or him a more comfortable and customary environment, which encourages more dialogue. Such Bible and/or theological studies are taking place in local haunts, including community rooms, libraries, cafés, and even pubs. One pastor leads a gathering in a pub with a vision "to gather in a natural setting and engage with folks who may not come to us."[19]
- Churches are developing Bible studies and sermons that tackle formerly taboo topics. Theologically delicate topics such as homosexuality, infidelity, spiritual insincerity, and so forth are being discussed in open and non-discriminatory forums. Dan Kimball surveyed the Vintage Faith congregation to solicit topics for a five-week sermon series called "Q-5: Questions of Theology and Culture." Topics included Christian prejudice, the reliability of the Bible, homosexuality, and why does a loving God kill people.[20] A result is that topics once avoided as too controversial are being addressed so that learning can result.

Discussing difficult topics through two-way communication in local environments requires Christians to go out among non-churchgoers. Genuine dialogue is weakened when it takes place in unfamiliar environs or only in church facilities. The best dialogue takes place when the church goes out and explains the *missio Dei* in person to those whom God is seeking to reconnect.

MILLENNIAL ATTITUDE 3: GATHERING IS A SUPERNATURAL ENCOUNTER.

While the modern approach is often to focus on the minutiae of planning and management in hopes of orchestrating a supernatural encounter, the millennial reaction is to spend more time in spiritual preparation. I have noticed that millennial churches spend more time in spiritual disciplines such as prayer and fasting when planning worship gatherings. Some have even characterized such an emphasis on spiritual preparation as a part of a "new monasticism" where young people on their spiritual journeys find that solitude, prayer, fasting, and meditation better prepare them for worship than selecting a liturgy or choosing the perfect illustration for a sermon.[21]

Here are some characteristics I have noticed in churches with a focus on supernatural experience:

- More preparatory time for worship celebrations, small-group meetings, and so forth is spent in prayer, fasting, silence, and meditation than in physical planning.
- The goal of a worship celebration is that everyone will *experience* God. We saw in chapter 5 that the Hebrew word for worship means a close encounter with a king that fosters reverence, respect, and praise.[22] And thus, the purpose of our worship celebrations should be to usher congregants into such a close personal encounter with the God who created

them. After all, since the *missio Dei* is God's quest to reconnect with his errant offspring, an appropriate goal for our worship encounters should be to accommodate that God-on-one connection.

• The Holy Spirit—not a liturgy or the order printed in the bulletin—is allowed to lead a worship encounter. Doug Pagitt leads an innovative church in Minneapolis. I was surprised when attending the church to find that they often practice improvisation in worship. "Some people think improvisation takes less work, but it takes more because you've got to have everything ready," Doug told me. "The key is that you let the Holy Spirit arrange how it unfolds when you get to Sunday evening."[23] To encourage improvisation, the Solomon's Porch worship team prepares four to five songs, the preacher prepares a sermon, someone else prepares a verse to share, and another person prepares a prayer. But when they start their Sunday evening celebration, no one knows in which order these elements will unfold. The worship team, speakers, and others wait until they feel God nudging them to go next. The result is what Pagitt calls improvisation but is really a Spirit-led structure for the elements they sense God has led them to prepare.[24]

NURTURING THE THREE ATTITUDES REGARDING INCARNATION

NURTURING MILLENNIAL ATTITUDE 1: GO IN PERSON.

1.a. *Provide opportunities for congregants to go to distant cultures.* Churches are discovering the power of congregants being involved personally in ministering to the needs of far-off cultures. This can take place in mission trips over holidays or summers. But such opportunities should not be limited to young people. Many retirees and second-career missionary workers are emerging. One of Youth with a Mission's most successful programs is called Crossroads, which features a discipleship training school for not-so-youthful people over age thirty.

All of these avenues are intended to get congregants from a First World culture to work alongside residents of a Two-thirds World culture in solving problems. Churches are already doing this to an extent, but the grave needs of most of the world's emerging nations mean that the great wealth of the haves is not yet reaching the have-nots.

> "There was so much need that a food pantry or a clothing shelf just couldn't make a dent. So, we don't do that now. Instead, we adopt a half dozen families and we meet all of their needs."

1.b. *Provide opportunities for congregants to go into local, but dissimilar cultures.* Almost all communities today have new cultures moving in. In many rural locales that were for many years immune to unfamiliar cultures, an influx of migrant workers is occurring. The migratory nature of these families creates challenges connecting with them, but they, too, are part of the *missio Dei*. Today churches are discovering the power of sending congregants to do the work personally instead of throwing money at the needs of locally emerging cultures. Many churches are discovering the power of releasing congregants to be tutors over lunch breaks at local and struggling schools.

1.c. *Adopt people, not programs.* It is easy to pick out a program, even one that appears in this book, and try to apply it without checking compatibility with local needs. Thus, it is important to get feedback from people in need and build a ministry around their needs rather than a program. For example, Jay Height is the millennial leader of a once-struggling Church of the Nazarene in Indianapolis, Indiana. Jay was tired of not being able to meet the mushrooming needs of the impoverished neighborhood. "The need was too great," stated Jay.

> There was so much need that a food pantry or a clothing shelf just couldn't make a dent. So, we don't do that now. Instead, we adopt a half dozen families and we meet all of their needs. If they need food, we provide it. If they need a better job, we help them get it. Whatever they need, the church has adopted them, so we help them get it. Because the need is so great, you can't just do a program and hope to meet everyone's need....A program makes people dependent on a program and not a person. Therefore, we just adopt families and our congregation takes care of all of their needs.[25]

NURTURING MILLENNIAL ATTITUDE 2: TEACH AND BE TAUGHT.

2.a. *Encourage dialogue, questions, and disagreement when discussing spiritual topics.* The key to learning is more discussion. We've all seen at one time or another that being unable to ask a question has stopped us in our exploration of a theme and thwarted learning. When we welcome discussion and listen, the teacher can learn more too. Figure 7.2 suggests five rules that can help discussants be "critical and creative at the same time".[26]

Figure 7.2. Five rules for discussion and learning

Focus and Time Allotment	The Five Rules
Presentation of the topic (25 percent of allotted time)	1. The leader presents an overview of the topic.
Discussion (50 percent of allotted time)	2. Listeners share their thoughts. • Critical or opposing discussion is welcome. • Combinations of ideas are sought. • Proposing or hearing an opinion does not mean accepting it.

Conclusions (25 percent of allotted time)	3. Leader summarizes the previous discussion. 4. Leader and participants conclude the discussion by noting areas of agreement. 5. Further discussion of the topic is scheduled, or discussion is considered complete.

2.b. Go out to places where non-churchgoers are comfortable, and dialogue with them there. The *missio Dei* is the reconnection that people are seeking. But Dan Kimball in his book *They Like Jesus but Not the Church* offers a sobering reminder that people today are often leery of Christians who bring that message of reunification. The message can be more palatable if the hearers are in a locale in which they are familiar and comfortable. Therefore, consider holding discussion groups at

- local cafés, coffee bars, and restaurants,
- public buildings such as libraries and community centers,
- private facilities such as rooms in health clubs, athletic clubs, and cultural associations, and
- homes of sociable and amicable people (for example, Jesus attended a party given by a tax gatherer named Matthew [Matt. 9:9-13]).

The best place to create dialogue with non-churchgoers about God's mission may be not in the unfamiliar (to them) confines of the church building but in the haunts and meeting places of the local community.

2.c. Allow God to do the work of the missio Dei, *and do not try to force a conclusion.* Sometimes because a Christian recognizes the eternal magnitude of God's *missio Dei*, he or she may try to force a conclusion. But this is God's mission. God directs its pace. Jürgen Moltmann described it as "not the church that has a mission of salvation to fulfill in the world; it is the mission of the Son and the Spirit through the Father that includes the church."[27] Therefore, if it is God's mission and it is the Holy Spirit that brings people to the point of conversion (John 6:44, 65), it is improper and presumptuous for a Christian to force a conclusion. I've written two books on the journey of faith and the time it takes for some people to navigate that journey. I've also interviewed twelve national Christian leaders about their spiritual journeys and described how they took different routes at different paces to meet God. Because God is the one leading the seeker forward and the route for each traveler can be so different, we must be careful not to allow our concern to overcompensate for God's patience.

NURTURING MILLENNIAL ATTITUDE 3: GATHERING IS A SUPERNATURAL ENCOUNTER.

3.a. *Spend more time in spiritual preparation for worship than in physical planning.* Since the Hebrew word for worship means "a close encounter with a king that fosters reverence, respect, and praise,"[28] this should be an aim of our worship gatherings. As such, preparation for spiritual encounter should be lengthier than preparation for physical planning. Yet the opposite is too often true. I have noticed many clients who plan profusely for the physical aspects of a worship gathering with bulletins, perfectly synchronized Scriptures, liturgical exactness, and fitting sermon examples. Yet we often do so with little regard for the spiritual dynamics involved. The best remedy is to simply spend more time in spiritual preparation for worship gatherings than in physical planning. Now, you may be saying, "I cannot lessen my preparation. A certain amount of time is required." If that is the case, then measure how much time you spend in physical preparation and designate a corresponding amount of time to pre-worship preparations. Below are just a few examples:

- prayer
- fasting
- meditation
- confession
- absolution

3.b. *Evaluate worship gatherings in light of how well people connected with God.* We have seen that the focus of worship should be encounter, and we should evaluate it based on this criterion. In other words, ask yourself the questions found in figure 7.3 after each worship celebration.

Figure 7.3. Five phases of worship evaluation

The Five Phases	Evaluative Actions
Phase 1: Experiences of encounter	Did people enter into a worship encounter during the worship celebration? What was happening and when? Why do you think this occurred?
Phase 2: Absence of encounter	Were there times when you and/or others sensed it was hard to connect with God? What was happening and when? Why do you think this occurred?

Phase 3: Possible changes	What can be changed: to foster more encounter? to foster less distraction? Are there some areas that cannot be changed and should be left in God's hands? Make a list and write down your responses.
Phase 4: Review three days before next worship celebration	Take out your list at least three days before the next worship celebration. Read it. Pray over it. Apply changes as warranted and guided.
Phase 5: Measurement	Track your time to spend equal amounts of time in spiritual preparation and in physical preparation.

Though some of these examples point to a corporate worship gathering, most are adaptable to any worship gathering, such as that in a small group. The important principle to remember in our chapter on incarnation is that God seeks to meet face-to-face with people. And not surprisingly, people seek God in the same way. Therefore, God's coming to earth in the flesh established a principle for how we partner with God's *missio Dei*. So we, too, must go personally in the flesh to connect with people, beginning authentic dialogue with them and together encountering their Creator.

MOVING TOWARD MILLENNIAL LEADERSHIP: QUESTIONS FOR PERSONAL REFLECTION AND/OR GROUP DISCUSSION

The following questions are for personal reflection but can also be used in a group setting.

1. *For personal and group reflection:* create an organix leadership journal by
   - selecting two items from each box, and
   - writing in it what you will begin to do over the next thirty days to move toward millennial leadership in these two areas.

I	**Nurturing Millennial Leadership**
Incarnation	1. Go in person. 1.a. *Provide opportunities for congregants to go to distant cultures.* 1.b. *Provide opportunities for congregants to go into local, but dissimilar cultures.* 1.c. *Adopt people, not programs.*
	2. Teach and be taught. 2.a. *Encourage dialogue, questions, and disagreement when discussing spiritual topics.* 2.b. *Go out to places where non-churchgoers are comfortable, and dialogue with them there.* 2.c. *Allow God to do the work of the missio Dei, and do not try to force a conclusion.*
	3. Gathering is a supernatural encounter. 3.a. *Spend more time in spiritual preparation for worship than in physical planning.* 3.b. *Evaluate worship gatherings in light of how well people connected with God.*

2. *For group reflection:*

- Share your responses to the chart above with your group (omitting answers/plans that are overly personal).
- Take notes in your journal on the following:
    a. Does your group agree or disagree with your assessments and plans?
    b. What input did they give you regarding moving toward millennial leadership?
- Then rewrite your plans in your journal using their input.

3. *For personal and group reflection:*

- Revisit your notes in your journal every month for six months. Ask yourself:
    a. Are there areas where I am making progress? If so, describe them.
    b. Are there areas where I am still weak? What will I do to address them?
- At the end of six months reread the chapter and update your plans.

Let's break through to the real reasons for growth or non-growth. . . . Let's put diagnostic tools into the hands of pastors, people . . . so they will see, clearly and scientifically the real situation.

—*Donald McGavran, Dean Emeritus, Fuller Seminary*[1]

	Modern Leadership	Millennial Leadership
Measure	1. Measure a church's growth in conversion and attendance.	1. Measure a church's growth in maturity.
		2. Measure a church's growth in unity.
		3. Measure a church's growth in favor among non-churchgoers.
		4. Measure a church's growth in conversion.

WHEN THINGS ADD UP

Jerry was preparing to hire two staff members. Though he looked forward to adding new staff at First Church, he always felt uncomfortable with the interviews. He was taken aback when he heard the sounds of merriment and laughter coming from the waiting room. *This is some way to start an interview,* Jerry thought as he opened the door.

In the waiting room Jerry found an older gentleman, a thirtyish young man, and a middle-aged woman laughing and chatting with such excitement that he could scarcely interject a word. Finally, Jerry blurted out, "Who is here for the job interview for pastor to senior adults?" The young man and the older gentleman raised their hands. "Well, who is here for the position of young adult pastor?" All three raised their hands. Spontaneously, they all broke into laughter again. "You see," said Joan, "we've known one another for years, but we had no idea we were applying for the same two jobs. I haven't seen Gordon and Joel for years, and I guess we just got carried away by the reunion."

To Jerry, there was something comforting in their camaraderie. "Well, we can start this interview together and then break out separately," Jerry suggested. They all thought that was a good idea. They moved to Jerry's office, and he began to read their résumés. "Joan, it says here you pastored at Aldersgate Church. I pastored there years ago."

"I followed you, I think," Joan replied.

"Aldersgate, that was a hard nut to crack," Jerry observed. "But eventually, when they let me start counting spiritual progress and stop tracking attendance so closely, we began to grow."

"What do you mean?" interjected Joel, who had always been a bit impolite when his interest was piqued.

"You see," Jerry continued, "after a few years at Aldersgate Church, things weren't adding up. Positive things were happening, but it wasn't reflected in our attendance numbers. The congregants were more unified than they'd been in a decade. And a growing ministry to the Hispanic community had been positive, with a nearby Hispanic church growing because of their generosity. I thought, *There's got to be a better way to measure a church's growth.* One night I sat down at my computer and sent an e-mail to a young pastor friend in Atlanta, describing Aldersgate's situation. Before I turned in for the night, I found this reply from Aaron: 'Before you go to bed tonight read Acts 2:42-47. I'll call you in the morning.'"

For the next hour Jerry recounted how Aaron's suggestion had led him to measure a church's health by spiritual metrics, not attendance numbers. Jerry had inherited a badly divided church at Aldersgate, but his hard work had brought about an improvement in unity. Jerry recalled, "One woman said, 'We're much more united than we were before Jerry came. If that is all we got out of his leadership . . . well, maybe that's enough.'" To track the growing unity, Jerry regularly asked people if they sensed the church was more or less unified than last year. Jerry also tracked the number of congregants in small groups such as Sunday school classes, Bible study groups, and even committees. "I wanted to see if people were growing in their devotion to Bible study, fellowship, meals together, and prayer gatherings, as it says in Acts 2:42. These things seemed more important to measure than how many people I could get to show up on Sunday morning."

As Jerry continued to explain, Joan, Gordon, and Joel peppered him with questions and impressions. Before long, all had lost track of the time. Finally, a knock at the door interrupted their lively discussion.

Jerry's assistant appeared. "I'm leaving now. It's the end of the workday. Do you want me to schedule more interviews next week?" Suddenly, Joan, Gordon, and Joel were brought back to reality. There were three of them and only two jobs.

"No, don't schedule any more for next week. I think I've found our staff members," Jerry told him. With that the assistant departed, but for Joan, Gordon, and Joel, anxiety took his place. Neither wanted to take the other's position, but all relished the idea of working with a creative pastor like Jerry.

After some uncomfortable minutes of silence, Jerry spoke again: "I've made my decision, if the church board agrees. I think Joel would make an excellent young adult pastor." Both Gordon and Joan smiled, and Joan winked at Joel. After all, Joan and Gordon had only suggested themselves for the job because of what they had learned through Joel's friendship. "And for the senior adult pastor, I will suggest Gordon to the board," Jerry continued. Now elation was tempered. Both Joel and Gordon felt that Joan had been their pastor, and she had been in the ministry longer. Spontaneously, they hugged, and tears of joy and sorrow began to flow down Gordon's face. Within a few minutes, they composed themselves, and Joan congratulated the two men.

After an awkward silence, Jerry said, "I don't know what you are getting all weepy about, and I don't know where we'll find the money, but I think we should create a new position of pastor to adults for Joan. I've needed help for some time, and I think your experiences and your spirits are right for this church. Welcome home."

With that, four circular routes reconnected and resulted in fruitful years of ministry. At First Church, lessons learned in so many diverse congregations and locales had come together to spread ever increasingly the good news of God's mission.

✖ IS FOR "MEASUREMENT"

This chapter discusses measurement: ways to measure spiritual growth and its relationship to effective leadership. Church leaders often cringe when the words *spiritual* and *measurement* are linked. Such phrases give the impression of either excessive scrutiny or oversimplification. Consider this short investigation into the rationale for measuring spiritual growth.

IS MEASUREMENT SPIRITUAL?

The Scriptures are full of examples of appraisal and assessment, especially when describing how spiritual seekers mature along their spiritual journeys. The numberings in Numbers 1:2; 26:2 reminded a Jewish nation that a lack of pre-exodus faith had resulted in many of them forfeiting the blessings of the promised land. And Luke's numberings in Acts 1:15; 2:41; 4:4 reminded the Christian church that even amid persecution, the Christian community matured and spread from the imperial backwaters of Jerusalem to the Roman capital.

Still, some argue against counting, claiming that David was punished for ordering a census of Israel (1 Chron. 21:1-30). A closer look reveals that in the face of an overwhelming opponent, David sought to count his men to bolster his faith rather than trust in God's assistance. David's error was not his counting per se, but his counting for inappropriate reasons. Yet the story of David's inappropriate counting can be a warning for all who would count today. If you are counting because you need to bolster your faith, your error is the same as David's. Measurement should be not a substitution for faith, but an indication of God's movement among God's people.

Modern leadership and millennial leadership differ in their approaches to measurement. This comparison can help tomorrow's leaders see what should be counted and what should not.

A PERIL OF MODERN LEADERSHIP REGARDING ✖ (MEASUREMENT)

	Modern Leadership	Millennial Leadership
Measure	1. Measure a church's growth in conversion and attendance.	1. Measure a church's growth in maturity.
		2. Measure a church's growth in unity.
		3. Measure a church's growth in favor among non-churchgoers.
		4. Measure a church's growth in conversion.

MODERN MISCUE 1: MEASURE A CHURCH'S GROWTH
IN CONVERSION AND ATTENDANCE.

Just one modern miscue is investigated in this chapter because it contrasts significantly with four more organic measurements. The modern miscue is to put too much reliance on measuring conversion and attendance as an indicator of leadership effectiveness.

1.a. *Counting conversion*. First, let me say that conversion is a critically important experience for every spiritual traveler.[2] Let's define what we are talking about using an accepted definition by psychologist and philosopher William James: "[Conversion is] the process, gradual or sudden, by which a self hitherto divided, and consciously wrong, inferior and unhappy, becomes unified and consciously right, superior and happy, in consequence of its firmer hold upon religious realities."[3]

Such conversion is an important response to God's mission (the *missio Dei*), for it describes a second birth where a person begins a new life reunited with her or his heavenly Father. The Bible states, "What we see is that anyone united with the Messiah gets a fresh start, is created new. The old life is gone; a new life burgeons! Look at it!" (2 Cor. 5:17 *THE MESSAGE*).

Such changes are countable, but there are two caveats to counting conversion:

1. Conversion can happen gradually or suddenly, so counting is difficult. A sudden conversion to Christianity is easily noted, while a more gradual conversionary experience is harder to count. Let's look at how the Bible describes both types of conversion and therefore how effectively counting all conversions becomes difficult.
   - *Sudden conversion*. Today when people think of conversion, they usually think of a sudden conversion like that of Paul on the road to Damascus (Acts 9:1-19). Many people, including this author, have experienced conversion in this abrupt and unmistakable way.
   - *Progressive conversion*. But if we look at how most of Jesus' disciples were converted, we see a more gradual progression. Fuller Seminary's Richard Peace emphasizes that "what Mark sought to communicate in his Gospel was the process by which these twelve men gradually turned, over time, from their culturally derived understanding of Jesus as a great teacher to the amazing discovery that he was actually the Messiah who was the Son of God."[4]

Scot McKnight adds that "for many Christians conversion is a process of socialization,"[5] meaning that it is in the company and companionship of other Christians that many people gradually convert to Christ.

2. Counting conversion is difficult because it is a supernatural work of God's spirit and occurs on God's timetable. Conversion involves a

143

God who declares, "My ways [are] higher than your ways and my thoughts than your thoughts" (Isa. 55:9 NIV). As Jesus pointed out, trying to tally up conversions is like trying to count the wind:

So don't be so surprised when I tell you that you have to be "born from above"— out of this world, so to speak. You know well enough how the wind blows this way and that. You hear it rustling through the trees, but you have no idea where it comes from or where it's headed next. That's the way it is with everyone "born from above" by the wind of God, the Spirit of God. (John 3:8 *THE MESSAGE*)

When Luke describes the growth of the early church, he stresses God's involvement: "And the Lord added to their number daily those who were being saved" (Acts 2:47 NIV). The scriptural emphasis is that being saved from the penalty of one's sin happens when the Holy Spirit and a human's free will intersect. Subsequently, counting conversions is not a good indicator of leadership, for it happens at different paces and as the result of a divine intersection.[6]

1.b. *Counting attendance.* Perhaps because conversion is such an inscrutable intersection, counting church attendance has become the common alternative. Yet attendance at an event, worship celebration, or something similar can be artificially skewed by many factors. Figure 8.1 includes just a few temporary factors that can artificially skew attendance growth, making it an inconsistent measurement.

Figure 8.1. Temporary types of attendance growth

Forces affecting temporary attendance growth	Actions that can create temporary growth
Curiosity	New facility is built. New pastor is hired. New program is initiated.
Entertainment	Special musical guest(s) perform. Special speaker(s) make appearances. Church becomes the "it" church, meaning it is inordinately popular, and thus people associate with it.[7]

: *Measure*

Population changes	Growing neighborhood surrounds the church. Church attracts an emerging culture (ethnic, age group, etc.) from the neighborhood.
In the examples above, temporary and artificial reasons, not leadership, may be driving attendance growth.	

Therefore, if modern ways of measuring leadership by counting conversion and attendance are difficult to decipher at best, perhaps Luke has given hints of better indicators. Let's look at the verses preceding Acts 2:47 and see if more relevant measurement tools emerge.

FOUR ATTITUDES OF MILLENNIAL LEADERSHIP REGARDING (MEASUREMENT)

	Modern Leadership	Millennial Leadership
Measure	1. Measure a church's growth in conversion and attendance.	1. Measure a church's growth in maturity.
		2. Measure a church's growth in unity.
		3. Measure a church's growth in favor among non-churchgoers.
		4. Measure a church's growth in conversion.

MILLENNIAL ATTITUDE 1: MEASURE A CHURCH'S GROWTH IN MATURITY.

In Acts 2:42-47 Luke described Jerusalem's reaction to Peter's first sermon.[8] A fresh Spirit-infused community came into being, and thus measuring it (as Luke always liked to do) required new metrics.[9] Luke wrote that as a result of Peter's sermon, they devoted themselves

- to the apostles' teaching
- and to fellowship,
- to the breaking of bread
- and to prayer. (Acts 2:42 NIV)

> What a refreshing metric! Luke was not measuring bodies, but hunger for knowledge, unity, community, and prayer. In the new millennium measurement is not about how many warm bodies show up at an event, but how much committed community emerges.

Devoted comes from two Greek words: *pros-* (a goal striven toward)[10] and *karterountes* (steadfast, to hold out, to endure).[11] The New International Version translates this as "devoted," but the King James Version translates it more accurately as "continued steadfastly." A compromise might be to say that they "steadfastly strove for the goals of..."

The four descriptive phrases indicate goals of this steadfast striving: learning, fellowship, communal dinners, and prayer. What a refreshing metric! Luke was not measuring bodies, but hunger for knowledge, unity, community, and prayer. In the new millennium measurement is not about how many warm bodies show up at an event, but how much committed community emerges.

Growth in maturity is one way to label this growth. But we shall see shortly that growth in maturity is not easily measured. Yet if we calculate it in the same way year after year (for instance, count the number of people involved in Bible studies and prayer groups), we can catch a glimpse of Luke's intent: to measure how God grows within and through God's followers. Before we look at tools that can measure growth in maturity, let's investigate three more measurements that Luke described in Acts 2:42-47.

MILLENNIAL ATTITUDE 2: MEASURE A CHURCH'S GROWTH IN UNITY.

Acts 2:44-45 describes a growing trust within the fledgling church. This resulted in their selling of their possessions to help one another. Some throughout history have taken this passage to suggest that true discipleship is only to be found by living a communal lifestyle where all possessions are shared.[12] However, if communal living was to be the norm for the Christian church, Paul, Peter, James, and others would have admonished churches in Corinth, Antioch, Philippi, Jerusalem, and elsewhere to adopt a communal lifestyle. Scholar Everett Harrison adds an interesting insight: "This was not the forsaking of the principle of private ownership, since the disposal and distribution of their possessions was occasioned 'as anyone might have need.' When the need became known, action was taken based on loving concern."[13] Luke emphasized heightened trust and unity growing in the church. Followers were becoming confident they could rely on one another, even in things they formerly valued most: their money and assets.

Such actions describe a deeper unity and trust among believers than they had known before. This is a second type of church growth and makes more sense to track than conversions or attendance. Growth in unity is one way to label this emerging inter-reliance. Again, measuring this will be subjective and require some effort to calculate. But a simple congregational questionnaire administered yearly and anonymously can glean congregational perceptions of whether unity is growing or waning.

Degree of unity is an important measurement that is often overlooked by denominational measurement methods too. For instance, in this chapter's story Pastor Jerry had inherited a badly divided congregation. His hard work had brought about an improvement in unity, as exemplified in a congregant's comment that "we're much more united than we were before Jerry came. If that is all we got out of his leadership . . . well, maybe that's enough." However, because the church was experiencing a plateau in attendance and the denomination was not tracking growth in unity, Jerry's progress was not evident to the denomination. We might ask ourselves, "Was Pastor Jerry growing the church?" Yes. "Was he growing it in a way that was helpful and valuable?" Yes. "But was this growth evident to the denomination?" No. Herein lies the problem. We are measuring things like conversion and attendance, which human leadership has only limited ability to influence, and we are overlooking important metrics of church growth, such as a church growing in unity. In the next section we will look at tools that can measure growth in unity as well.

MILLENNIAL ATTITUDE 3: MEASURE A CHURCH'S GROWTH IN FAVOR AMONG NON-CHURCHGOERS.

The Acts 2:47 phrase, "and enjoying the favor of all the people" (NIV), describes in concise terms a growing appreciation for the church among community residents. Here we see that manifold connections and service to the community result in favor, esteem, and a good opinion from people outside the congregation. The community does not regard members of the church as mongers, dogmatists, or self-absorbed elitists. Instead, the church seems to have been serving the community with such joyful enthusiasm that people

> We are measuring things like conversion and attendance, which human leadership has only limited ability to influence, and we are overlooking important metrics of church growth, such as a church growing in unity.

genuinely respected and valued its presence. Here is another refreshing metric that Luke chose to describe.

Measuring growth in favor among non-churchgoers can ascertain whether community favor is increasing or declining. But there is a caveat. Growing in favor does not mean catering to immoral elements in a community in hopes of currying their favor. Rather this verse describes what happens when a church applies biblical principles of love, fairness, truth-telling, and compassion in a non-churchgoing community. This results in the community returning to them favor and respect. Such regard can be seen in an observation of the early church leader Tertullian, who wrote that non-Christians often commented, "Behold, how they love one another."[14] We shall now see how measuring a church's impact and esteem in a community is an effective tool to measure leadership.

MILLENNIAL ATTITUDE 4: MEASURE A CHURCH'S GROWTH IN CONVERSION.

Millennial leaders are raised in a culture where change occurs frequently and intensely. It is little wonder they have always known personal change to be a part of life's odyssey. But they also know that personal change can be faked or fleeting. Subsequently, I have found it refreshing to see that while millennial leaders measure conversion too, they do it in the reverse manner to the way modern leadership tracks conversion. Let me explain.

> Millennial leaders are raised in a culture where change occurs frequently and intensely. . . . But they also know that personal change can be faked or fleeting.

On the one hand, modern leaders spend a considerable amount of time and emphasis tracking conversion at an altar or a prayer room. This often fosters an emphasis upon the new convert's altar testimonial or their verbal declarations as proof of spiritual change. However, little tracking is conducted after conversion to confirm this change.

On the other hand, millennial leaders spend more time and energy tracking the results of conversion, looking to build a case for what happened at the altar. They realize that a conversion is less likely to be faked or fleeting this way. This millennial attitude is akin to that of Luke in Acts 2:42-47, who built a case for conversion by first citing examples of the changed lives and actions of the new followers. Thus, millennial leaders look to long-term results, which can confirm a conversion, resonating with James's admonition that,

> what good is it if people say they have faith but do nothing to show it? Claiming to have faith can't save anyone, can it? Imagine a brother or sister who is naked and never has enough food to eat. What if one of you said, "Go in peace! Stay warm! Have a nice meal!"? What good is it if you don't actually give them what

their body needs? In the same way, faith is dead when it doesn't result in faithful activity.

Someone might claim, "You have faith and I have action." But how can I see your faith apart from your actions? (James 2:14-18 CEB)

NURTURING THE FOUR ATTITUDES REGARDING (MEASUREMENT)

Growth in favor is similar to maturity growth and unity growth, in that all three must rely on subjective assessment. As noted, this may be why modern leaders often take the easy route of counting physical attributes of attendance and conversion. But subjective measurement is a reliable tool if consistent and commonsense questionnaires are employed. After years of applying the following assessment tools among client churches and students, I have found that these tools are a helpful starting place.

NURTURING MILLENNIAL ATTITUDE 1: MEASURE A CHURCH'S GROWTH IN MATURITY.

This is one of the easier types of growth to measure. Acts 2:42 describes how the young church steadfastly strove for goals of "the apostles' teaching...fellowship,...the breaking of bread and...prayer." Every church has groups that center on these purposes. Thus by counting the percentage of people involved in small groups where teaching takes place, fellowship takes place, shared meals take place, and prayer takes place, a church can begin to get a general picture of spiritual progress (or regress).

1.a. *Count all of your small groups.* Figure 8.2 suggests typical small groups and how they might correlate to the categories mentioned in Acts 2:42. When counting groups, limit yourself to small groups as defined in chapter 3 as "less than twenty people meeting one or more times a month."[15] Measuring changes in participation in these small groups can be a general indicator of changes in how many congregants are actively striving for learning, fellowship, communal dinners, and prayer.

Figure 8.2. Groups that might exemplify growth in maturity

"They devoted themselves to...	Small groups in a church that might exemplify this

the apostles' teaching...	Bible studies Sunday school classes Newcomer classes Membership classes Confirmation classes Baptism classes Any regular gathering or class encouraging Christian education
to fellowship...	Hobby groups Sport teams Any regular gathering or class primarily fostering Christian fellowship
to the breaking of bread...	Lunches together Dinners together Any gathering promoting Christian community with a meal
and to prayer."	Prayer meetings Participation in prayer programs (prayer triplets, prayer covenants, etc.)[16] Participation at prayer times (at the altar, in the prayer room, etc.)

Still, measuring all groups in figure 8.2 could be cumbersome for many churches due to the large number of groups involved. One alternative is to limit the count to small groups that are easier to detect, that is, those oriented around biblical teaching or engaged in prayer.[17]

1.b. *Track your church's growth in maturity* (figure 8.3). A church's emerging

150

spiritual maturity could be estimated and changes tracked by counting the number of participants in groups that are focused on Bible study or prayer. Figure 8.3 shows how to tally the number of participants in these groups and track changes from year to year.

Figure 8.3. Tracking growth in maturity

	Number of People Involved				Composite Maturation Number	
	Bible study groups (adult) Sunday schools Any small group with a Bible focus	Prayer groups (adult) Prayer meetings and events Prayer programs			Total involvement *divided by* church attendance	
Years			Total involvement	Church attendance[18]		% of change
2008	34	16	50	200	25%	
2009	45	18	63	203	31%	+ 6%
2010	49	23	72	199	36%	+ 5%

The goal of figure 8.3 is to see movement toward a higher percentage of congregants involved in Bible study groups and prayer groups. In the example above, the church has been plateaued for three years. But by computing the composite maturation number, we find that involvement in prayer and Bible study groups has actually grown 6 percent and then 5 percent per year (for a total of 11 percent). This growth in maturity demonstrates that something good is happening, but unless the composite maturation number is tracked, a denomination will not usually notice this.

In addition, because each church is unique, a church should not try to compare its scores with any other church but itself. This score will show you only if you are changing in the number of people who are participating in groups that focus primarily on Bible study or prayer. Therefore, compare them only with yourself to gauge year-by-year changes in congregational commitment to Bible study and prayer.

NURTURING MILLENNIAL ATTITUDE 2: MEASURE A CHURCH'S GROWTH IN UNITY.

2.a. *Track a church's growth in unity* (figure 8.4). Congregants usually have a good sense of whether unity in the congregation is improving or waning. A simple Likert-type scale with two questions (figure 8.4) can be administered to congregants once a year, and improvement or deterioration in a church's perceptions of unity can be tracked.[19]

Figure 8.4. Tracking a church's perceptions of growth in unity

Growth in Unity		
Our church is more unified than last year.		
1. 2. 3. 4. 5.		
strongly disagree disagree neither agree nor disagree agree strongly agree		
I trust our church leadership more than last year.		
1. 2. 3. 4. 5.		
strongly disagree disagree neither agree nor disagree agree strongly agree		
Given:	*Given when:*	*Results:*
once per year	at each worship celebration	Movement toward higher numbers is preferred.

2.b. *Track unity of congregants with one another and with leadership.* The purpose of tracking growth in unity is not to score high, but to move higher. And each question above measures a different attribute of unity that should be increasing.

Question 1 assesses perceptions of unity among congregants.

Question 2 assesses perceptions of unity of the congregation with church leadership.

Again these numbers should not be bandied around between congregations.

These scales are not relevant to boasting or bravado. Rather these scales measure progress (or regress) in congregational unity. For example, a church that has a low self-esteem may initially score poorly on this scale. But in subsequent years if the numbers move upward, the congregation's perception of its unity is increasing. This does not mean unity has always increased, but it does indicate that something is going on that is increasing a congregational sense of unanimity.

NURTURING MILLENNIAL ATTITUDE 3: MEASURE A CHURCH'S GROWTH IN FAVOR AMONG NON-CHURCHGOERS.

3.a. *Measure opinion makers in the community who do not attend your church* (figure 8.5). A Likert-type questionnaire is helpful here, too, for it measures changes in attitudes. Here we will poll not the congregation, but the non-churchgoing community. I use the term *non-churchgoers* in an attempt to be sensitive to labels, for these are people who may go to another church, synagogue, temple, or mosque but who are not churchgoers at your place of worship. They include community leaders and opinion makers, such as community officials, school principals/superintendents, business people, community leaders, and so on.

3.b. *Poll the same people/positions each year for consistency.* When possible, attempt to poll the same people every year to ensure that you are tracking changes in perception among the same local opinion makers. Figure 8.5, when given to community leaders, can help track changing perceptions of favor toward a local church.

Figure 8.5. Tracking the perception of growth in church favor among non-churchgoers

Growth in Favor		
In your view (name of church) is more favorably regarded within this community than last year.		
1. strongly disagree 2. disagree 3. neither agree nor disagree 4. agree 5. strongly agree		
Given: once per year	*Given to:* community officials/leaders school and business leaders local opinion makers	*Results:* Movement toward higher numbers is preferred.

NURTURING MILLENNIAL ATTITUDE 4: MEASURE A CHURCH'S GROWTH IN CONVERSION.

Though we have seen that conversion is difficult to track, it can still be a help-ful measurement and less likely to be faked or fleeting when evaluated in light of the above metrics: growth in maturity, growth in unity, and growth in favor among the community. In addition, Luke tracked conversion, as we see from an abbreviated record from the book of Acts:[20]

- "Those who accepted his message were baptized, and about three thou-sand were added to their number that day" (Acts 2:41 NIV).
- "The Lord added to their number daily those who were being saved" (Acts 2:47b NIV).
- "Many who heard the message believed; so the number of men who believed grew to about five thousand" (Acts 4:4 NIV).
- "More and more men and women believed in the Lord and were added to their number" (Acts 5:14 NIV).
- "So the word of God spread. The number of disciples in Jerusalem increased rapidly, and a large number of priests became obedient to the faith" (Acts 6:7 NIV).

Thom Rainer summarizes, "Luke writes Acts in rapid-fire sequences, demon-strating that believers were persistently active in prayer, evangelism, and service."[21] Punctuating this rapid-fire account is Luke's repeated emphasis on conversions taking place at the mystical intersection of God's will and human choice. As we noted earlier, because of God's involvement, counting conversion is like counting the wind (John 3:8). But Luke still tracks it, even though out-comes of conversion may be less tied to the leader's skill. So, we should count growth in conversion, for it is a valid metric to signify God's movement. And though conversion is the apex of one's spiritual journey before eternity, we must always remind ourselves that this number is less indicative of effective leadership and more indicative of God's sovereign workings in the *missio Dei*. The cross in organix reminds us that conversion is the heart of God's *missio Dei*.

Though evaluating leadership by counting conversion is difficult because of the supernatural nature of conversion, it is also problematic to underemphasize conversion. Conversion is the penultimate experience that God wants all his off-spring to experience:

- "He [Jesus] said: "Truly I tell you, unless you change and become like little children, you will never enter the kingdom of heaven" (Matt. 18:3 NIV).
- "Very truly I tell you, no one can see the kingdom of God unless they are born again. . . . You must be born again" (John 3:3, 7 NIV).
- "Repent, then, and turn to God, so that your sins may be wiped out, that times of refreshing may come from the Lord" (Acts 3:19 NIV).
- "What we see is that anyone united with the Messiah gets a fresh start,

is created new. The old life is gone; a new life burgeons! Look at it!" (2 Cor. 5:17 THE MESSAGE).

Thus the X in organix has at its heart the icon of a cross. The small crosses in each quadrant stand for four valid types of measurement derived from Acts 2:42-47. Yet the X in the center[22] reminds us that Christ's death and resurrection have offered humanity the prospect of conversion. This conversion, as a turning from trust in self to trust in God,[23] is central to God's mission, the *missio Dei*. God wants his offspring to go in the opposite direction, reunite with him in his mission, and lovingly join others on the way back to a relationship with him.

MOVING TOWARD MILLENNIAL LEADERSHIP: QUESTIONS FOR PERSONAL REFLECTION AND/OR GROUP DISCUSSION

The following questions are for personal reflection but can also be used in a group setting.

1. *For personal and group reflection*: create an organix leadership journal by

- selecting two items from each box, and
- writing in it what you will begin to do over the next thirty days to move toward millennial leadership in these two areas.

	Nurturing Millennial Leadership
Measurement	1. Measure a church's growth in maturity.
	1.a. *Count all of your small groups.*
	1.b. *Track your church's growth in maturity* (figure 8.3).
	2. Measure a church's growth in unity.
	2.a. *Track a church's growth in unity* (figure 8.4).
	2.b. *Track unity of congregants with one another and with leadership.*

	3. Measure a church's growth in favor among non-churchgoers. 3.a. *Measure opinion makers in the community who do not attend your church* (figure 8.5). 3.b. *Poll the same people/positions each year for consistency.*
	4. Measure a church's growth in conversion.

2. *For group reflection:*

- Share your responses to the chart above with your group (omitting answers/plans that are overly personal).
- Take notes in your journal on the following:
  a. Does your group agree or disagree with your assessments and plans?
  b. What input did they give you regarding moving toward millennial leadership?
- Then rewrite your plans in your journal using their input.

3. *For personal and group reflection:*

- Revisit your notes in your journal every month for six months. Ask yourself:
  a. Are there areas where I am making progress? If so, describe them.
  b. Are there areas where I am still weak? What will I do to address this?
- At the end of six months reread the chapter and update your plans.

THE MISSIO MESH

MESHING

Today's electronic world is making it increasingly easy to link together different people, tactics, principles, and products to create new associations never thought of before. A church can link in real time with a sister congregation halfway around the world. Church leaders can video-conference with colleagues to gain immediate input. Churches can culti-vate online communities with very lit-tle financial expenditure. And congre-gations can instantaneously help needy people in more places more efficiently and successfully. The speed and cost-effectiveness of participating in the *missio Dei* have never been greater.

> **The speed and cost-effectiveness of participating in the *missio Dei* have never been greater.**

Two new metaphors have emerged to describe such organic fusions in this new networked world: *the mesh* and *meshing*. A *mesh* can be thought of as a con-stantly evolving but effective lattice of leadership tactics. And *meshing* is the art of creating this net of leadership practices. Lisa Gansky defines a mesh this way:

> [In a mesh] the core offering is something that can be shared.... Every part is connected to every other part, and they move in tandem.... [Mesh organiza-tions] are knotted to each other and to the world, in myriad ways.... This is the first time in human history when this kind of far-reaching, always-on, and rela-tively inexpensive connectivity has existed.[1]

Gansky's description of a mesh mirrors Mary Jo Hatch's conditions of an organism: organic dependency on its environment, organic harmony among the parts, organic adaption to the surroundings, and organic uniqueness from other organisms.[2] Yet Hatch prefers to describe such organic leadership as a leadership *collage*, that is, an artistic compilation of different tactics.[3] Hatch's terminology, while attractive, is influenced by artistic expressions, but Gansky's term is influ-enced by electronic modes of communication. Therefore, in today's environment Lisa Gansky's image of a *mesh* is more relevant and appealing.

CREATING YOUR MINISTRY MESH

Picture your *mesh* as a fishing net that adapts and stretches to ensure nothing falls through. You create your *ministry mesh* by picking the best and most relevant ideas from each chapter of this book. And you must also be careful not to over-look any chapter's organic theme. The following three elements will help ensure your *ministry mesh* is holistic and appropriate:

1. *Meshing starts by incorporating each and every one of the chapter topics in this book.* It is important that your ministry mesh does not leave out any chapter's organic focus. To do so would be to create holes in your mesh. For instance, if a church embraced all the topics in this book except the multicultural sensitivities of the graffiti chapter, that church might be doing good work but still be hindered by a cultural bias. *Meshing means weaving a net without gaps.*

> It is important that your ministry mesh does not leave out any chapter's organic focus. To do so would be to create holes in your mesh.

2. *Meshing means choosing specific tactics within each chapter that are best for you and your ministry environment.* This requires investigation, dis-section, and experimentation to ensure the tactics you are selecting are right for your organizational context. Remember, those whom you serve will be the best sounding board for tactical effectiveness.

3. *Meshing means being flexible, willing to change, and doing so with an appropriate promptness.* I describe this as an "appropriate" promptness because research shows that if you change things too quickly, you will often doom the adoption of new ideas.[4] For new ideas to be success-fully adopted, you must go slow and build consensus, and then you will succeed.[5] Still, it is important to accomplish progress. Therefore, maintain a moderate pace, but ensure that you are still moving forward.

Such actions create a ministry mesh that is comprehensive, evolving, and flexible but also messy. Some churches will chafe at such integration and elas-ticity. But churches that will launch new tactics or nurture new congrega-tions will find that participating in the *missio Dei* requires such suppleness. The result is messy, but also an increas-ingly effective and elastic set of princi-ples and strategies.

> Some churches will chafe at such integration and elasticity. But churches that will launch new tactics or nurture new congregations will find that participating in the *missio Dei* requires such suppleness.

This book's purpose has been to focus in each chapter on one key organic component on which churches can cre-ate their own unique ministry mesh. An effective ministry mesh means a church is providing a safety net for the needy in the name of the *missio Dei* through lead-ership strategies that evolve and adapt.

HOW TO USE ORGANIC WORD CLOUDS

To help the reader weave one's own organic ministry mesh, the following pages include clouds of words drawn from each chapter, accompanied by a short summation of that chapter. These word clouds are helpful in three ways:

1. Ask yourself, Which concepts in the word cloud are we accomplishing? Use the visual word cloud from each chapter as a discussion starter to ask, "How many concepts are we effectively addressing in each cloud?"

2. Ask yourself, Which concepts in the word cloud are we failing to accomplish? Use the visual word cloud from each chapter as a discussion starter to ask, "How many concepts are we not addressing in each cloud?"

3. Word clouds can serve as "content pages" to help you return to the appropriate chapter more quickly. Word clouds can help visual learners quickly see which chapter addresses which topics.

Let's now look at each chapter's word cloud. Each word cloud is an arrangement of randomly positioned words with larger fonts indicating the most important organic concepts from each chapter.

CHAPTER 1: O

Integrity **Needs** Community Culture
Others Social justice Disenfranchised poor
Live among them. **Sift a culture.** Live a simple life.
Nurture Solicit input. **Humility**
Social action **Live a life that models the *missio Dei*.**
Learning is as important as performance. See the potential in others.
Learn from them. Others should complement your weaknesses.
Live a well-thought-out life. **Live a natural life.**
Live a life of honesty about faults.

In chapter 1 we saw that a new and organic leadership paradigm is founded on meeting the needs of others and not necessarily the needs of the leader. Here are suggestions to nurture these attitudes:

1. Others and their needs drive the leader:
   a. Live among them.
   b. Learn from and with them.
   c. Because good and bad are in each culture, "sift" out the bad.

2. Others are souls to be nurtured:
   a. Look for and nurture the potential in others.
   b. See learning in others as important as their performance.
   c. Others should have input, so solicit it.
   d. Others should complement your weaknesses.

3. Others are led by integrity:
   a. Live a simple life.
   b. Live a natural life.
   c. Live a well-thought-out life.
   d. Live a life of honesty and openness about faults.
   e. Live a life that models the *missio Dei*.

CHAPTER 2: Θ

God strengthens the leader for the work.   Journaling
God's will is your food.   **Spiritual filling**   Meditation
God examines the leader's participation in the *missio Dei*.
God   Strengthened through others   **Fasting**
Theos   **Strengthened through worship**
Expect the scrutiny of God.
Strengthened through God's word   **Prayer**
Expect the scrutiny of others.   God's presence is a sign of the leader's need.
Submit to open and honest accountability.

In chapter 2 we discovered that God is the source behind our compassion for others and the one who gives us the strength to meet their needs. And we learned that to muster the strength to meet others' needs, we must maintain a close and nurturing relationship with God through prayer, worship, learning, others, and refilling. The following are suggestions to nurture these attitudes:

1. God strengthens the leader for the work
   a. through God's word.
   b. through worship.
   c. through others.

2. God's presence is a sign of the leader's need:
   a. Regular times of fasting, journaling, and silence connect us with God.
   b. Spiritual filling is an ongoing process; seek refilling.

3. God examines the leader's participation in the *missio Dei*:
   a. Embrace prayer as a time of humility and openness before God.
   b. Expect the scrutiny of God, his church, and his creation.
   c. Make knowing God's will your food.
   d. Submit to honest and authentic accountability.

CHAPTER 3: ℞

Community   **Healthy people**
Accountability   **Small groups** Honest evaluation
Mentoring leaders   UP-IN-OUT discipleship
     Missional-ize small groups
Healthy churches   **Small-group leaders**
   UP   **Fitting goals**
     Leaders assess needs of emerging leaders.
IN ⟍⟋ **OUT**   Spiritual direction via small groups

In chapter 3 we discovered that healthy people lead to healthy churches (and not the other way around). And we saw that most people gain spiritual health through the accountability and community of personal discipleship *and* small groups. We also learned that when small groups join together into Missional-Nets, they can better meet the needs of others outside the organization. Attitudes include these:

1. The prescription for a healthy church is healthy people:

   a. Small-group leaders assess the needs and health of emerging leaders.
   b. Small-group leaders foster spiritual direction and service via the small group.
   c. Small-group leaders help emerging leaders establish fitting goals.
   d. Small-group leaders offer emerging leaders honest evaluation.

2. The prescription for spiritual health results from a personal and communal effort:
   a. Locate all of your small groups.
   b. Create healthy people by practicing UP-IN-(OUT) discipleship in small groups.
   c. Missionalize your small groups by practicing (UP-IN)-OUT discipleship.

3. The prescription for volunteer health is a network of small groups:

a. The Groups-MissionalNets-Cultures approach creates healthy people by clearly defining routes into accountability and leadership.
b. The Groups-MissionalNets-Cultures approach shares the good news with those outside a church via MissionalNets.

CHAPTER 4: G

Practice reconciliation. Liturgical acts of reconciliation
Graffiti–colorful, risky, improvisational and led by passion
Public acts of reconciliation
White male privilege **Mosaic churches**
Risk taking   Listen to voices that challenge you.
Embracing risk as a contrast community **Relocation**
Grow cultural subcongregations
Redistribution   Internal church planting
Anger by the non-privileged is understandable.
"The end is...reconciliation." –MLK Jr.

Chapter 4 was a very important chapter, for we saw that people blindness and unearned privilege can create walls between people even in the body of Christ. We learned that churches must take risks, practice reconciliation, and create colorful mosaic networks and churches. The following are suggestions to nurture such attitudes:

1. Graffiti leadership embraces risk:
   a. Take risks for the sake of the good news.
   b. Contrast with the usual way of doing things.
   c. Undertake such actions publicly.

2. Graffiti leadership practices and repeats reconciliation:
   a. Liturgical acts of reconciliation.
   b. Public acts of reconciliation.
   c. Personal acts of reconciliation.
   d. Listen regularly to voices that challenge you.

3. Graffiti leadership grows mosaic churches:
   a. Balance autonomy and partnership to grow a mosaic church.
   b. Unify different cultures within a mosaic church.

CHAPTER 5: ⚠

Acknowledge and address sin.
Preserve traditional worship.
Worship–a culturally relevant encounter **Recycle**
Recycle people.　　Watch your temptations.
Recycle defective people. **Recycle finances.**
　　　　　　　Chart a course for return
Glocal　　**Recycle worship.**
Honor tradition with ancient-future.　Recycle facilities.

In chapter 5 we observed that a modern tactic was to discard damaged people and assets, but the millennial reaction is to recycle them to their original purpose when possible. We discovered steps to recycling people, assets, and even worship. Here are suggestions to nurture recycling attitudes:

1. Recycle defective people to honor their creation in the image of God:
   a. Emphasize the good before contrasting it with the bad.
   b. Acknowledge and address the sin.
   c. Chart a route for return.
   d. Those who help must watch over their own inclinations.

2. Recycle resources glocally.
   a. Recycle facilities.
   b. Recycle finances.

3. Recycle worship.
   a. Preserve traditional worship celebrations to create stability for older congregants.
   b. Embrace ancient-future elements to honor traditional worship and build unity.
   c. Recapture the original purpose of worship: a culturally relevant encounter.

CHAPTER 6:ℵ

Social networks & the *missio Dei*   eWorld
Restrictions   Relational networks
Networks   Democratization of evangelism
Network sabbaticals   Accessible networks
Online communities should supplement face-to-face communities.
Instantaneous feedback   The accessible church
Historical networks   Online communities
Free-based access

Chapter 6 discusses how leaders can respond to the growing electronic and social networks that connect people more quickly, more efficiently, and more globally than ever before. We learned that churches must be more accommodating of technology and that churches can foster robust and spiritual online communities. Yet with more networking comes more exposure to good and bad, and thus spiritual discernment and network sabbaticals are needed. The following are suggestions to nurture these attitudes regarding networks:

1. Networks of relationships are just as important as organizational networks:
   a. Online networks supplement but do not replace traditional face-to-face networks.
   b. Use social networks as bridges of God to discuss faith.
   c. Every church should use new networks because communication is cheaper and easier.

2. Networks should be accessible:
   a. The accessible church creates networks that reach out to people in need.
   b. The accessible church offers free-based access to knowledge.
   c. The accessible church fosters instantaneous feedback and research at teaching venues, including during the sermon.
   d. The accessible church provides online communities to augment its offline fellowship.

3. Network restrictions may be personal, but are necessary:
   a. Restrict yourself to those networks for which you are gifted and called.
   b. Avoid perverse elements of networks.
   c. Take network sabbaticals.

CHAPTER 7: ¡

Individuals teach, but also are taught.
"in the flesh"
Gatherings as supernatural encounters
Go personally   Incarnation
Local but dissimilar cultures   Long-term relationships
Adopt people, not programs.
Distant cultures
Jesus' personal coming
Dialogue, disagreement, and questions lead to learning.
Do not force a conclusion.   **Go where they are comfortable.**

The *i* icon of chapter 7 stands for *incarnation*, which is derived from the Greek word meaning "in the flesh." This describes what Jesus accomplished by taking on the flesh of a human to better communicate with us. It reminds us that the church must personally go to serve and help others. And by going personally to those in need, we develop long-term relationships through which we can tell others about the *missio Dei*, God's desire to reconnect with his offspring. Jesus' personal coming likewise reminds us that gathering in his name should result in supernatural and personal encounters with him. The following are suggestions to nurture incarnational experiences:

1. Go in person:
    a. Provide opportunities for congregants to go to distant cultures.
    b. Provide opportunities for congregants to go into local but dissimilar cultures.
    c. Adopt people, not programs.

2. Teach and be taught:
    a. Encourage dialogue, questions, and disagreement when discussing spiritual topics.
    b. Go out to places where non-churchgoers are comfortable, and dialogue with them there.
    c. Allow God to do the work of the *missio Dei*, and do not try to force a conclusion.

3. Gathering is a supernatural encounter:
    a. Spend more time in spiritual preparation for worship than in physical planning.
    b. Evaluate worship gatherings in light of how well people connected with God.

CHAPTER 8: ✖

The Jerusalem Cross
                    Growth in favor among non-churchgoers
  Poll community opinion makers.
        Growth in maturity   Service to the community
  Measurement   Spiritual maturity   **Sacrifice**
                    Growth in unity
              Increasing involvement in prayer opportunities.
  Growth in conversions   **Acts 2:42-47**
  Devoted to fellowship and meals together

In this final chapter, we learned that progress must be measured if we are to ensure that movement forward is taking place. But we also saw that measuring church attendance can be flawed because attendance is influenced by many factors other than leadership. Therefore, we turned to Acts 2:42-47 and found four growth measurements that are still relevant today. We discussed a formula to measure a church's changes in spiritual maturity and looked at congregational questionnaires that can track improvement in church unity and service to the community. Yet our metrics have at their center a cross, reminding us that dying to the old self and rising into a new life are the ultimate indication of God's work. The following are suggestions for gauging changes in leadership effectiveness and ensuring our increasing partnership with the *missio Dei*:

1. Measure a church's growth in maturity:
   a. Count all of your small groups.
   b. Track your church's growth in maturity (figure 8.3).

2. Measure a church's growth in unity:
   a. Track a church's growth in unity (figure 8.4).
   b. Track unity of congregants with one another and with leadership.

3. Measure a church's growth in favor among non-churchgoers:
   a. Measure opinion makers in the community who do not attend your church (figure 8.5).
   b. Poll the same people and/or positions each year for consistency.

4. Measure a church's growth in conversion.

NOTES

INTRODUCTION

1. Quoted anonymously by James P. Wind, "Building Congregations in an Anti-Institutional Age," *Congregations* (Summer 2009): 5.

2. Though there are seven icons, the first icon comprises of two symbols: an ◯ for others and a ⊖ for God.

3. The term *emerging leadership* has been more popular in the church than it has been in the field of organizational leadership. However, some organizational change experts have implied the term indirectly; see Edwin E. Olson and Glenda H. Eoyang, *Facilitating Organization Change: Lessons from Complexity Science* (Hoboken, N.J.: Wiley & Sons, Pfeiffer, 2001). More recently management researchers Sherry Penney and Patricia Neilson have used the term in the same way as I have in *Next Generation Leadership: Insights from Emerging Leaders* (New York: Palgrave Macmillan, 2010). Of all the books in the church realm, especially insightful is the research into emerging leadership by prominent sociologist Dean R. Hoge with Marti R. Jewell in *The Next Generation of Pastoral Leaders: What the Church Needs to Know, Emerging Models of Pastoral Leadership* (Chicago: Loyola, 2010).

4. Here again, the church has embraced this term more readily than the organizational leadership field. Still, the definitive work on emerging leadership by a management researcher is Mary Jo Hatch's *Organization Theory: Modern, Symbolic, and Postmodern Perspectives* (Oxford: Oxford University Press, 1997).

5. For more of the positives and negatives of postmodern viewpoints, see Bob Whitesel, *Inside the Organic Church: Learning from 12 Emerging Congregations* (Nashville: Abingdon Press, 2006), xxiii–xxiv; David S. Dockery, ed., *The Challenge of Postmodernism: An Evangelical Engagement* (Wheaton, Ill.: Bridgepoint Books, 1995); and Chuck Smith Jr., *The End of the World . . . as We Know It* (Colorado Springs: WaterBrook, 2001).

6. For examples of the rising importance of millennial leadership in the field of business management, see Jeanne C. Meister and Karie Willyerd, *The 2020 Workplace: How Innovative Companies Attract, Develop, and Keep Tomorrow's Employees Today* (New York: Harper Business, 2010); and Ron Alsop, *The Trophy Kids Grow Up: How the Millennial Generation Is Shaking Up the Workplace* (Hoboken, N.J.: Jossey-Bass, 2008). For examples in the church leadership field, see Thom S. Rainer and Jess Rainer, *The Millennials: Connecting to America's Largest Generation* (Escondido, Calif.: Hovel, 2010); and M. Rex Miller, *The Millennium Matrix: Reclaiming the Past, Reframing the Future of the Church* (Hoboken, N.J.: Jossey-Bass, 2004).

7. *Command and control* is a general way to describe a modern leadership approach that relies heavily on authority and manipulation to control subordinates. See Adam Smith, *The Wealth of Nations* (1776; reprint, Chicago: University of Chicago Press, 1976), books

1 and 4. The foundational modern element in this approach is that the task, objective, and/or organization come first and not the person. The fallacy of this approach will be explored in chapter 3, ℞.

8. Harrison Monarth, *Executive Presence: The Art of Commanding Respect Like a CEO* (New York: McGraw-Hill, 2009), 55. In his best seller, Monarth recognizes the deficiencies of command and control leadership but attempts to replace it with a modern strategy of fostering control through esteem and reverence rather than through position. Perhaps a small step toward millennial leadership, Monarth's approach is heavily leadercentric.

9. For the sake of brevity this overview of modernism is very short. However, the reader wishing more information on the rise of modernism and its leadership principles should consult Lawrence E. Cahoone, *From Modernism to Postmodernism: An Anthology* (Hoboken, N.J.: Wiley-Blackwell, 2003); and James K. A. Smith, *Who's Afraid of Postmodernism? Taking Derrida, Lyotard, and Foucault to Church*, The Church and Postmodern Culture (Grand Rapids: Baker Academic, 2006).

10. For an overview and rationale for the rise of postmodernism, see Whitesel, *Inside the Organic Church*, xxiii–xxiv; and Thomas C. Oden, "The Death of Modernity and Postmodern Evangelical Spirituality," in *The Challenge of Postmodernism: An Evangelical Engagement*, ed. David S. Dockery (Wheaton, Ill.: Bridgepoint Books, 1995).

11. In times of crisis, command and control leadership has been shown to be effective and therefore warranted. For warfare examples, see Neville A. Stanton, Chris Baber, and Don Harris, *Modelling Command and Control*, Human Factors in Defence (Farnham, UK: Ashgate, 2008), and for illustrations from firefighters, see Vincent Dunn, *Safety and Survival on the Fireground* (Tulsa, Okla.: Pennwell Books, 2002).

12. For a summary see Richard W. Hallstein, *Memoirs of a Recovering Autocrat: Revealing Insights for Managing the Autocrat in All of Us* (San Francisco: Berrett-Koehler, 1993).

13. Command and control grew out of Frederick Taylor's "scientific management" approach to leadership, where the worker was to be manipulated in order to produce the desired outcome, or in Taylor's words, "the worker must be trimmed to fit the job." Quoted by Daniel Boorstin, *The Americans: The Democratic Experience* (New York: Vintage, 1974), 369.

14. Hallstein, *Memoirs of a Recovering Autocrat*.

15. Though younger segments of Gen X embrace millennial leadership, we will describe this rising phenomenon as *millennial leadership* because the millennial generation best represents emerging leadership attitudes.

16. Figure A.2 uses accepted generational segments (the nineteen-year periods preferred by demographers). For more on generational differences and the labels associated with each, see Bob Whitesel and Kent R. Hunter, *A House Divided: Bridging the Generation Gaps in Your Church* (Nashville: Abingdon Press, 2000), 13–25. For an exhaustive survey of these generations in American history and life, see William Strauss and Neil Howe, *Generations: The History of America's Future, 1584 to 2069* (New York: Quill, 1991).

17. Strauss and Howe, regarded as the landmark writers on generational differences, follow the growing custom of using the millennial designation over the Generation Y label. *Generations*, 335–43.

18. Alastair Davidson, *Antonio Gramsci: Towards an Intellectual Biography* (London: Merlin Press, 1987).

19. James Engel, *Contemporary Christian Communication: Its Theory and Practice* (New York: Thomas Nelson, 1979), 93–95.

20. See, for example, Neil Cole, *Organic Church: Growing Faith Where Life Happens* (Hoboken, N.J.: Jossey-Bass, 2005); and Whitesel, *Inside the Organic Church.*

21. Howard Snyder, *The Problem of Wineskins* (Downers Grove, Ill.: InterVarsity Press, 1975), 73–75.

22. Charles B. Singletary, "Organic Growth: A Critical Dimension for the Church," in *Church Growth: State of the Art*, ed. C. Peter Wagner, with Win Arn and Elmer Towns (Wheaton, Ill.: Tyndale, 1988), 114.

23. Alan Roxburgh, "Missional Leadership: Equipping God's People for Mission," in *Missional Church: A Vision for the Sending of the Church in North America*, ed. Darrell L. Guder (Grand Rapids: Eerdmans, 1998), 193.

24. Neil Cole, response to the question by Keith Giles, "What is your definition of organic church?" "What Is Organic Church? An Interview with Neil Cole and Frank Viola," Church Multiplication Associates Resources, September 20, 2010, www .cmaresources.org/article/organic-church_n-cole_f-viola.

25. Frank Viola, response to the question by Keith Giles, "What is your definition of organic church?" Ibid. Cole's and Viola's perspectives, while laudable for their emphasis on community, tend to emphasize kinship at the expense of the *missio Dei*. We shall see that a more holistic definition by Mary Jo Hatch stresses the missional aspect of organic dependency on its environment. Hatch, *Organization Theory*, 53–54.

26. Frank Viola, "Why Organic Church Is Not Exactly a Movement," *Christianity Today* (January 13, 2010).

27. Hatch, *Organization Theory*, 53–54.

28. And thus the organization must do so or die.

29. Hatch, *Organization Theory*, 54.

30. For an interesting comparison of modern leaders who have a penchant for unwavering rules (whom he calls "hedgehogs") and millennial leaders who favor elastic leadership styles (whom he calls "foxes"), see Abraham Zaleznik, *Hedgehogs and Foxes: Character, Leadership, and Command in Organizations* (New York: Palgrave Macmillan, 2008).

31. The following chapters correspond to the four conditions: chapters 1 and 8—organic dependency on its environment; chapters 2 and 5—organic harmony among the parts; chapters 3 and 6—organic adaption to the surroundings; and chapters 4 and 7—organic uniqueness from other organisms.

32. *Missio Dei* was first used in this sense by missiologist Karl Hartenstein to describe God's mission in contrast to Karl Barth's emphasis on God's action (the *actio Dei*). For an overview of these terms, their history, and their implication for the millennial leader, see John Flett's *The Witness of God: The Trinity, Missio Dei, Karl Barth, and the Nature of Christian Community* (Grand Rapids: Eerdmans, 2010).

33. David J. Bosch, *Transforming Mission: Paradigm Shifts in the Theology of Mission* (Maryknoll, N.Y.: Orbis, 1991), 390.

34. Flett, *Witness of God*, 5.

35. William H. Willimon, *Pastor: The Theology and Practice of Ordained Ministry* (Nashville: Abingdon Press, 2002), 239–40.

36. The active verb, and hence the purpose of Jesus' Great Commission in Matthew 28:19, is "to make disciples." For the etymology of this phrase, see Bob Whitesel, "Organizational Behavior: Grasping the Behavior and Personality of a Church," in Bruce L. Petersen, Edward A. Thomas, and Bob Whitesel, *Foundations of Church Administration:*

Professional Tools for Church Leadership (Kansas City, Kans.: Beacon Hill, 2010), 83–84.

37. For a synopsis of the *imago Dei*, see Millard J. Erickson, *Christian Theology*, 2nd ed. (Grand Rapids: Baker, 1998), 517–36.

38. Note that chapter 8 will present only one modern leadership attribute for comparison. However, three millennial reactions will be discussed, each of which contrasts with the modern leadership attribute.

39. Wind, "Building Congregations in an Anti-Institutional Age," 5.

1.O

1. Shane Claiborne and John Perkins, *Follow Me to Freedom: Leading as an Ordinary Radical* (Ventura, Calif.: Regal, 2009), 97.

2. Though chapters 2 through 7 will deal with only one symbol each, this first icon will be given two chapters because the O symbol requires a ⊖ symbol in response.

3. Here as elsewhere in these illustrations, a pseudonym has been used.

4. The stories that begin each chapter are based on actual client stories and conversations. However, to maintain a degree of anonymity for my clients, the names have been changed, and various stories have been combined and edited to demonstrate a range of problems. However, this quotation is an actual quotation from a client pastor.

5. See Ken Blanchard, *Leading at a Higher Level: Blanchard on Leadership and Creating High Performing Organizations* (Upper Saddle River, N.J.: Financial Times Press, 2009); Malcolm Gladwell, *Outliers: The Story of Success* (New York: Little, Brown, 2008); Marshall Goldsmith and Mark Reiter, *What Got You Here Won't Get You There: How Successful People Become Even More Successful* (New York: Hyperion, 2007). Though these books address the necessity of motivating followers, the basic thrust of each book is to view followership as that which defines the leader's success. I will argue shortly that such goals are a trait of modern leadership.

6. See W. G. Rowe, *Cases in Leadership* (Thousand Oaks, Calif.: Sage Publications, 2007); and John Maxwell's discussion of the pioneer myth in *The 21 Irrefutable Laws of Leadership* (Nashville: Thomas Nelson, 2007). The inference here and in chapter 5 in Maxwell's book is that the numerical size of the leader's followers attests to leadership. Such suppositions are historically refutable (see Riccardo Orizio's *Talk of the Devil: Encounters with Seven Dictators* [New York: Walker & Company, 2004] for a discussion of how the magnitude of followers does not necessarily signify leadership, but can signify control).

7. Barbara Kellerman, "What Every Leader Needs to Know About Followers," *Harvard Business Review*, December 2007.

8. Maxwell, *21 Irrefutable Laws of Leadership*, 49.

9. Frederick Taylor, *The Principles of Scientific Management* (New York: Harper & Row, 1913).

10. Quoted by Daniel Boorstin in *The Americans: The Democratic Experience* (New York: Vintage, 1974), 363.

11. Elton Mayo first described the negative effects of scientific management in *The Social Problems of an Industrial Civilization* (Abingdon, UK: Routledge, 1949). Building on this, psychologist Frederick Herzberg laid the foundation for human resource management with Bernard Mausner and Barbara Bloch Snyderman in *The Motivation to Work* (New York: John Wiley & Sons, 1959).

12. Alexander Hill, *Just Business: Christian Ethics for the Marketplace* (Downers Grove, Ill.: InterVarsity Press, 1997), 155–56.

13. In 1939 this style of leadership was labeled "autocratic leadership" by Kurt Lewin and his coauthors Ronald Lippitt and Ralph K. White in "Patterns of Aggressive Behavior in Experimentally Created Social Climates," *Journal of Social Psychology* 10 (1939): 271–330. Lewin and his colleagues compared this style to the "democratic" and the "laissez-faire" (or "hands-off") styles. Lewin and his colleagues found that the democratic style was the most productive.

14. See "The Circuit Riders Dismount and Democracy Wanes" and "Affluent Methodists," in Roger Finke and Rodney Stark, *The Churching of America 1776–1990: Winners and Losers in Our Religious Economy* (New Brunswick, N.J.: Rutgers University Press, 2000), 153–54, 159–63.

15. For more on the "experience trap," see David L. Dotlich and Peter C. Cairo, *Unnatural Leadership: Going Against Intuition and Experience to Develop Ten New Leadership Instincts* (San Francisco: Jossey-Bass, 2002), 75–78.

16. Leonard Sweet, speech to the Academy for Evangelism in Theological Education (Ashland Theological Seminary, Ashland, Ohio, October 6, 2007).

17. This is not to say these books are not helpful in the right circumstances. However, some of these books imply that fine-tuning a mission or vision statement will directly lead to church growth, a connection I have not witnessed in my research.

18. This passage emphasizes that pruning is necessary in an individual's life, not necessarily in the corporate church life. In other words, God prunes the leader of sin to make the leader more fruitful. The interpretation that God is cutting away people from a church to make the church more productive is forcing the text. See Leon Morris, *The Gospel According to John* (Grand Rapids: Eerdmans, 1995), 668–70.

19. A modern leader may also cite Old Testament passages about the commanding vision of Abraham, Moses, and a host of other Old Testament heroes to bolster one's interpretation of John 15:1. But what is often downplayed is that Old Testament leaders led in a time before the guidance of the Holy Spirit was available to all Christians who ask for it. The Old Testament prophet Joel forecast that one day the Holy Spirit would be made available to all believers (Joel 2:28-29). Peter interpreted the day of Pentecost as this fulfillment, saying, "This is what was spoken by the prophet Joel" (Acts 2:16 NIV). Subsequently, from then until today the Holy Spirit's guidance is given not just to a mega-leader, but to a degree is bestowed on many in the congregation too. This is not to imply that a congregation should be tyrannical. But neither should be the leader; since the day of Pentecost, leadership is a delicate synthesis between a leader's vision and the vision of other godly leaders, both paid and volunteer.

20. *People blindness* has been defined as a church illness that prevents a congregation from seeing important cultural differences between groups of people who live in close geographical proximity to the church. C. Peter Wagner, "Principles and Procedures of Church Growth: American Church Growth" (lecture, Fuller Theological Seminary, Pasadena, California, January 31–February 11, 1983). However, an inability to see the cultural differences between leadership and followership is another important cultural chasm that affects many of today's leaders. It could thus be described as a type of people blindness within the church.

21. For more on generational ideas and behaviors, see William Strauss and Neil Howe's landmark research in *Generations: The History of America's Future, 1584 to 2069* (New York: Quill, 1991).

22. That a minister might cling to a ministry one no longer suitably serves might seem far-fetched. However, in my consulting practice I have seen a number of experienced leaders who hang on to their positions long after they know they are unsuitable because of concerns about pensions, promised compensation, and so on. Since traveling with Christ is a journey of faith (Phil. 1:6), it should not be surprising that the journey requires this reliance from start to finish.

23. In *Church Quake!: The Explosive Power of the New Apostolic Reformation* (Ventura, Calif.: Regal Books, 1999), chap. 4, C. Peter Wagner argues that effective leaders should emulate his pastor, who controls 65 percent of a $5 million church budget. I have known Dr. Wagner for years and consider him a mentor. However, I have also observed that rapid church growth associated with autocratic leadership works best during times of crisis (e.g., start-up processes such as church planting, unexpected catastrophes, and so on).

24. This initial growth that an autocratic leader can bring to a church in crisis, in my opinion, misleadingly led Pete Wagner to conclude that such autocratic style is usually preferred for church growth to occur.

25. For more on how conflict often leads to group exits in autocratically led churches, see Bob Whitesel, *Staying Power: Why People Leave the Church over Change and What You Can Do About It* (Nashville: Abingdon Press, 2002).

26. This can be a hands-off approach (i.e., laissez-faire) or an autocratic style of leadership. See Lewin, Lippitt, and White, "Patterns of Aggressive Behavior in Experimentally Created Social Climates," 271–330.

27. Under the *G* in organix, we shall see that blending together a collage of different backgrounds, ideas, and interests is the way the millennial leader creates consensus and innovative routes forward.

28. See Bill George, David Gergen, and Peter Sims, *True North: Discover Your Authentic Leadership* (Hoboken, N.J.: Jossey-Bass, 2007); Kevin Cashman, *Leadership from the Inside Out: Becoming a Leader for Life* (San Francisco: Berrett-Koehler, 2008); and Christopher Bones, *The Cult of the Leader: A Manifesto for More Authentic Business* (Hoboken, N.J.: John Wiley & Sons, 2011).

29. Bruce J. Avolio and William L. Gardner, "Authentic Leadership Development: Getting to the Root of Positive Forms of Leadership," *The Leadership Quarterly* 16, no. 3 (June 2005): 315–38.

30. David Apgar, *Relevance: Hitting Your Goals by Knowing What Matters* (New York: Jossey-Bass, 2008).

31. For more examples of authenticity sightings, see Larry Osborne's story and interview in Bob Whitesel's *Spiritual Waypoints: Helping Others Navigate the Journey* (Indianapolis: Wesleyan Publishing House, 2010), 201–11.

32. Dan Kimball, lecture in a course for Wesley Seminary at Indiana Wesleyan University, taught with Bob Whitesel (Santa Cruz, California, June 24, 2010).

33. See the chapter "Missteps with Staff Influence" in Bob Whitesel, *Growth by Accident, Death by Planning: How NOT to Kill a Growing Congregation* (Nashville: Abingdon Press, 2004).

34. David L. McKenna, ed., *The Urban Crisis* (Grand Rapids: Zondervan, 1969), 138.

35. John M. Perkins, *Radix* (March–April 1997): 7.

36. Roger Finke and Rodney Stark, *The Churching of America, 1776–1990: Winners and Losers in Our Religious Economy* (New Brunswick, N.J.: Rutgers University Press, 2000),

and Roger Finke and Kevin Dougherty, "The Effects of Professional Training: The Social and Religious Capital Acquired in Seminaries," *Journal for Scientific Study of Religion* 41 (2002): 103–20.

37. This often results because seminaries that require pastors to leave their local churches to attend three years of schooling so remove pastors from the people they serve that afterward seminary pastors will implement ideas that are out of touch with the people back home.

38. For more on this and an interview with Roger Finke, see Bob Whitesel, *Growth by Accident, Death by Planning.*

39. Aaron Norwood, pastor of the Bridge, e-mail message to author, November 30, 2010.

40. This requires seminarians to learn *from* congregants. Often called "action research," this is research that is co-generated by both the leader and the follower, for it involves the active participation of followers. See Davydd J. Greenwood and Morten Levin, *Introduction to Action Research: Social Research for Societal Change* (Thousand Oaks, Calif.: Sage, 1998). Two seminaries that practice this include Denver Seminary (see an analysis and interview in *Growth by Accident, Death by Planning,* 121–31) and Wesley Seminary at Indiana Wesleyan University, www.wesley.indwes.edu.

41. Michael Fullan, *Leading in a Culture of Change* (New York: Jossey-Bass, 2007), 1.

42. Eddie Gibbs, *I Believe in Church Growth* (Grand Rapids: Eerdmans, 1981), 92.

43. Sifting occurs because "conscientious Christians will have to 'sift' through the various *behaviors, ideas* and *products* of a culture. This means Christians who are missionaries to other cultures must ascertain what cultural elements are impure and reject them, while also retaining elements that agree with the teachings of Christ." Bob Whitesel, *Preparing for Change Reaction: How to Introduce Change in Your Church* (Indianapolis: Wesleyan Publishing House, 2008), 60–61.

44. Gibbs, *I Believe in Church Growth,* 120.

45. Joanne Martin, Martha S. Feldman, Mary Jo Hatch, and Sim B. Sitkin, "The Uniqueness Paradox in Organizational Stories," *Administrative Science Quarterly* (September 1983): 442–43.

46. Aaron Norwood, e-mail message to author, November 30, 2010.

47. Jonah Lehrer, "The Power Trip," *Wall Street Journal,* August 14, 2010.

48. Barbara Kellerman, *Followership: How Followers Are Creating Change and Changing Leaders* (Boston: Harvard Business School Press, 2008), 97–212. Especially helpful is Kellerman's identification of five types of followers based on their level of engagement (isolate, bystander, participant, activist, and diehard).

49. Warren Bennis, "Followership," *USC Business Magazine* (Summer 1994).

50. For examples, see Bob Whitesel, *Inside the Organic Church: Learning from 12 Emerging Congregations* (Nashville: Abingdon Press, 2006).

51. Strategic, tactical, and operational leadership is a meta-theory that explains leadership as a mixture of three traits. Used by the military for designating leadership traits (see Sun Tzu, *The Art of War,* trans. Samuel B. Griffith [Oxford: Oxford University Press, 1971]), it is one of the most helpful ways to efficiently categorize leaders. Though all leaders are a mixture of these three traits, some traits dominate each leader. Here is an overview:

Strategic leadership—leadership by vision
Tactical leadership—leadership by analysis
Operational leadership—leadership by relationships

For more on strategic, tactical, and operational leadership, see Bob Whitesel, *Preparing for Change Reaction*, 29–48.

52. See Adrian Gostick and Chester Elton, *The Orange Revolution: How One Great Team Can Transform an Entire Organization* (New York: Free Press, 2010); Dave Logan, John King, and Halee Fischer-Wright, *Tribal Leadership: Leveraging Natural Groups to Build a Thriving Organization* (New York: HarperBusiness, 2008); and Larry Osborne, *Sticky Teams: Keeping Your Leadership Team and Staff on the Same Page* (Grand Rapids: Zondervan, 2010).

53. Jimmy Long, *The Leadership Jump: Building Partnerships Between Existing and Emerging Christian Leaders* (Downers Grove, Ill.: InterVarsity Press, 2008), 52.

54. Dietrich Bonhoeffer, *The Cost of Discipleship* (New York: Touchstone, 1995), 89–90.

55. In a collage, "objects and pieces of objects are arranged together to form something new." Mary Jo Hatch, *Organization Theory: Modern, Symbolic, and Postmodern Perspectives* (Oxford: Oxford University Press, 1997), 53.

56. Aaron Norwood, e-mail message to author, November 30, 2010.

57. In a group setting, precautions should be taken to ensure sensitivities and/or vulnerabilities are handled appropriately. If such precautions are instituted, sharing your reflections with others can foster an intimate and helpful sounding board.

2. Θ

1. Alexander Carmichael, *Carmina Gadelica* (Edinburgh: Floris Books, 1992), 35.

2. The story that begins this chapter is a continuation of the story begun in chapter 1. For the sake of continuity and storytelling, each chapter will build on the story in the chapter before. In chapter 1 we first encountered Joan as the pastor who led Clarkston Church from a dying church of forty attendees into a growing congregation of more than one hundred. Joan's successor, Gordon, struggled at Clarkston Church because his leadership style was less millennial and more modern than Joan's. In this chapter we will explore how Joan almost lost her organic leadership style at her new church: Aldersgate Church.

3. For an overview of the prosperity movement and its influence on modern church leadership, see Simon Coleman, *The Globalization of Charismatic Christianity: Spreading the Gospel of Prosperity* (Cambridge: Cambridge University Press, 2000). And for an interesting examination of prosperity in African American congregations, see Stephanie Y. Mitchem, *Name It and Claim It? Prosperity Preaching in the Black Church* (Cleveland: Pilgrim Press, 2007).

4. See Kenneth Hagin, *Biblical Keys to Financial Prosperity* (Tulsa, Okla.: Faith Library Publications, 2009); Gloria Copeland, *God's Will Is Prosperity* (Fort Worth: Kenneth Copeland Publications, 1996); and Frederick K. C. Price, *Prosperity* (Lake Mary, Fla.: Creation House, 2007).

5. The Amplified Bible is customarily cited by the prosperity movement because its amplifications emphasize the eminence of the blessing. See Joyce Meyer, *Prepare to Prosper: Moving from the Land of Lack to the Land of Plenty* (New York: FaithWords, 2003), 10. Meyer rightly notes that when God bestows his bounty, it is usually accompanied by a responsibility to help the needy (23). But this book does not address charitable opportunities and tactics to any great degree.

6. For a comparison of blessings and buffetings in 2 Corinthians, see Alan Redpath's *Blessings Out of Buffetings: Studies in II Corinthians* (Old Tappan, N.J.: Revell, 1985).

7. Examining whether buffetings are sent by God, allowed by God, or autonomous work of the devil is beyond the scope of this book. Readers who want to study this topic further may wish to start with these books: C. S. Lewis, *The Problem of Pain* (New York: HarperOne, 2001); Philip Yancey, *Where Is God When It Hurts?* (Grand Rapids: Zondervan, 2002); and Timothy Keller, *The Reason for God: Belief in an Age of Skepticism* (Boston: Dutton Adult, 2008).

8. Joyce G. Baldwin, *1 and 2 Samuel: An Introduction & Commentary* (Downers Grove, Ill.: InterVarsity Press, 1998), 231. Baldwin describes David's actions with the term *droit de seigneur*, a feudal right that allowed a lord to justify doing whatever he pleased.

9. Thomas à Kempis, *The Imitation of Christ* (Chicago: Moody Publishing, 1980), 114–15.

10. Richard N. Ostling, Barbara Dolan, and Michael P. Harris, "Religion: Raising Eyebrows and the Dead," *Time* (July 13, 1987).

11. Henri J. M. Nouwen, *In the Name of Jesus: Reflections on Christian Leadership* (New York: Crossroad Publishing, 1989), 51–53.

12. For more on case studies about how leaders distance themselves from congregational worship and prayer as a church grows, see Bob Whitesel, *Growth by Accident, Death by Planning: How NOT to Kill a Growing Congregation* (Nashville: Abingdon Press, 2004).

13. Dietrich Bonhoeffer, *The Cost of Discipleship* (New York: Touchstone, 1995), 89, 91.

14. Henri J. M. Nouwen, *The Wounded Healer: Ministry in Contemporary Society* (New York: Image, 1979), 82.

15. Bonhoeffer, *The Cost of Discipleship*, 202.

16. Karen Ward, *About*, 2005, www.apostleschurch.org.

17. Merrill F. Unger and William White Jr., *Nelson's Expository Dictionary of the Old Testament* (Nashville: Thomas Nelson, 1980), 482.

18. Dan Kimball, *Emerging Worship: Creating Worship Gatherings for New Generations* (Grand Rapids: Zondervan, 2004).

19. Quoted by Eddie Gibbs and Ryan Bolger, *Emerging Churches: Creating Community in Postmodern Cultures* (Grand Rapids: Baker Academic, 2005), 105.

20. St. Thomas's Church, Sheffield, UK, 2010, www.stthomascrookes.org/daily prayers.

21. Tickle explains fixed-hour prayer as growing out of historical periods where "in the cities of the Empire, the forum bell rang the beginning of that day at six o'clock each morning (*prime* or 'first' hour); noted the day's progress by striking again at nine o'clock (*terce* or third hour); sounded the lunch break at noon (*sext* or sixth hour); called citizens back to work by striking at three o'clock (*none* or ninth hour); and closed the day's markets by sounding again at six o'clock in the afternoon (*vespers* or evening hour)." Phyllis Tickle, *The Divine Hours: Prayers for Summertime* (New York: Image, 2006), ix.

22. For more on St. Thomas's Anglican Church and its millennial leadership, see Paddy Mallon, *Calling a City Back to God* (Eastbourne: Kingsway Communications, 2003); and Bob Whitesel, *Inside the Organic Church: Learning from 12 Emerging Congregations* (Nashville: Abingdon Press, 2006).

23. Examples of prayer triplets can be found in Whitesel, *Growth by Accident, Death by Planning*, 49.

24. Gibbs and Bolger, *Emerging Churches*, 105.

25. Richard J. Foster, "Spiritual Formation," *Heart-to-Heart Pastoral Letter* (January 18, 2004).

26. For a collection of historical Wesleyan writings on sanctification, see the volume edited by Matt LeRoy and Jeremy Summers, *The Way Forward: Discovering the Classic Message of Holiness* (Indianapolis: Wesleyan Publishing House, 2007); and George G. Hunter III, *To Spread the Power: Church Growth in the Wesleyan Spirit* (Nashville: Abingdon Press, 1987).

27. David A. Womack, ed., *Pentecostal Experience: The Writings of Donald Gee: Settling the Question of Doctrine Versus Experience* (Springfield, Mo.: Gospel Publishing House, 1994).

28. Thomas Smith, "Cultivating the Fruit of the Spirit, Part II," *Catholic News Agency* (January 12, 2009).

3. ℞

1. Paul A. Wright, *Mother Teresa's Prescription: Finding Happiness and Peace in Service* (Notre Dame, Ind.: Ave Maria, 2006), 20.

2. Stuart Anderson, *Making Medicines: A Brief History of Pharmacy and Pharmaceuticals* (London: Pharmaceutical Press, 2005), 77–78.

3. Quoted by Ed Stetzer, "The Evolution of Church Growth, Church Health, and the Missional Church: An Overview of the Church Growth Movement from, and Back to, Its Missional Roots" (address, American Society for Church Growth, Fuller Theological Seminary, Pasadena, California, November 9, 2003), www.edstetzer.com/2008/11/14/Churchgrowth.pdf.

4. Ed Stetzer, "The Evolution of Church Growth."

5. The Greek word for church is *ekklesia*, which denotes not an organization but an assemblage of people called out on a regular basis for civic duty. Walter Bauer, *A Greek-English Lexicon of the New Testament and Other Early Literature*, ed. William F. Arndt and F. Wilbur Gingrich (Chicago: University of Chicago Press, 1957), 240–41. Therefore, though the term *church* can be used to describe an organization, it is best thought of as a collective group of citizens called out to participate in a community task, such as the *missio Dei*.

6. Rick Warren, *The Purpose Driven Church: Growth Without Compromising Your Message and Mission* (Grand Rapids: Zondervan, 1995), 27.

7. Emil Brunner, *The Misunderstanding of the Church*, trans. Harold Knight (London: Lutterworth Press, 1952), 15–18.

8. Ibid.

9. David S. Luecke and Samuel Southard, *Pastoral Administration: Integrating Ministry and Management in the Church* (Waco, Tex.: Word, 1986), 56–57.

10. See, for example, Robert Basevorn's classic treatise on preaching, where he admonishes the pulpiteer to see an attribute or *conditiones* of preaching as "including an impeccable moral character." Quoted by Alastair Minnis, *Fallible Authors* (Philadelphia: University of Pennsylvania Press, 2007), 36. On the rise and influence of heroic leadership, see Jimmy Long, *The Leadership Jump: Building Partnerships Between Existing and Emerging Christian Leaders* (Downers Grove, Ill.: InterVarsity Press, 2008), 47–49.

11. For examples of how group exits in churches can occur because of unhealthy relationships, see Bob Whitesel, *Staying Power: Why People Leave the Church over change and What You Can Do About It* (Nashville: Abingdon Press, 2002).

12. Greg L. Hawkins and Cally Parkinson, *REVEAL: Where Are You?* (South Barrington, Ill.: Willow Creek Association, 2007), 36.

13. Bill Hybels, Leadership Summit, South Barrington, Illinois, August 9, 2007.

14. Tom Albin, interviewed by Tim Stafford, "Finding God in Small Groups: Tom Albin's Doctoral Research Reveals Why Wesley's System Worked So Well," *Christianity Today*, August 2003, 44.

15. *Christianity Today*'s blog, Out of Ur, October 18, 2007, www.outofur.com/archives /2007/10/willow_creek_re.html (accessed July 11, 2011).

16. Ibid.

17. Bob Whitesel, *Inside the Organic Church: Learning from 12 Emerging Congregations* (Nashville: Abingdon Press, 2006), xvii–xix, 26–27.

18. John Marsh, personal interview with author, St. Thomas's Church, Sheffield, UK, June 9, 2009.

19. Not surprisingly, being a leader of a small group rather than an organizer of the church is often the highest calling in the millennial world. See Bob Hopkins and Mike Breen, *Clusters: Creative Mid-sized Missional Communities* (Sheffield, UK: 3D Publishing, 2007), 32–34. We shall see shortly that millennial leaders flatten the leadership structure by emphasizing small-group leadership. In millennial churches, the leaders who mentor others in small groups are actually more numerous and more lauded due to the critical and foundational nature of their roles.

20. It is interesting that Leith Anderson embraces a more modern leadership opinion that "small groups are not for everyone," since in his experience even churches that heavily promote small groups rarely see more than 50 percent of their congregation involved. Leith Anderson, *A Church for the 21st Century* (Minneapolis: Bethany House, 1992), 36. However, Larry Osborne, stressing the more millennial stickiness factor of small groups, states that his church has "reached an 80 percent participation rate in our small group program." Larry Osborne, *Sticky Church* (Grand Rapids: Zondervan, 2008), 94.

21. Osborne, *Sticky Church*, 41–46.

22. Ibid., 34–35.

23. Thom Rainer, *Surprising Insights from the Unchurched and Proven Ways to Reach Them* (Grand Rapids: Zondervan, 2001), 120.

24. Whitesel, *Inside the Organic Church*, 26–27.

25. Ibid., 28–29.

26. Robert Clinton, *The Making of a Leader* (Colorado Springs: NavPress, 1988), 35.

27. Ibid., 94.

28. Randy D. Reese and Keith R. Anderson, *Spiritual Mentoring: A Guide for Seeking and Giving Direction* (Downers Grove, Ill.: InterVarsity Press, 1999), 35.

29. Helmut Thielicke, *How the World Began: Man in the First Chapters of the Bible*, trans. John W. Doberstein (Philadelphia: Fortress Press, 1961), 112.

30. Osborne, *Sticky Church*, 53–58; Rainer, *Surprising Insights from the Unchurched and Proven Ways to Reach Them*, 120; Eddie Gibbs and Ryan K. Bolger, *Emerging Churches: Creating Christian Community in Postmodern Cultures* (Grand Rapids: Baker Academic, 2005), 109–10.

31. Albin, "Finding God in Small Groups," 43.

32. Ibid., 44.

33. Clinton, *The Making of a Leader*, 94.

34. Amy Frykholm, "Reinventing Leadership: Shepherds in Training," *Christian Century*, February 23, 2010, 26–27.

35. Bob Whitesel, *Growth by Accident, Death by Planning: How NOT to Kill a Growing Congregation* (Nashville: Abingdon Press, 2004), 139–40. Though this definition is more inclusive than many, it helps ensure that no groups are left out. This is necessary because it is within these small, interpersonal gatherings that attendees and the leaders hold one another accountable as well as where spiritual health is fostered.

36. Bob Whitesel and Kent R. Hunter, *A House Divided: Bridging the Generation Gaps in Your Church* (Nashville: Abingdon Press, 2000), 26.

37. Though small groups "may on occasion be comprised of more than 12 individuals, the cell group's cohesiveness is rarely found in meetings of more than 20 individuals" (Whitesel, *Growth by Accident, Death by Planning*, 140). And research by John N. Vaughn found that as small groups become larger (more than twenty), growth of the groups slows. "Trends Among the World's Largest Churches," in *Church Growth State of the Art*, ed. C. Peter Wagner (Wheaton, Ill.: Tyndale, 1986), 132. Thus, the optimum size for a small group may be less than twenty participants.

38. Gibbs and Bolger, *Emerging Churches*, 109, italics mine.

39. George G. Hunter III, "Emerging Trends in Church Growth" (course lecture, Marion, Indiana, Wesley Seminary, 2010).

40. Gordon Cosby, quoted by Frykholm in "Reinventing Leadership," 26–27.

41. Bauer, *A Greek-English Lexicon of the New Testament and Other Early Literature*, 317–18.

42. For a comparison of conversion and how liturgical, evangelical, and mainline churches describe this differently see Charles Kraft, "Christian Conversion as a Dynamic Process," *International Christian Broadcasters Bulletin*, Second Quarter (1974); Scot McKnight, *Turning to Jesus: The Sociology of Conversion in the Gospels* (Louisville: Westminster John Knox, 1997), 171–72; and Richard Peace, "Conflicting Understandings of Christian Conversion: A Missiological Challenge," *International Bulletin of Missionary Research* 28, no. 1 (2004): 8.

43. Clinton, *The Making of a Leader*, 94.

44. Billy Graham, *Peace with God: The Secret of Happiness* (New York: Thomas Nelson, 1953, 2000), 237.

45. John Stott, ed., *Evangelism and Social Responsibility: An Evangelical Commitment* (Lausanne Committee for Evangelism and the World Evangelical Fellowship, 1982), 23.

46. The IN element reminds small groups that interpersonal dialogue, accountability, and sharing are critical. The UP element of small groups maintains a focus on the heavenly convener of the meeting. And the OUT element reminds every small group that its members should be reaching out with evangelism (i.e., sharing the good news) on a regular basis to those outside the church.

47. Accountability and candidness are two by-products of healthy small groups. St. Thomas's Church in Sheffield, England, uses the Groups-MissionalNets-Cultures approach among nine different cultures (which they call "celebrations"). See Hopkins and Breen, *Clusters*.

48. Whitesel and Hunter, *A House Divided*, 26.

49. Paul Hiebert, *Cultural Anthropology* (Grand Rapids: Baker, 1976), 25.

50. For examples of various cultures, see (for ethnic cultures) *The World Factbook: CIA Edition*, rev. ed. (Washington, D.C.: Potomac Books, 2006; (for ethnic cultures) David Jaffee's *Levels of Socio-economic Development Theory* (New York: Praeger 1998) and *Organization Theory* (New York: McGraw-Hill, 2001); (for affinity cultures) Bob Whitesel, *Preparing for Change Reaction: How to Introduce Change in Your Church* (Indianapolis: Wesleyan Publishing House, 2007), 56–58; and (for generational cultures) Whitesel and Hunter, *A House Divided*, 56–81.

51. The church as organizational entity is sometimes called the "membership circle" (Lyle E. Schaller, *Growing Plans: Strategies to Increase Your Church's Membership* [Nashville: Abingdon Press, 1983], 26) and includes everyone who officially belongs to a church. But most healthy churches will also have subcongregations (George G. Hunter III, *The Contagious Congregation* [Nashville: Abingdon Press, 1979], 63) with different cultural worship expressions. These various subcongregations (see Whitesel and Hunter, *A House Divided*, 25–27) will in turn compose MissionalNets and within each MissionalNet two to five small groups.

52. Albin, "Finding God in Small Groups," 43.

53. Gibbs and Bolger, *Emerging Churches*, 110.

54. In a group setting, precautions should be taken to ensure sensitivities and/or vulnerabilities are handled appropriately. If such precautions are instituted, sharing your reflections with others can foster an intimate and helpful sounding board.

4.6

1. Spotted by Ronald Wright, *A Short History of Progress* (Cambridge, Mass.: Da Capo, 2005), 7.

2. Soong-Chan Rah, *The New Evangelicalism: Freeing the Church from Western Cultural Captivity* (Downers Grove, Ill: InterVarsity, 2009).

3. Marva Dawn, *Reaching Out Without Dumbing Down: A Theology of Worship for This Urgent Time* (Grand Rapids: Eerdmans, 1995). Though this is a beneficial book, the choice to study this book by the leaders of Smith Street Church demonstrated the modern, provincial, and overly programmatic approach they were taking toward connecting with the African American neighborhood.

4. For a look at graffiti's influence on the international art world, see Henry Chalfant and James Prigoff, *Spraycan Art* (London: Thames & Hudson, 1987), 7.

5. Nicholas Ganz, *Graffiti World Updated Edition: Street Art from Five Continents*, 2nd ed. (New York: Abrams Books, 2009), back cover. Although types of graffiti have existed since ancient times (see Scape Martinez, *GRAFF: The Art and Technique of Graffiti* [Atascadero, Calif.: Impact, 2009], 6–8), graffiti in its current state of art is a product of the 1960 East Coast urban street culture.

6. For the classic introduction to the influence of graffiti as an art, see Norman Mailer and Jon Naar's *The Faith of Graffiti*, new ed. (New York: IT Books, 2009).

7. Martinez, *GRAFF*, 6.

8. Ibid.

9. Michel Crouhy, Dan Galai, and Robert Mark, *The Essentials of Risk Management* (New York: McGraw-Hill, 2005), 1.

10. Barbara Kellerman, "The Abiding Tyranny of the Male Leadership Model: A Manifesto," *Harvard Business Review*, April 27, 2010.

11. Barry A. Kosmin and Ariela Keysar, *The American Religious Identification Survey* (Hartford, Conn.: Trinity College Press, 2008), 11.

12. Maureen E. Fielder, *Breaking Through the Stained Glass Ceiling* (Harrisburg, Pa.: Church Publishing, 2010), xvii.

13. Ibid.

14. David Murrow, *Why Men Hate Going to Church* (Nashville: Thomas Nelson, 2004), 4.

15. Peggy McIntosh, "White Privilege: Unpacking the Invisible Knapsack," in *White Privilege: Essential Readings on the Other Side of Racism*, ed. Paula S. Rothenberg, 3rd ed. (New York: Worth Publishers, 2002), 97–102; and Robert Jensen, "White Privilege Shapes the U.S.," in *White Privilege: Essential Readings on the Other Side of Racism*, 103–6.

16. Stephanie M. Wildman with Adrienne D. Davis, "Making Systems of Privilege Visible," in *White Privilege: Essential Readings on the Other Side of Racism*, 92.

17. Jensen, "White Privilege Shapes the U.S.," 129.

18. Wildman with Davis, "Making Systems of Privilege Visible," 112.

19. Kellerman, "Abiding Tyranny of the Male Leadership Model."

20. Philip A. Klinkner and Rogers M. Smith, *The Unsteady March: The Rise and Decline of Racial Equality in America* (Chicago: University of Chicago Press, 2002), 317.

21. Quoted by Harvard Sitkoff and John Hope Franklin, *The Struggle for Black Equality* (New York: Hill & Wang, 2008), 38.

22. Based on the disciplines of linguistics, theology, sociology, and history, "organic" may be the most fitting metaphor for a healthy church. See Bob Whitesel, *Inside the Organic Church: Learning from 12 Emerging Congregations* (Nashville: Abingdon Press, 2006), xxiv–xxviii.

23. Missiologists have long shown that it is a biblical and relevant strategy to contextualize worship for different cultures. For a helpful book on the rationale for adding worship celebrations, see Charles Arn's *How to Start a New Service: Your Church CAN Reach New People* (Grand Rapids: Baker Books, 1997).

24. Patrick Lencioni defines a *silo* as "nothing more than the barriers that exist between departments within an organization, causing people who are supposed to be on the same team to work against one another." *Silos, Politics and Turf Wars: A Leadership Fable About Destroying the Barriers That Turn Colleagues into Competitors* (Hoboken, N.J.: Jossey-Bass, 2006), 175.

25. Although a siloed church with little interaction is not desirable, it may still be preferable to a church split that forces a dissimilar culture to leave the church and plant a church down the street. At least in a siloed church, some cross-cultural communication may take place because of proximity. The worst-case scenario is a split-off silo where cross-cultural pollination will rarely take place. For practical tactics to create a mosaic or networked church with several multicultural congregations under the same local church umbrella, see Bob Whitesel, "The New Network Approach: The Missing Side of Church Planting," *Church Executive*, October 2010.

26. Mary Jo Hatch, *Organization Theory: Modern, Symbolic, and Postmodern Perspectives* (Oxford: Oxford University Press, 1997), 9.

27. Lois Barrett, "Pattern 3: Taking Risks as a Contrast Community," in *Treasures in Clay Jars: Patterns in Missional Faithfulness* (Grand Rapids: Eerdmans, 2004), xiii.

28. Ibid.

29. Lewis A. Drummond, *Reaching Generation Next: Effective Evangelism in Today's Culture* (Grand Rapids: Baker Books, 2002), 179.

30. Barrett, "Pattern 3: Taking Risks as a Contrast Community," 74–83.

31. Ibid., 78.

32. Ibid., 75.

33. Edward Gilbreath, *Reconciliation Blues: A Black Evangelical's Inside View of White Christianity* (Downers Grove, Ill.: InterVarsity, 2006), 9, 11, 18.

34. Jo Ann Robinson, quoted by Sitkoff and Franklin, *Struggle for Black Equality*, 37.

35. Charles Marsh and John M. Perkins, *Welcoming Justice: God's Movement Toward Beloved Community* (Downers Grove, Ill.: InterVarsity, 2009), 28–31.

36. Ron Sider, *Rich Christians in an Age of Hunger: A Biblical Study* (Downers Grove, Ill.: InterVarsity, 1977), 105, 193.

37. John M. Perkins, *A Quiet Revolution: The Christian Response to Human Need, a Strategy for Today* (Pasadena, Calif.: Urban Family Publications, 1976), 220.

38. Phil Yancey quoting Martin Luther King Jr. in the foreword to *Welcoming Justice*, by Marsh and Perkins 13–14.

39. For more on these types of churches, see "Types of Multiracial Churches" in George Yancey's *One Body, One Spirit: Principles of Successful Multiracial Churches* (Downers Grove, Ill.: InterVarsity, 2003), 51–64; and "St. Thomas' Church, Sheffield, England," in Whitesel's *Inside the Organic Church*, 1–12.

40. See Whitesel, "The New Network Approach."

41. Ibid.

42. Walter Brueggemann, "Always in the Shadow of the Empire," in *The Church as Counterculture*, ed. Michael L. Budde and Robert W. Brimlow (Albany: State University of New York Press, 2000), 54.

43. Anthony B. Robinson and Robert W. Wall, *Called to Be Church: The Book of Acts for a New Day* (Grand Rapids: Eerdmans, 2006), 223.

44. Lois Barrett, *Treasures in Clay Jars: Patterns in Missional Faithfulness* (Grand Rapids: Eerdmans, 2004), xiii.

45. These questions for risk taking were taken from an interview with Randy Komisar by Frances Hesselbein and Rob Johnson in *On Creativity, Innovation, and Renewal: A Leader to Leader Guide* (San Francisco: Jossey-Bass, 2002), 72–73. For more on Kosimar's insights into realistic risk taking, see his *The Monk and the Riddle: The Art of Creating a Life While Making a Living* (Boston: Harvard Business Press, 2001).

46. Though I belong to the Wesleyan Church now, I grew up in the Church of God (Anderson, Indiana), which regularly practices foot washing.

47. Leon Morris, *The Gospel According to John* (Grand Rapids: Eerdmans, 1995), 544.

48. These are Scriptures in which Jesus' words as prayer for the unchurched are recorded. There are many more examples where Jesus' words are not recorded, but his action of prayer for the unchurched is documented. See John Wimber and Kevin Springer's *Power Evangelism*, rev. ed. (Ventura, Calif.: Regal Publishers, 2009), for a detailed look at Jesus' prayers for those who were not yet following Christ.

49. Bob Whitesel and Kent R. Hunter, *A House Divided: Bridging the Generation Gaps in Your Church* (Nashville: Abingdon Press, 2001), 224–25; and Bob Whitesel, *Growth by Accident, Death by Planning: How NOT to Kill a Growing Congregation* (Nashville: Abingdon Press, 2004), 50.

50. These are guidelines given students at Wesley Seminary at Indiana Wesleyan University so that prayers for people not present respect their privacy and confidentiality. (From the "Email Usage Policy" directive, October 30, 2006, revised April 26, 2010. Approved by the President's Cabinet. Used by permission.)

Items sent to the Prayer list should be intended to draw from the power of the Indiana Wesleyan University prayer community for various needs. Please use caution when describing the nature of the circumstance requiring prayer out of respect for all individuals involved. See "Medical Information Guidelines."
Medical Information Guidelines
i. Information shared about medical diagnoses/prognoses can provide potential challenges in light of the Americans with Disabilities Act (ADA), and the Health Insurance Portability and Accountability (HIPAA) Privacy standards. This applies to medical conditions of students, job applicants and employees, and may even hold true with other outside constituents. When sharing prayer requests, please use generalities only instead of condition-specific information.
Non-Preferred: Please pray for [employee name]. S/he was just rushed to Marion General Hospital suffering severe chest pains. The emergency medical technicians believed it was a heart attack, and [Employee name]'s spouse is very concerned since [employee name] previously had bypass surgery and angioplasty.
Preferred (Initial): Please pray for [employee name]. S/he was just rushed to Marion General Hospital with health concerns.
Preferred (Follow-up): Thank you to those who prayed for [employee name]. The doctors were able to stabilize the condition and [employee name] is resting comfortably at MGH.

51. Jason Brian Santos, *A Community Called Taizé: A Story of Prayer, Worship and Reconciliation* (Downers Grove, Ill.: InterVarsity Books), 53–67. Note that the Taizé community comprises primarily small communities serving the poor in some of the most destitute neighborhoods in the world.
52. Brother Roger Shutz, the founder of the Taizé community, was tragically killed in 2005 by a disturbed woman. The Liturgy of Reconciliation given at his funeral (http://fullhomelydivinity.org/reconciliation.htm) is a moving example of reconciliation in liturgical form. The Coventry Litany of Reconciliation is another helpful liturgy on reconciliation (www.coventrycathedral.org.uk/about-us/our-reconciliation-ministry/coventry-litany-of-reconciliation.php).
53. Since this is a long process that will never be met (in this lifetime), such events must be recurring in addition to being authentic.
54. Perkins, *A Quiet Revolution*, 219–20.
55. Rah, *The New Evangelicalism*, 120.
56. John L. Drury, e-mail message to the author, August 11, 2010.
57. Alejandro Portes and Ruben G. Rumbaut suggest that selective acculturation results in less conflict and a more harmonious blend of cultures. *Immigrant American: A Portrait* (Berkeley and Los Angeles: University of California Press, 1996), chap. 7.
58. Ruben G. Rumbaut, "Acculturation, Discrimination, and Ethnic Identity Among Children of Immigrants," in *Discovering Successful Pathways in Children's Development: Mixed Methods in the Study of Childhood and Family Life*, ed. Thomas S. Weisner (Chicago: University of Chicago Press, 2005), 8. See also Eddie Gibbs, *I Believe in Church Growth* (Grand Rapids: Eerdmans, 1981), 92; and Charles Kraft, *Christianity in Culture: A Study of Dynamic Biblical Theologizing in Cross-Cultural Perspective* (Maryknoll, N.Y.: Orbis, 1979), 113.

59. See Bob Whitesel, "Communicating the Good News Across Cultural Divides," in *Preparing for Change Reaction: How to Introduce Change in Your Church* (Indianapolis: Wesleyan Publishing House, 2008), 62–68.

60. Brian Schrag and Paul Neeley, eds., *All the World Will Worship: Helps for Developing Indigenous Hymns* (Duncanville, Tex.: EthnoDology Publications, 2007).

61. C. Peter Wagner traces such blending through history as an "assimilationist model" that seeks "Anglo-conformity" in *Our Kind of People: The Ethical Dimensions of Church Growth in America* (Atlanta: John Knox, 1979), 45–49.

62. Such committees might include trustees, financial, staff-parish (HR), and so on.

63. Sociologists, however, refer to this as the "new pluralism" or "structural pluralism." See Milton Gordon, "Assimilation in America," *Daedalus* 90, no. 2 (1961): 263–85.

64. George G. Hunter III, *The Contagious Congregation* (Nashville: Abingdon Press, 1979), 63.

65. *Mosaic* is a term that has been applied to multiethnic churches largely due to the popularity of some megachurch models. See Erwin Raphael McManus, *An Unstoppable Force: Daring to Become the Church God Had in Mind* (Colorado Springs: Group Publishing, 2001).

66. The melting pot imagery can be traced to Israel Zangwill's popular play *The Melting-Pot* (1908) where the protagonist cries, "Germans and Frenchmen, Irishmen and Englishmen, Jews and Russians—into the crucible with you all! God is making the American." Quoted in Winthrop S. Hudson, ed., *Nationalism and Religion in America: Concepts of American Identity and Mission* (New York: Harper & Row, 1970), 127. C. Peter Wagner, who wrote his dissertation on models of assimilation and pluralism, defined *new pluralism* as "a model in which America is seen as a nation that maintains group diversity, within national unity." *Our Kind of People*, 50.

67. Nathan Moynihan and Daniel Patrick Glazer, *Beyond the Melting Pot* (Boston: MIT Press, 1984).

68. Andrew M. Greeley, "Catholics Prosper While the Church Grumbles," *Psychology Today* (June 1976): 44.

69. Indiana University scholar Gerardo Marti has written extensively on Mosaic Church in Southern California (led by Erwin McManus) and believes that its multiethnicity is produced in part by "playing down" ethnic differences and uniting around evangelicalism. For more on Marti's analysis, see *A Mosaic of Believers: Diversity and Innovation in a Multiethnic Church* (Bloomington: Indiana University Press, 2009).

70. Wagner, *Our Kind of People*, 51.

71. Whitesel, *Inside the Organic Church*, 56–57.

5. ♲

1. Barry Commoner, *Orion Nature Quarterly* (1990).

2. Lucas Bretschger and Sjak Smulders, *Sustainable Resource Use and Economic Dynamics* (New York: Springer, 2010), 1.

3. Sharon Astyk, *Depletion and Abundance: Life on the New Home Front* (Gabriola Island, B.C.: New Society Publishers, 2008), 6.

4. See Rebekah Simon-Peter, *Green Church: Reduce, Reuse, Recycle, Rejoice!* (Nashville: Abingdon Press, 2010); and *Seven Simple Steps to Green Your Church* (Nashville:

Abingdon Press, 2010); Daphna Flegal and Suzann Wade, *Green Church: Caretakers of God's Creation* (Nashville: Abingdon Press, 2010); and even a "green" Bible that will "equip and encourage you to see God's vision for creation and help you engage in the work of healing and sustaining it" (*Green Bible* [New York: HarperOne, 2008], front flap).

5. Bill McKibben, *Eaarth: Making a Life on a Tough New Planet* (New York: Times Books, 2010), 212.

6. As noted, this discussion should not imply that repurposing is not warranted at times. Repurposing is often necessary if the original material or intent has been so damaged that a return to the original purpose is no longer viable. This is especially evident in repurposing and recycling people.

7. J. Hudson, Archibald Hart, G. McKinney, K. Larson, and S. Smith, "How Sexually Healthy Must a Pastor Be?" *Leadership* 16, no. 3 (1995): 26.

8. Ibid.

9. Avoidance of repurposing, in favor of recycling, is not a hard-and-fast rule. Rather, it is an inclination I have observed in churches founded on modern leadership principles.

10. I have written elsewhere explaining that generations are cultures and the modern approach at abandoning the traditional worship celebration does not retain a worship expression for older members. See Bob Whitesel, *Inside the Organic Church: Learning from 12 Emerging Congregations* (Nashville: Abingdon Press, 2006); and *Staying Power: Why People Leave the Church over Change and What You Can Do About It* (Nashville: Abingdon Press, 2002).

11. Effective and unifying blended worship is extremely hard to develop. In fact, in my consulting career I have rarely seen it work, and in each case the church became less evangelistic because a blended format appealed primarily to Christians and not to unchurched people. Visitors from a non-churchgoing background often find blended services too unfocused and jumbled.

12. Recycling leaders is not appropriate for all cases. Certain circumstances in which abuse of people or things occurs may preclude a leader from being recycled to his or her original purpose. Still, the modern leader's propensity to embarrass/plunder/forbid usually fails to honor God's redemptive power and purpose (Prov. 10:12; 17:9; 1 Pet. 4:8).

13. Jerry Falwell and Elmer Towns, *Capturing a Town for Christ* (Old Tappan, N.J.: Revell, 1973), 67.

14. George F. Ritzer, *The McDonaldization of Society*, 6th ed. (Thousand Oaks, Calif.: Pine Forge, 2010), 168–74.

15. For more on St. Thomas's organic network of nine different worship celebrations, see Whitesel, *Inside the Organic Church*, 1–12.

16. Karen Ward, pastor of Church of the Apostles, an ancient-future congregation in the Fremont section of Seattle, emphasizes that "ancient-future speaks to postmodern generations. It draws equally on ancient (hymns, chants, candles, communion) as well as techno-modern sources (alternative rock, art, ambiance, projections, video)." *Karen Ward Campus Residency*, 2008, www.ssw.edu/news/view/karen-ward-campus-residency (accessed July 13, 2011).

17. These steps are but broad categories, and due to the seriousness of leadership failure, a more extensive approach to restoration of leaders should be embraced. The Assemblies of God and The United Methodist Church are two denominations that have robust and holistic approaches to leadership failure.

18. Hudson et al., "How Sexually Healthy Must a Pastor Be?" 26.

19. Earl D. Wilson et al., *Restoring the Fallen: A Team Approach to Caring, Confronting, and Reconciling* (Colorado Springs: InterVarsity, 1997), 133.

20. Lewis B. Smedes, *The Art of Forgiving: When You Need to Forgive and Don't Know How* (Nashville: Moorings, 1996), 27.

21. Gordon MacDonald, *Rebuilding Your Broken World* (Nashville: Thomas Nelson, 2004), 216.

22. Joel Comiskey, *Wesley's Small Group Organization* (Moreno Valley, Calif.: Comiskey Group, 1997), 5.

23. For examples of *lectio divina*, see Tim Guptill, *Listening for God Through 1 & 2 Peter* (Kansas City, Mo.: Beacon Hill, 2006); and Robin Maas and Gabriel O'Donnell, eds., *Spiritual Traditions for the Contemporary Church* (Nashville: Abingdon Press, 1990).

24. Francis Brown, S. R. Driver, and Charles A. Briggs, *A Hebrew and English Lexicon of the Old Testament Based on the Lexicon of William Gesenius* (Oxford: Clarendon, 1974), 1005.

25. The original "purpose" of worship is retained when each generation, ethnicity, or affinity culture experiences a worship encounter in its own artistic and cultural form.

6. N

1. Lon Safko and David K. Brake, *The Social Media Bible* (Hoboken, N.J.: Wiley, 2009), 3–4.

2. Tim Wu, *The Master Switch: The Rise and Fall of Information Empires* (New York: Knopf, 2010), 168–70. See also J. C. R. Licklider's visionary paper, "Man-Computer Symbiosis," in *In Memoriam: J. C. R. Licklider: 1915–1990*, ed. R. W. Taylor (Palo Alto, Calif.: Digital Systems Research Center Reports, 1990).

3. Paul Hiebert, *Cultural Anthropology* (Grand Rapids: Baker, 1976).

4. For an examination of different types of cultures, see David Jaffee (socioeconomic cultures) *Levels of Socio-economic Development Theory* (New York: Praeger, 1998) and *Organization Theory* (New York: McGraw-Hill, 2001); and William Strauss and Neil Howe (generational), *Generations: The History of America's Future, 1584 to 2069* (New York: Quill, 1991).

5. Kathleen A. Begley, *Face-to-Face Communication: Making Human Connections in a Technology-Driven World* (Mississauga, Ont.: Crisp Learning, 2004).

6. Howard Rheingold, "A Slice of Life in My Virtual Community," in Linda Harasim, ed., *Global Networks: Computers and International Communication* (Cambridge, Mass.: MIT Press, 1995).

7. *Mesh* and *meshing* are recent terms used to describe networks that depend on other networks to function. For more information on meshing, see Linda Gansky, *The Mesh: Why the Future of Business Is Sharing* (New York: Portfolio, 2010).

8. David Morgan, "The Allure of Electronic Media and the Study of Religion," *Religion and American Culture: Journal of Interpretation* 16, no. 1 (2006): 7.

9. Ibid., 7–8.

10. Ibid., 7.

11. Rheingold, "A Slice of Life in My Virtual Community," 58; and Howard Rheingold, *The Virtual Community: Homesteading on the Electronic Frontier* (Boston: Addison Wesley, 1993), xx.

12. Heidi Campbell and Patricia Calderon, "The Question of Christian Community Online: The Case of the 'Artist World Network,'" *Studies in World Christianity* 13, no. 3 (2007): 263.

13. See Neville A. Stanton, Chris Baber, and Don Harris, *Modeling Command and Control*, Human Factors in Defense (Farnham, UK: Ashgate, 2008); and Vincent Dunn, *Safety and Survival on the Fireground* (Tulsa: Pennwell Books, 2002).

14. John Seddon, *Freedom from Command and Control: Rethinking Management for Lean Service* (New York: Productivity Press, 2005).

15. Michael Crosby, *The Paradox of Power: From Control to Compassion* (New York: Crossroad Publishing, 2008).

16. See Stephen R. Conway, "War of American Independence," in James C. Bradford, ed., *A Companion to American Military History*, vol. 1 (Hoboken, N.J.: Wiley-Blackwell, 2009), 23–48.

17. Quoted by Daniel Boorstin, *The Americans: The Democratic Experience* (New York: Vintage, 1974), 368–69.

18. Rusty Rueff (lecture, Wesley Seminary at Indiana Wesleyan University, offsite course held in Santa Cruz, California, 2006).

19. Tim Wu, interview by Brooke Gladstone, National Public Radio, November 12, 2010. Transcript available at www.onthemedia.org/transcripts/2010/11/12/05 (accessed July 13, 2011).

20. There is nothing wrong with such alternatives, but they may garner less usage and reach a smaller population segment because of their narrow focus.

21. Wayne Parry, "Pastor to NJ Church Leaders: Thou Shall Not Facebook," Associated Press, November 17, 2010, http://latimesblogs.latimes.com/technology/2010/11/pastor cedric-miller-thou-shall-not-facebook-living-word-christian-fellowship-church-in -neptune-new-jersey.html.

22. Christopher De Hamel, *A History of Illuminated Manuscripts*, 2nd ed. (London: Phaidon, 1997).

23. Chris Anderson and Michael Wolff, "The Web Is Dead: Long Live the Internet," Wired, August 17, 2010, www.wired.com/magazine/2010/08/ff_webrip/all/1 (accessed July 13, 2011).

24. Indiana Wesleyan University, "Wesley Seminary Hosts Conference on 'Outreach in an eWorld,'" press release, November 30, 2010. The release can be found at www.indwes.edu/News/2010/Wesley-Seminary-Hosts-Conference-on-Outreach-in-an -eWorld/ (accessed July 21, 2011).

25. Russ Gunsalus, personal conversation with author, Marion, Indiana, December 6, 2010.

26. Russ Gunsalus, "New Life in Second Life: Can the Church Grow in Virtual Worlds?" (paper, Great Commission Research Network, Wesley Seminary, Indiana Wesleyan University, Marion, Indiana, November 10, 2010).

27. Morgan, "The Allure of Electronic Media and the Study of Religion," 10.

28. Gunsalus, "New Life in Second Life."

29. Rusty Rueff, lecture, Great Commission Research Network, Wesley Seminary, Indiana Wesleyan University, Marion, Indiana, November 10, 2010.

30. Bob Whitesel, *Inside the Organic Church: Learning from 12 Emerging Congregations* (Nashville: Abingdon Press, 2006), xxxiii.

31. Ibid., 110–15.

32. Ibid., 22–26.

33. Lon Safko, *The Social Media Bible*, 2nd ed. (Hoboken, N.J.: Wiley, 2010), 5.

34. The United Methodist Church Large Church Initiative Conference (University United Methodist Church, San Antonio, April 12–15, 2010); and The Great Commission Research Network Annual Conference (Wesley Seminary, Indiana Wesleyan University, Marion, Indiana, November 10–11, 2010).

35. Quentin J. Schultze and Robert H. Woods Jr., eds., *Understanding Evangelical Media: The Changing Face of Christian Communication* (Downers Grove, Ill.: InterVarsity, 2008), 23.

36. Mark Silk et al., "News Filter: Navigating the New Media," *Christian Century*, September 22, 2009, 25.

37. Richard Niebuhr, *Christ and Culture* (New York: Harper & Row, 1956). For a helpful expansion of Niebuhr's categories regarding Christ and culture, see Paul Hiebert, *Cultural Anthropology* (Grand Rapids: Baker, 1976), 45–82; and Charles Kraft, *Christianity in Culture: A Study of Dynamic Biblical Theologizing in Cross-Cultural Perspective* (Maryknoll, N.Y.: Orbis, 1979), 105–6.

38. Niebuhr, *Christ and Culture*, 190–95.

39. Eddie Gibbs, *I Believe in Church Growth* (Grand Rapids: Eerdmans, 1981), 120.

40. Heidi Campbell and Patricia Calderon, "The Question of Christian Community Online: The Case of the 'Artist World Network,'" *Studies in World Christianity* 13, no. 3 (2007): 262, italics mine.

41. Morgan, "The Allure of Electronic Media and the Study of Religion," 13.

42. To identify social networks of friends, relatives, acquaintances, and neighbors, see Bob Whitesel and Kent R. Hunter, *A House Divided: Bridging the Generation Gaps in Your Church* (Nashville: Abingdon Press, 2000), 195–98.

43. Donald A. McGavran, *The Bridges of God* (New York: Friendship, 1955).

44. Donald A. McGavran, *Understanding Church Growth* (Grand Rapids: Eerdmans, 1980), 395.

45. Win Arn and Charles Arn, *The Master's Plan for Making Disciples* (Grand Rapids: Baker, 1998), 48.

46. Walter Bauer, *A Greek-English Lexicon of the New Testament and Other Early Literature*, trans. William F. Arndt and F. Wilbur Gingrich (Chicago: University of Chicago Press, 1957), 562–63.

47. Michael Green, *Evangelism in the Early Church*, rev. ed. (Grand Rapids: Eerdmans, 2004), 321.

48. *Oikos* is the Greek word for "household," and *evangelism* is derived from the Greek word for "good news." We saw in chapters 1 and 2 that *evangelism* should be thought of as more than just conversion, for a person receives good news about God when someone gives a cup of cold water to a parched person in God's name. Thus, a more relevant term might be *household good news*.

49. Portions of this paragraph are taken from an interview with the author (Bob Whitesel) and published in *Christian Post*. Michelle Vu, "Democratizing Evangelism in an eWorld," *Christian Post*, November 15, 2010.

50. The sol café (the name is not capitalized) is a church plant of the Christian and Missionary Alliance in Canada.

51. Stan Toler, personal conversation with author, Church of the Nazarene District Superintendents' Retreat, St. Augustine, Florida, February 8, 2010.

52. Silk, "News Filter," 27.

53. Campbell and Calderon, "The Question of Christian Community Online," 263.

54. Robert Schuller tells the story of Rosie, whose husband stated, "'She's been sitting in your drive-in church every Sunday since the beginning. . . . She can't walk and she can't talk. She can only grunt and drop a tear. You see,' her husband explained with moist eyes, 'my wife Rosie had a stroke a few years ago. And the drive-in church was just the answer for our needs.'" *Your Church Has a Fantastic Future* (Ventura, Calif.: Regal, 1986), 32–33. Since that time Schuller vowed to maintain a drive-in service because, like online communication today, it offered accessibility.

55. Heidi Campbell, *Exploring Religious Community Online: We Are One in the* Network (New York: Peter Lang, 2005).

56. Campbell and Calderon describing Campbell's conclusions, "The Question of Christian Community Online," 262.

57. Colin McAlister, "The Church and Modern Media," *Modern Believing* 51, no. 2 (April 2010): 41.

58. Ibid., 46.

59. Rodney Clapp makes the argument that this story of Alypius warns against sinning in virtual worlds and thinking it makes no difference in the real world. Clapp summarizes, "Judging by its effects on the psyche, is there any real difference between doing something in virtual reality and doing it in actual reality? Virtual stalking (cyber-voyeurism) may not land us in jail, but it may grievously wound our souls" (Rodney Clapp, "Our Stalker Culture," *Christian Century*, November 17, 2009, 45).

60. Augustine, *Confessions*, trans. R. S. Pine-Coffin (London: Penguin Classics, 1961), 122.

61. Ibid.

62. Rogers, "Navigating the New Media News Filter," 25.

63. William Powers, *Hamlet's BlackBerry: A Practical Philosophy for Building a Good Life in the Digital Age* (New York: Harper, 2010), 223–33.

64. Yancey, "'O, Evangelicos!' We Need Not Abandon Our Name—Just Live Up to It," *Christianity Today*, November 2009, 65.

65. Editorial, "Media in Motion: Evangelicalism's Mission and Message Outlast Evolving Technologies," *Christianity Today*, October 2006, 38.

7. ∬

1. Carlton T. Lewis, *Latin Dictionary* (Oxford: Oxford University Press, 1996), 112.

2. N. T. Wright, "Incarnation and Establishment" (sermon, Durham, UK: Cathedral Church of Christ, December 25, 2008).

3. David J. Bosch, *Transforming Mission: Paradigm Shifts in the Theology of Mission* (Maryknoll, N.Y.: Orbis, 1991), 390.

4. Mary Jo Hatch, *Organization Theory: Modern, Symbolic, and Postmodern Perspectives* (Oxford: Oxford University Press, 1997), 25–54.

5. The term *postmodern* was coined by Federico de Onis in the 1930s but was not widely used to depict a growing dissatisfaction with the modern experiment until the 1960s. Eddie Gibbs, *Church Next* (Downers Grove, Ill.: InterVarsity Press, 2000), 23.

6. For more on the differences between modernism and postmodernism, see Bob Whitesel, *Inside the Organic Church: Learning from 12 Emerging Congregations* (Nashville: Abingdon Press, 2006), x–xii, xxviii–xxxiii. See also Jean-François Lyotard, *The Postmodern Condition: A Report of Knowledge*, trans. Geoff Bennington and Brian Massumi, Theory and History of Literature, vol. 1 (Minneapolis: University of Minnesota Press, 1984).

7. James Emery White, "Evangelism in a Postmodern World," in David S. Dockery, ed., *The Challenge of Postmodernism: An Evangelical Engagement* (Wheaton, Ill.: Bridgepoint Books, 1995), 359–73.

8. Kathryn L. Ludwigson, "Postmodernism: A Declaration of Bankruptcy," in David S. Dockery, ed., *The Challenge of Postmodernism: An Evangelical Engagement* (Wheaton, Ill.: Bridgepoint Books, 1995), 281–92.

9. Whitesel, *Inside the Organic Church*, x–xii, xxviii–xxxiii.

10. Joel Bezaire, "When Church Signs Suck," September 13, 2006, www .churchmarketingsucks.com/2006/09/when-church-signs-suck (accessed July 13, 2011).

11. Bob Kauflin, *Worship Matters: Leading Others to Encounter the Greatness of God* (Wheaton, Ill.: Crossway, 2008), 36.

12. Pat Hannon, Associate Dean of Students, Indiana Wesleyan University, personal correspondence with author, December 17, 2010.

13. Bob Whitesel, *Spiritual Waypoints: Helping Others Navigate Their Journey* (Indianapolis: Wesleyan Publishing House, 2010), 113–14, 119–20.

14. Shane Claiborne, "How Many People Are Part of the Community?" www .thesimpleway.org/about/faq.

15. The Simple Way Community, "Our Expressions," www.thesimpleway.org/about/ our-expressions.

16. Ron Sider, personal interview with author, April 12, 2009.

17. Charles Marsh and John M. Perkins, *Welcoming Justice: God's Movement Toward Beloved Community* (Downers Grove, Ill.: InterVarsity, 2009), 28–31.

18. For an overview of how varying degrees of interaction and learning arrangements can foster learning, see Tessa H. S. Eysink, Ton de Jong, Kirsten Berthold, Bas Kolloffel, Maria Opfermann, and Pieter Wouters, "Learner Performance in Multimedia Learning Arrangements: An Analysis across Instructional Approaches," *American Educational Research Journal* 46, no. 4 (December 2009): 1107–49.

19. Daron Earlewine, personal conversation with author, December 14, 2010. Earlewine is a pastor on staff with the megachurch East Ninety-first Christian Church and regularly leads a pub theology, www.east91st.org/event/2010-11-20-pub-theology.

20. Personal visit with author, Vintage Faith Church, Santa Cruz, California, June 24, 2010.

21. Carl Turner examines examples of how new monastic churches in the Fresh Expressions Movement in England view spiritual preparation as "essential" and physical preparation as "not so essential." "Liturgical Issues and Fresh Expressions" in *Ancient Faith, Future Mission: Fresh Expressions in the Sacramental Tradition*, ed. Steven Croft, Ian Mobsby, and Stephanie Spellers (Norwich, UK: Canterbury, 2009), 93–95.

22. Francis Brown, S. R. Driver, and Charles A. Briggs, *A Hebrew and English Lexicon of the Old Testament Based on the Lexicon of William Gesenius* (Oxford: Clarendon Press, 1974), 1005.

23. Doug Pagitt, personal conversation with author, Solomon's Porch Church, Minneapolis, Minnesota, 2005.

24. See figure 9, "A Comparison Between Institutionalism and Improvisation," in Bob Whitesel, *Inside the Organic Church*, 119–20.

25. Jay Height, Executive Director of Shepherd Community Center, personal conversation with author, Marion, Indiana, September 15, 2010.

26. These rules are based on brainstorming principles as originally conceived by A. F. Osborn, *Applied Imagination: Principles and Procedures of Creative Problem-Solving* (New York: Scribner, 1963). The rules also incorporate ideas for a teaching format by Sy Landau, Barbara Landau, and Daryl Landau in *From Conflict to Creativity: How Resolving Workplace Disagreements Can Inspire Innovation and Productivity* (Hoboken, N.J.: Jossey-Bass, 2001), 128–29.

27. Jürgen Moltmann, *The Church in the Power of the Spirit: A Contribution to Messianic Ecclesiology* (Philadelphia: Fortress Press, 1993), 64.

28. Brown, Driver, and Briggs, *A Hebrew and English Lexicon of the Old Testament*, 1005.

8. ✖

1. Donald A. McGavran and Winfield C. Arn, *Ten Steps for Church Growth* (New York: Harper & Row, 1977), 3.

2. There are various types of conversion, such as secular conversion (for example, when a drug addict is transformed to a drug-free lifestyle) or religious conversion (for example, when a Sikh converts to Hinduism). Richard Peace gives a good overview of these kinds of conversion and the relevant literature in *Conversion in the New Testament: Paul and the Twelve* (Grand Rapids: Eerdmans, 1999), 7–11. We will limit our discussion to conversion to a Christian worldview as defined by Peace.

3. William James, *The Varieties of Religious Experience* (London: Longmans, 1902), 114.

4. Peace, *Conversion in the New Testament*, 4.

5. Scot McKnight, *Turning to Jesus: The Sociology of Conversion in the Gospels* (Louisville: Westminster John Knox, 2002), 5.

6. The modern inclination to count conversions, while insightful to the wind of the Spirit, may include too many divine and unperceived factors, making its usage as a leadership indicator deficient.

7. This is not to say there is not something, like a supernatural and indescribable *it*, that people seek to encounter in a church. Craig Groeschel, in his book *It: How Churches and Leaders Can Get It and Keep It* (Grand Rapids: Zondervan, 2008), describes it not as a trendiness but as a profound encounter with the supernatural.

8. Luke's emphasis is jarring, for most secular writers at the time reveled in the scale of the followers, and not on new passions for learning, fellowship, communal dinners, and prayer.

9. The four types of church growth described by Luke may be divinely inspired metrics or simply part of a biblical narrative. Yet they suggest relevant and helpful measurement of tools.

10. Walter Bauer, *A Greek-English Lexicon of the New Testament and Other Early Literature*, trans. William F. Arndt and F. Wilbur Gingrich (Chicago: University of Chicago Press, 1957), 716–18.

11. Ibid., 406.

12. The most prevalent historical examples of communal living would be the monastic movements.

13. Everett F. Harrison, *Acts: The Expanding Church* (Chicago: Moody, 1975), 66.

14. Leon Morris, *The Gospel According to John*, New International Commentary on the New Testament (Grand Rapids: Eerdmans, 1971), 485.

15. Some may wish to measure attendance in all church worship celebrations in lieu of small groups. This may yield a less reliable result, since in a large worship gathering, it is easier to attend without a steadfast striving for goals of the apostles' teaching and so on. In addition, it is harder to attend a small-group setting without this commitment since in a small group, accountability is stronger.

16. For examples of prayer triplets, neighborhood prayer centers, prayer covenants, and prayer chapels, see Bob Whitesel and Kent R. Hunter, *A House Divided: Bridging the Generation Gaps in Your Church* (Nashville: Abingdon Press, 2000), 230–37.

17. If your church has organized regular fellowship groups (for example, sports teams, hobby groups, etc.), and/or your church has regular times where congregants dine together (recurring evening dinners/lunches, a "dinners of eight" program, etc.), these groups can be included in your assessments. The key is for each church to include groups that have as a goal the development of spiritual maturity.

18. Church attendance is valid to track here since the pivotal number is the percentage of church attendees who are involved in Bible study groups and prayer groups.

19. Growth in unity and growth in community favor are based on perceptions. Yet subjective scales have been proved to be valid and reliable. See Rensis A. Likert, "A Technique for the Measurement of Attitudes," *Archives of Psychology* 22, no. 140 (1932): 55.

20. Further examples include Acts 9:42; 11:24; 13:43, 48-49; 17:12; 19:18-20.

21. Thom S. Rainer, "Church Growth and Evangelism in the Book of Acts," *Criswell Theological Review* 5 (September 1, 1990): 67.

22. The cross at the center of these four measurements also reminds us that progress is God's doing and that we only participate in his *missio Dei*.

23. Bauer, *A Greek-English Lexicon of the New Testament and Other Early Literature*, 301.

9. AFTERWORD

1. Lisa Gansky, *The Mesh: Why the Future of Business Is Sharing* (New York: Portfolio Penguin, 2010), 16–17.

2. Mary Jo Hatch, *Organization Theory: Modern, Symbolic, and Postmodern Perspectives* (Oxford: Oxford University Press, 1997), 53–54.

3. Ibid.

4. Bruno Dyck and Frederick A. Starke, "The Formation of Breakaway Organizations: Observations and a Process Model," *Administrative Science Quarterly* 44 (1999): 792–822; Frederick A. Starke and Bruno Dyck, "Upheavals in Congregations: The Causes and Outcomes of Splits," *Review of Religious Research* 38 (1996): 159–74.

5. For more on how to introduce new ideas in a unifying manner and thwart group exit, see Bob Whitesel, *Staying Power: Why People Leave the Church over Change and What You Can Do About It* (Nashville: Abingdon Press, 2002).